THE EDUCATION OF
CLARENCE THREE STARS

A Lakota American Life

Philip Burnham

University of Nebraska Press
LINCOLN

Portions of the text were previously published, in different form, as "'We Consider Ourselves Human Beings': The Education of Clarence Three Stars," *South Dakota History* 50, no. 2 (Summer 2020): 146–79. Used with permission.

Manufactured in the United States of America

The University of Nebraska Press is part of a land-grant institution with campuses and programs on the past, present, and future homelands of the Pawnee, Ponca, Otoe-Missouria, Omaha, Dakota, Lakota, Kaw, Cheyenne, and Arapaho Peoples, as well as those of the relocated Ho-Chunk, Sac and Fox, and Iowa Peoples.

∞

Library of Congress Cataloging-in-Publication Data
Names: Burnham, Philip, author.
Title: The education of Clarence Three Stars: a Lakota American life / Philip Burnham.
Other titles: Lakota American life
Description: Lincoln: University of Nebraska Press, [2024]. | Includes bibliographical references and index.
Identifiers: LCCN 2023032808
ISBN 9781496238047 (hardback)
ISBN 9781496239419 (epub)
ISBN 9781496239426 (pdf)
Subjects: LCSH: Three Stars, Clarence, 1864–1931. | Lakota Indians—Biography. | BISAC: SOCIAL SCIENCE / Ethnic Studies / American / Native American Studies | LCGFT: Biographies.
Classification: LCC E99.T34 B885 2024 | DDC 978.004/9752440092 [B]—dc23/eng/20231106
LC record available at
https://lccn.loc.gov/2023032808

Set in Quadraat by A. Shahan.

For my teachers,
lettered and not

Contents

Illustrations

PHOTOGRAPHS

Following page 116

MAPS

Preface

Clarence Three Stars likely never saw battle, counted coup, or hunted buffalo. He was a fighter and "full-blooded" Lakota of a modern age. He debated government agents, challenged draft boards, contested government treaties.

Like thousands of other Native boys and girls, he underwent a boarding-school education full of sacrifice and toil. And he survived.

Educated by family, tribe, and school, he ushered hundreds of Lakota students into a world where he taught them that learning can fundamentally change a life.

Today, Native people often appear in our histories as famous warriors or hopeless victims.

Clarence Three Stars, "Wicapi Yamni," was neither.

Acknowledgments

The idea for this book originated at a National Endowment for the Humanities summer institute, "The View from the East," held at George Mason University in 2014.

I thank Rebecca Chief Eagle and Elton Three Stars Sr., great grandson of Clarence Three Stars Sr., who offered kind words of encouragement early in my research. Darryl Kooiman and his wife, Rose Bordeaux, great-granddaughter of Jennie Dubray's sister Mary, offered important family details and unswerving support. Deb Cordier, another relative of Jennie's, provided genealogical help with the family tree.

A special thanks to Alvon Little White Man, Jackie Eagle Heart, and Dorothy Thunder Bull, who made possible my visit to Little Wound Middle School; to Tim Wardell and congregation for welcoming me at the Pass Creek Church of God in Allen; and to Joyce Wilson for her tour of the Martin historical museum.

Archives and libraries played a major role in uncovering the life of a man few people remember. I'm grateful to the staff of Oglala Lakota College Archives and Library, especially Tawa Ducheneaux for her insight and unwavering encouragement. At the National Archives in Washington, I thank Rebecca Sharp, Mary Frances Ronan, and especially Rose Buchanan, who helped me obtain many key documents at project's end. Joyce Burner at the NARA (National Archives and Records Administration) branch in Kansas City was very helpful in accessing the regional archives. I salute the efforts of Virginia Hanson, Halley Hair, and Matthew Reitzel of the South Dakota State Historical Society Archives. The staff at the Beinecke Library was efficient and ever helpful, as were those at the

Historical Society of Pennsylvania and at the Cumberland County Historical Society in Carlisle, including Cara Curtis and the legendary Barbara Landis. The National World War I Museum and Memorial in Kansas City offered useful assistance. I'm also deeply grateful to the mammoth task that Dickinson College has undertaken in scanning archival documents about the Carlisle boarding school at the National Archives and making them available online. Frank Vitale IV of the Carlisle Indian School Project offered much valuable advice, and his colleague Jim Gerencser provided sage and useful suggestions about my chapter on Carlisle and the school's history overall.

Elsewhere, Jean Kelley of Windover Historical Research located and retrieved many documents for me during the pandemic. Rebecca Klaudt, county clerk at the Bennett County courthouse, was welcoming and supportive. Cristina Stanciu of Virginia Commonwealth University pointed me in the direction of HathiTrust and the Beinecke, and Linda Waggoner's early enthusiasm was important in convincing me the project was worthwhile. I thank Jessie Matthews for sharing her knowledge of Carlisle and for her strong support as my supervisor at George Mason University. Rod Ross, as always, offered warm encouragement. Charles Evans-Gunther imparted valuable advice about the mystery of the two Sam Lone Bears. Richmond Clow and Elliott West were timely, generous, and gracious in their support. And a special shout-out to Harold Compton, who has always—somehow, somewhere—obtained valuable documents I couldn't otherwise find.

Many collaborators made the actual task of writing easier. Carla Joinson offered fine advice on the Canton chapter. My peer reviewers at the University of Nebraska Press were exacting and thoughtful. Greg Burnham gave his usual wise counsel. *South Dakota History* published a pilot essay about Clarence Three Stars that forced me to organize my research and consider the entire scope of his life. None of this is to forget Nawana Salimbeni, who planted the seed for the book years ago, perhaps unknowingly, when she told me that her history students only had examples of Native people who were warriors or victims, what I soon took to be a challenge when I set out to write this book.

The book's final version, in published form, owes much to my editor, Matt Bokovoy, who urged from the beginning that this should be a single biography, not an anthology of lives, and whose guidance steadied me from start to finish. Heather Stauffer skillfully mentored me through a consuming submission process; Sara Springsteen deftly managed production; the copyedit by Ellen Hurst was thorough, sensible, and astute. And the maps by Erin Greb shed light on this topic in ways I only could have done with a ton of words.

As always, friends and family have been patient and encouraging. I wish there were space to name them all. But my first reader and first responder, my better half and loving partner, devoted mother of brave Mallory, is Michele, without whom I couldn't have undertaken this journey.

With thanks to all, I claim any errors or oversights that follow for my own.

THE EDUCATION OF CLARENCE THREE STARS

Prologue

High Forehead

There was a story he used to hear as a young boy. "What I'm going to tell you," his father would say, "is about all of us." He started it the same way every time. "About the white man, about our people, and even about you, though it happened long before you were born."

It began, he said, during the Moon When the Cherries Turn Black. A band of hungry Lakotas was camped near the white man's fort, waiting for rations. One day a wagon train plodded by the camp, and an old lame cow, driven by a white man in a big hat, wandered among the tipis pitched along the trail.

A warrior named High Forehead took him for an intruder. He wanted revenge because the year before two of his brothers had been killed by white men. So he drew his bow on the man and fired, but his mark was wide. High Forehead launched a second arrow that felled the cow, whose carcass he dragged back to his tipi to feed his family. When they cut it up all they found was a sack full of gristle and bones, barely enough for the little ones to gnaw on.

The Lakota chief, named Conquering Bear, rode to nearby Fort Laramie to pay for the butchered cow and avoid any trouble. That was how the whole thing should have ended.

But the officer at the fort said they didn't want payment; they wanted the cow killer himself. They picked out an interpreter and called up twenty-nine soldiers and told a lieutenant named Grattan to go arrest him. Grattan told his men he "hoped to God they would have a fight." They marched out of that fort with a caisson hauling two cannons behind them.

It seemed like an awful lot of trouble for a lame cow.

The lieutenant stopped at the trading post on his way to the Indian camp, host to almost five thousand souls. "You tell the Bear I have come down here for that man," Grattan barked at the trader, "and I'll have him or die." When they got to the camp, the Bear pointed out High Forehead's tipi. The warrior held two guns in his arms as he stood before his home and said he would rather die than surrender.

No one knew what to do. Grattan's interpreter, a "mixed-blood" Frenchman, was drunk and scared. The more the two sides talked, the more their words got scrambled. Soon the interpreter, crazy with whiskey, sneered at the Lakotas and promised that he "would eat their hearts raw."

That's when some of the soldiers should have been getting ready to die.

The Bear told Grattan he couldn't give up one of his own people, not unless the request had been made, in the Lakota way, four times. But the lieutenant said no.

And so it was settled. Grattan ordered the cannons to fire, maybe just to scare the women and children, and the pieces boomed like a clap of thunder across the prairie. Conquering Bear crumpled to the ground, mortally wounded, and dozens of Lakotas rose up and returned fire.

In a few minutes all was quiet. There, on the ground, every one of the panicking bluecoats was dead or wounded. The boy listened closely, trying to imagine what all those bodies must have looked like.

They cut the throats of the dead soldiers; they chopped off their legs at the knee. They skewered the lieutenant's body with twenty-four arrows, one through the head. They stuffed his empty boots and a pile of manure in the mouth of a cannon. For days the bodies rotted under the sun before they were buried.

The white men called it "murder" and "massacre," the father told his boy. But how can it be murder when they aim a cannon in your face?

"And that man," he added, "the one who killed the cow . . . who fired the arrow that started the long war with the white people. That man was High Forehead, your grandfather."

The boy's father, called Yellow Knife, let that sink in for a moment. "So answer me something," he said to his son. "If the white people would send thirty troopers to avenge a dead cow . . . how many do you think they would send for a dead soldier?"

The boy, who was named Packs the Dog, and who one day would be known to the world as Clarence, just shrugged. He was only five years old.

"*Lila óta*," his father answered for him. "More than you will ever be able to count."[1]

I

The Iron Road

The children had no idea where they were going.

The wagons wound their way along the rutted trail that pushed across the Dakota prairie. It was almost the Moon of the Changing Season. The drivers of the teams were fathers and uncles and grandfathers all, chiefs and headmen of the tribe, who guided the plodding convoy toward what they called the Mud River. The wagon beds were laden with tipis for the nights they would spend on the road, but the elders were most concerned about the rest of the cargo they carried, neither dried beef nor cut boards nor rolls of bright calico—but their very sons and daughters. A few boys rode alongside on saddle mounts. It was almost two hundred miles to the river from Pine Ridge. Their spotted and prancing ponies were the last form of locomotion the children would even recognize on the longest trip of their lives.[1]

It had only been days before, at the agency, that some Indian boys dressed in strange clothes suddenly appeared. They were with white people who passed out candy to the children and promised them a new suit of clothes if they would go away to a place called *school*. They didn't force them, exactly. A loud white man walked around and made a long speech, asking permission of the parents and making a lot of big promises. Some were less trusting than others, but it wasn't long before most parents were watching as their children stood in line to be poked and prodded by a white man doctor. He looked in their eyes, listened to them breathe, checked their pulses, and each time made little black marks on a long roll of paper. They only picked the ones they thought would survive.[2]

The parents whose children were chosen gave away blankets and ponies to the needy of the tribe. Then they hitched their teams and headed east for the river, a journey that would take many days. But they arrived too early for the send-off. It was another day or two of waiting before the steamboat lumbered down the winding river from the north, pushing and paddling its way along the current like a big wooden swan belching black smoke and finally docking at the meeting place the Lakotas called the Black Pole and the white men knew as Rosebud Landing.[3]

It was already dusk. The boatmen put the gangplank down and called out their names: Plenty Kill! Packs the Dog! Cloud Shield! Makes Himself Run! One by one the young people from Pine Ridge and Rosebud walked up the plank, their parents and families weeping as they parted. Only about eighty were allowed to board. A white man would later remember unauthorized children stowing away on the ship to avoid detection, tribal runaways of a sort. The Lakotas would recall instead the youngsters who refused to go and stood timidly on the dock, frightened to take the first step in a journey that wouldn't end for a thousand miles. The two sides saw different things, as they always did and always would, while the boat pushed off from the Black Pole on a trip that wouldn't end until they reached the far side of the country.[4]

Where were they going? the children asked in their language. How many days would it take? What was waiting at the end of the river? The boys and girls, some as young as six or seven, huddled on deck in the shadow of the older ones, many in their late teens. Packs the Dog was fifteen, his future friend Plenty Kill, later known as Luther Standing Bear, was a little younger. They were hardly an entering class in the sense of a schoolroom, at least not yet, but were instead the handpicked elite of a generation chosen to redeem the wild ways of their ancestors. Just before they steamed away—almost as an afterthought—the crew brought an interpreter on board, the "mixed-blood" husband of Chief Spotted Tail's eldest daughter. The children hardly spoke a word of English. The white men would need a Lakota translator until they got to the school and the teachers could get their hands on them.[5]

The paddlewheel steamer plied the lazy course of the Missouri southward. The cottonwoods fluttered along each winding bend of the river.

The boys found a store on the boat where they cadged a few cigarettes; the schoolmaster, the loud man who liked to give speeches, bought the whole stock of four thousand and handed them out to the boys as a way to teach a lesson. They could smoke all they wanted until they got to their destination, he promised, but then they would have to quit. And he would quit with them. Their first taste of the white man's school—a smiling welcome followed by a stern prohibition—started a habit of mind that, for some, would last the better part of a lifetime.[6]

When they came to low water, a man in the bow placed a pole over the steamer's edge to make a sounding. He would yell it out to the pilot like a piece of song: "Mark Twain!" That meant two fathoms, or twelve feet, safe passage for the draft. The boys and girls would sing out the phrase, too, even when the man wasn't there anymore. "Quarter Twain!" they yelled at each other. "Marrrrrrrk Twain!"[7]

As the steamer plowed on, their enthusiasm gathered. When the boat finally docked, the children were ushered to a nearby yard with a platform high above them, which they reached by ascending a steep bank of stairs. On the platform they were escorted into a row of small wooden houses perched on a pair of iron rails. That was the train. Later it would seem like a foolish way to describe a train. But it was no more foolish than a white man from the city wondering how you cut a good tipi pole or butchered a buffalo bull or notched a box elder for the sweet juice it gave. A loud whistle sounded, and the train began to pull away. The frightened children gripped the seats, afraid the houses would topple over. Maza Canku, they called it, the "Iron Road." And "Mark Twain!" they might well have murmured over and again, more subdued and scared than they had been before, thinking of the boatman's song to keep them safe.[8]

It must have been the first train Packs the Dog ever rode. They stopped for food in Sioux City, and when they rolled into the station and pulled down the windows, a crowd of white people threw money at them. The smaller boys wanted to keep the coins, but no, the older ones said, give everything back or the strangers might write down their names and make trouble. The children were marched into a restaurant, surrounded by policemen, and mocked with war whoops by people who gawked and laughed at them from behind a big window. At the next stop, Chicago, they did an honor dance with a bass drum in a railroad waiting room. The people were so plentiful, said one boy, they scuttled around like a hill full of busy ants. They had never seen so many *wasicu* (white people) before, nor imagined that so many human beings—anywhere, of any tribe—could even exist. It was just as the father of Packs the Dog had warned him.[9]

The train whistled its way east, the children sleeping in fits and starts. The seats were stiff and uncomfortable. The passengers started to wonder if they would ever get to where the Captain (what people later called the schoolmaster) was taking them. Two nights later they passed the moon. It was in front of them one moment and behind them after they went to sleep. Some worried they would be killed because they passed the moon. But *hanwi*, as they called it, hadn't moved at all, one of the bigger boys explained—the train had just turned off and headed in a different direction. Every day, just like this, they acquired something new to sharpen their minds, having promised their families to learn and remember everything they could. They resolved they would know more about white people than they would let white people know about them.[10]

They were alone and far from home. Their grandparents had cried to see them go. Had their fathers ever been so far? Their people had a test they called *hanbleciya* (crying for a dream): this was when a boy or man would leave his family, instructed by a medicine man, and go up on a hill with a pipe. Four days and nights he would stay there and pray, with nothing to eat or drink, seeking a vision that would guide his life. When his time was done he would come down the hill and tell of what he saw, if anything at all. But this journey was no *hanbleciya*.

Any Lakota boy looking out the window at a town whose lights now flickered far away in the darkness would have known the truth: they had been gone more than four days. Packs the Dog had no pipe. There was no medicine man. And the boy had come too far to find his way home again without someone to tell him. It would be years before he could understand everything he had seen just in the last two days. How fast could the train run? What was in the thing they called a *school*? Would he ever see his mother and Uncle Three Stars again?[11]

They arrived at the place called Carlisle in early October, near midnight. The townspeople turned out by the hundreds to greet them. When the Lakota youth hopped off the train, they wore their buckskin leggings and dresses, their chokers and feathers, beads and long braids. The crowd gently walked the boys and girls a half mile up the lane to the "barracks," as the school was once called. The newer name, if the young people could have pronounced it, much less understood what it meant, had a ring both upright and ominous: the Carlisle Training School for Indian Youth. The Iron Road had led them to a solemn-looking place. They couldn't have guessed it then, but the days of their shaming had begun.[12]

At the front gates they separated boys from girls, eighty-four in all by official count. Upstairs in one dorm the boys found rooms with no beds. For weeks they slept on a hard floor, wrapped tightly under their blankets in the late autumn frost where the bare boards were colder than the earth had ever been at home. The older boys sang brave songs to give them courage, and many nights they could hear the girls crying from a nearby dorm. The boys cried, too, when they were called, one by one, into a classroom where their heads were shaved "with a machine," as one of them put it. It was hard not to cry in those early days. The first morning they had only bread and water to eat. After a little meat at noon, the fare got better. All of them realized by now that the day they left the Black Pole their childhoods had been cut short just as suddenly as their flowing hair had been shorn at the new school.[13]

Each Lakota child was given a pile of things to fill up their new world: bags stuffed with straw to sleep on; scratchy uniforms; a pencil and slate for class, a fork and plate at meals; a desk for writing and reading and sitting. Everything they touched was the same but separate. Yet nothing around them was theirs—all of it belonged to the school or was only good for wearing to school. And they better hold tight to everything they had, because to lose something was to break a rule, they were told, and if the rules were broken there would be a price to pay for it—whatever a *price* was, exactly—but it sounded like something they would have to give up or surrender even though they knew almost everything they owned had already been taken from them. For the boys, that included their hair.[14]

The last thing issued them was the most vital. On the assigned day Packs the Dog stood in a classroom and watched as the teacher pointed to a list of white marks scribbled on a dark board. She gave him the pointer, said something he didn't understand, then had her interpreter explain. The boy took the pointer and tapped, for no particular reason, on the word "Clarence," one of many written on the board. They wrote the name on a piece of tape and erased it from the board so nobody else could choose it. Then they sewed the tape like a sign on the back of his shirt. He learned soon enough how to recognize the sound when they shouted it out: "Clar-ence!" almost as much a taunt as a name. "Here," he would call out as he stood up whenever he heard it. "I am here!" Some of the younger ones, enamored of their new names, scrawled them in chalk across the walls and furniture, tracing out a mysterious line of letters they couldn't read.[15]

He knew it wasn't the Lakota way. Children at home were named for a rare feat, an odd event, a dream, an honored relation. A name was about something you could see or hear in the world, something alive, like Fire Thunder or Running Horse or Looking Woman . . . or Packs the Dog. But at Carlisle a name was just a line from a list of words. The boy had done nothing to earn it. It may have pointed at him, but it meant nothing. It was just a catch in the throat with a dying hiss ("Clarencesssss"), a sound that dangled meekly at the end of his lips, a name chosen, grudgingly, among strangers.[16]

And there was one more thing: just what kind of a Lakota boy would *name himself?*

2

Agency Boy

The sum total of everything we know about Clarence's family could probably fit on an oversized index card. He was born east of the Black Hills near Bear Butte, a sacred place in Lakota stories and legends. He later told census takers his birth year was 1864, known in various Lakota calendars as the Year Four Crow Indians Were Killed and the Year Two Faces Was Hanged. His father was Yellow Knife, a member of the Miniconjou subtribe of the Lakotas, or western Sioux, a leader well known to white authorities; his mother was Big Woman, said by some to be the daughter of Chief Smoke, a Brulé Lakota from Rosebud. At first the boy was likely given a name that signaled his position in the family birth order. By his early teens he had been given the name Packs the Dog, an image that recalled the days when a heavily loaded travois was drawn by a camp dog before the coming of the horse (*sunka wakan*, or "holy dog") transformed Lakota life.[1]

His father died when he was five, and Packs the Dog was adopted by his uncle Three Stars (*wicapi yamni* in Lakota). His uncle was a prominent man who headed a *wicoti* (camp), consisting of a dozen or so lodges. He had two wives, Bawling and Two Horses, who may have been sisters—plural marriage was common among prosperous Lakota men, who often married siblings to provide for a widow or spinster and expand family wealth. Another uncle was Black Bear, a significant leader renowned for his oratorical skills. Both uncles were followers of Little Wound, one of the great Oglala chiefs of the period and a leader of the Kiyuksa band of Lakotas. Born probably in the 1840s, Three Stars was old enough to remember what life was like before the big wagon trains started rumbling up the ruts of the Oregon Trail along the Platte River after the discovery of gold in California, and the great herds of buffalo began to disappear.[2]

The roots of the family name are a mystery. It seems unlikely that the elder Three Stars was born in or around the Year of Falling Stars (1833), the name given the Leonid meteor shower depicted in many annual Lakota calendars painted on animal hide. Perhaps his name referred to a constellation like Orion's Belt—what Lakotas saw as the spine of a bison—or any bright cluster that stood out in a prairie night sky densely packed with a cloud of stars. Or perhaps "Three Stars" recalled the nickname certain tribes had given U.S. Army officers like George Crook and Nelson Miles, so called, eventually, for the row of stars they wore on their shoulders. But would borrowing an army name have been a point of honor for an Oglala leader? Like many Indian names, Three Stars is only the faint glimmer of a family story that is barely visible today underneath a stack of yellowing census pages.[3]

Packs the Dog was born in the middle of the war that had begun the day his grandfather killed the cow at Fort Laramie—that is, the point when the *wasicu*, or white people, and Lakotas moved from being wary allies to bitter enemies. In 1864 the Powder River War and Little Bighorn Battle, both stunning victories for the boy's people, were still in the future. But powerful forces were arrayed against them: William Harney's scorched-earth campaign at Ash Hollow in 1855, the mounting rate of overland immigration, and the coming end of the Civil War, which would turn the military's focus to the west, all portended ill for the Lakotas. Most important, the *pte* were dying, the massive herds of buffalo that once moved across the land like a black shadow when seen from a distant rise, a moving forest that rumbled across the prairie in pursuit of something instinctive and unseen.

Packs the Dog, a child of that prairie, took his lessons the way Lakota boys did. There was hardly a day when school wasn't in session. They learned to give away food to a hungry elder. They learned that children weren't beaten—or even touched—in anger and would never run away from home. They learned how to listen so they could grasp a song by heart after hearing it only once. They learned to ride a horse by watching how their fathers did it. They learned how to make horseshoes of buffalo hide, how to ford a deep stream on a horse without drowning, how to mount a galloping mustang by grabbing its mane and going up with the thrust. They learned that the best swimmer or rider wasn't a rival to envy but a peer to admire. They learned not to complain about the weather and to remember that the wind had good intentions. In time they learned to listen to the dark but not be afraid of it. They learned not to stare at the moon or point at a rainbow. They learned there was no such thing as emptiness in the world, whether in the spreading sky or a balding stretch of badlands or the branches of the barest cottonwood in the Moon of Popping Trees. A Lakota boyhood was vigorous and sharp-eyed, shrewd and sensible. But by the time he reached puberty, Packs the Dog had become an agency boy tethered to store and stockade; it was a new way of life that compromised his school days on the prairie.[4]

The change began in early 1876, when many Lakota bands agreed to come into Red Cloud Agency, within the hunting grounds allotted them by treaty, to receive government rations and wait out the winter. Packs the Dog and his family were among them. A fortified outpost in northwestern Nebraska, the agency was where Little Wound and his followers would settle for months, even if the place wasn't held in high regard by many of its residents. By early June, in fact, close to two thousand agency Indians—Lakotas, Cheyennes, and Arapahos, many of whom were headed north where they would fight at the famous Battle of the Little Bighorn on June 25—had abruptly decamped from Red Cloud. Their encounter with General George Custer and the Seventh Cavalry ended as the Grattan episode of 1854 had: the main body of the army force was annihilated to a man, although the casualty count was almost ten times greater. Some 260 troopers attacked an Indian encampment along the Little Bighorn River but met their death among the nearby hills and hollows in a scrambling brawl later denounced as a "massacre" by the national press. As with the Grattan Fight, triggered by Packs the Dog's own grandfather, the army again set off on a brutal campaign to exact revenge on warriors and noncombatants alike.[5]

It is very doubtful his family fought in the summer of 1876 at Little Bighorn, since Little Wound's band was more inclined to cooperate with the government than contest it, deliveries of food and raiment being highly

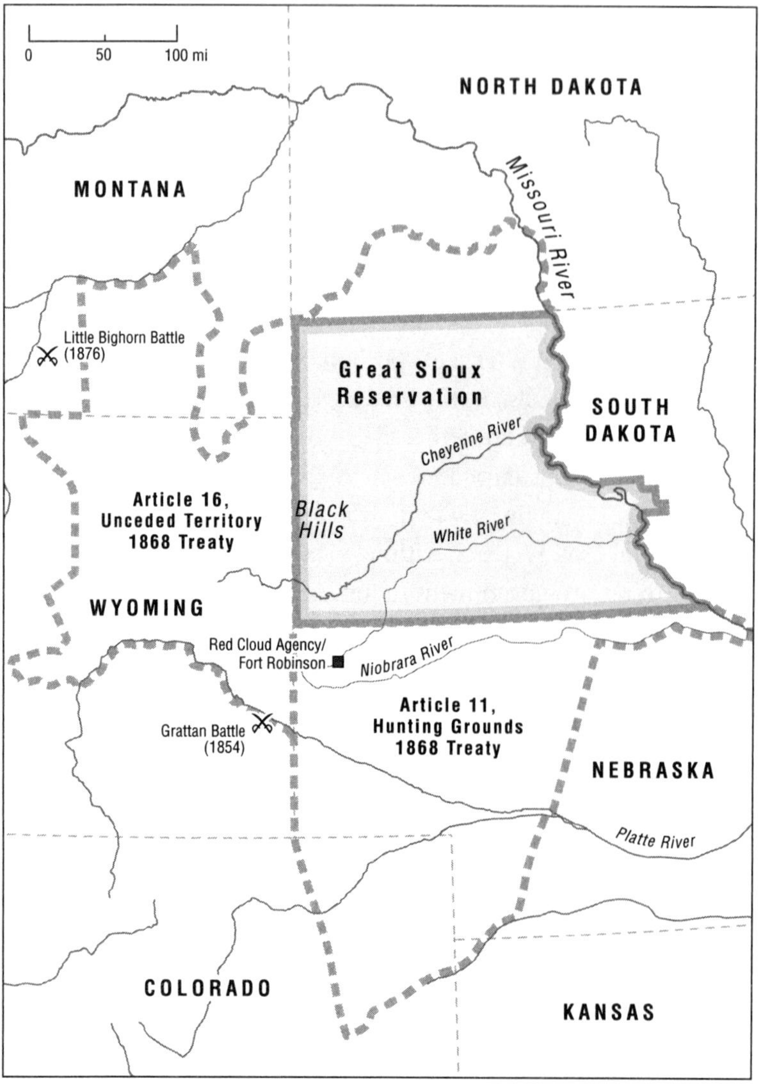

Map 1. The Lakota World, 1876. Erin Greb Cartography.

prized. We do know that in the fall of that year the elder Three Stars and his family were camped at Red Cloud Agency, like thousands of other Lakotas and their allies, under general orders to surrender to the government and end all resistance. Three Stars headed a family of eleven: three men, two women, and six children. Packs the Dog, one of three boys, was soon to come into his teens. They were still at Red Cloud the following February, drawing ration tickets for cattle that were slaughtered on the hoof by hungry Lakotas. Thirty people were eligible for one head of beef every ten days, what could have been a feast—or a famine—depending on the jib of the beast and how it was butchered. The Three Stars family was eating government beef before Packs the Dog was even old enough to hunt a buffalo, or, for that matter, court a woman.[6]

After Little Bighorn, the war against the white people went bad. Little Wound's people turned from disciplined nomads into fleeing refugees. Once they had roamed from the Platte River west to Fort Laramie and well up into Montana and Dakota Territory and all the way east to the Missouri River, a huge inland empire; it was a staggering expanse of perhaps one hundred thousand square miles where Clarence's mother tongue was a lingua franca. Now they found themselves camped near Red Cloud Agency, hundreds of feet below the rocky crags of clay that trimmed their horizon and overlooked a broad plain filled with canvas tipis. They had spread themselves along the flat of the land with their branch arbors, their beef-drying racks, the smaller play tipis for children, the hungry dogs, beaded cradles, the painted horses—what horses, that is, they were allowed to keep. Three Stars must have given up his ponies and guns just as the others did when they surrendered. The thought was slowly sinking in that they weren't going anywhere in the future without a white man saying yes. The government, rather than the chiefs and headmen, would choose their next home.[7]

The boy learned at Red Cloud, as his grandfather did at Fort Laramie, what it felt like to wait. And Red Cloud might as well have been a fort, too, bounded by a ten-foot wall of wooden planks that enclosed a corral and several buildings of hewn boards and shingled roofs. The soldiers who ran it spent their time counting Indians—Lakotas, Cheyennes, Arapahos—a job that never seemed to end. Every ten days or so, the men in uniform gave heads of family a paper ticket, warning them not to lose it. The next day, men like Uncle Three Stars would go back for family provisions and stand in line with hundreds of others, milling about like children waiting for school to open. They would call out his name, Three Stars would step forward, they would punch his ticket and shuttle him to the storeroom to get the family's measure of coffee, flour, bacon, sugar, and clothing. Next he went to the slaughter pen where the cattle were killed, some with guns the soldiers had given the Indians to shoot them. The meat was butchered and the hides removed on site. Then they hauled the rations back to the camp in wagons, some even slung over the headman's shoulder, and no one needed to say it was a far cry from the days when the leaders of a buffalo hunt would ride into camp shouting news of the killing harvest and the abundant feast to come.[8]

The fall and winter lingered long at Red Cloud. Families dug in and told stories about battles against the Crows, about how the Lakotas first emerged from the earth in the Black Hills, about the coming of the sacred pipe. They decorated their clothes with buttons and shells they bought from the trader. After first light a few children would file through the door of the wooden school. Some days the soldiers, stationed at nearby Fort Robinson (initially Camp Robinson), had horse races for entertainment, and a few times a man with a black box came and took pictures—the snout in front of the camera looked like a pointing gun, but even the children weren't afraid. Packs the Dog, barely twelve, would get used to photographers. He would also get used to seeing his people stand in line until their backs ached, get used to eating the white man's doughy grub, and to hearing the strange words of English the soldiers spoke. His people looked on, confused, as the sutler figured time by never even looking at the sun.[9]

The Kiyuksa band, which included the Three Stars family, took its name from a phrase that meant "cut off" or "divide by speaking," an apt description, it would seem, of how the government was working to isolate the many Oglala bands. Little Wound led the group of several extended families (*tiyospaye*) that numbered, in total, about a thousand people at Red Cloud, the bulk of them children. His people spent their months at the agency reconciling old ways and new. Adults prized the cloth shirts, dresses, and brass buttons the trader swapped, while the deerskin garments of the older generation began to disappear. The government gave out suits, shirts, and hats to the men and rolls of cloth to the women, pressing an outward conversion that would hopefully lead to an interior one. Their tipis were made of canvas now, not buffalo hides. Some had taken to burying their dead in wooden coffins on scaffolds built of board lumber instead of leaving the corpse of the dead perched in a tree hollow or lying on a branched scaffold as their ancestors did. Even the way they dealt with death was changing.[10]

In the meantime, Lakota resistance elsewhere had faltered. In May 1877 the legendary Crazy Horse, one of the heroes of the Little Bighorn triumph, surrendered to authorities at Fort Robinson, barely a mile from Red Cloud Agency. On September 5, as he was about to be confined in the guardhouse, the warrior was stabbed with a bayonet in a scuffle involving fort guards and fellow Lakotas, some of them political rivals. Crazy Horse was tended to by the fort's assistant surgeon, one Valentine McGillycuddy, who witnessed the fracas from a distance; after settling the victim in the adjutant's office and determining that his wound was fatal, he used a hypodermic syringe to inject him with morphine and ease the pain in his final hours. When Crazy Horse died later that night, the backbone of the main Lakota resistance was broken. McGillycuddy, whose life with the Lakotas was far from over, would soon become Indian agent to Little Wound's people and play a role in Packs the Dog's unlikely, and as yet unforeseen, education.[11]

Their sojourn at Red Cloud came to an end that fall. The Oglalas, including the Kiyuksas, who had camped far from any railhead or river landing, were given a stark choice by their overseers: either winter on the faraway Missouri River to get their rations or starve. And so they left, escorted by a corps of bluecoats, a column of some 5,000 Lakotas and 2,000 cattle with 120 wagons piled with rations, all of it stretching for miles across the prairie on a 250-mile trek to the Big Muddy. The next spring, granted permission by President Rutherford B. Hayes to pick their home base within the Great Sioux Reservation, they were escorted once again, this time back to the west, to camp along White Clay Creek in Dakota Territory near the Nebraska border, what would become Clarence's home agency for the rest of his life. At Red Cloud they had camped on treaty land reserved for Indian hunting, not settlement. But at Pine Ridge, as the new agency was called, they were safely inside the Great Sioux Reservation established in 1868. There was a catch in the fine print, however: the Oglalas were going to be living as prisoners in their own house.[12]

It was the next year, 1879, that the noisy white man with the combed-over hair came to talk to the families of Pine Ridge. He looked pale and puffed up, his manner consoling and strident by turns. He lectured the Oglalas about the benefits of education, and he did it by chiding them for giving up the Black Hills, which they had sold to the government three years before: "You signed that paper, knowing only what the interpreter told you it said," he hectored them. "If anything happened when the paper was being made up that changed its order, if you had been educated and could read and write, you could have known about it and refused to put your name to it. . . . Because you were not educated, the mountains, valleys, and streams have passed from you. . . . Cannot you see it is far, far better," he asked, "for you to have your children educated and trained as our children are so that they can speak the English language, write letters, and do the things which bring to the white man such prosperity?"[13]

Some of the elders decided he was right. The Black Hills had been taken from them by ruse and by force, and they had had no weapons to fight with. So the loud man wanted them to offer up their children to go away with him to a new school and learn to read and write. Red Cloud stepped forward and offered a grandchild. American Horse volunteered several children. Uncle Three Stars saw the matter the same way; he promised that Packs the Dog would leave Pine Ridge and be among the first to open the doors of the new school.[14]

The loud man didn't tell them everything, though. He didn't say that his strategy would be to mix Indians from different tribes to weaken their unity. He didn't say that the Indian Office had sent him to recruit Lakota children as "hostages" in the aftermath of the Custer battle. He didn't say the children were to be pawns in a strategy that would display the strength of the Great Father. And he didn't say the school was to be run as a house of correction and confinement, where life would be spartan, punishments harsh, and the children discouraged from going home even in summer.[15]

There was so much that the loud man, Richard Henry Pratt, didn't tell them.

3

School Days

Their first months at Carlisle were agony. Most of the students were homesick and hungry. The moon rose and set in the same sky, but the months had different names now. The trees were bare, the air biting. The temptation to resist was strong, especially among the older boys. In the eyes of his warders, Packs the Dog, now known as Clarence, was an unkempt, uncivilized, unfinished specimen of a boy.

That first year he became known as a troublemaker. He was smart and good with numbers, a skill that would stand him well in later life, and one day he decided that everyone in class should know about it. He talked out of turn, was disruptive and loud, and the teacher grew annoyed. After a minute or two of his antics she dispatched a student with a handwritten note to the superintendent. Minutes later he strode in, bluff and irritated, a Lakota interpreter on his heels. The teacher pointed out the boy. "Clarence, stand up. Hold up your head," the superintendent snapped. The boy was confused. Not until the translator parroted him in Lakota did young Clarence know to rise to his feet. "Put your hands down by your side, palms to the front." Clarence put his hands down.

The superintendent marked out each motion as he ordered it, like a man drilling a dog.

"Put your heels together," the interpreter barked. "Push your shoulders back." Their English wasn't very good yet, and Clarence could hardly grasp the master's words. "What is the matter?" snapped the superintendent. The students were frozen in their seats. Clarence fought back tears. He was starting to explain himself, in Lakota, but his voice was shaking. "If you are so brave," classmate Robert American Horse taunted him, in Lakota, "what makes your voice shake so?" Clarence couldn't answer. The biting words cut him like a whip. He fell silent, ashamed and exposed. "I guess things will go all right now," said the superintendent, who turned on his heels and marched out of the room as everyone looked on in disbelief.[1]

The boy stood there like a saddled pony. His people would never have shamed a child in front of others. He had lost honor before friends and peers, a man-child doing times tables in a white man's classroom stuck in a military barracks more than a thousand miles from home—and ridiculed for the effort! His life in Dakota seemed farther away now than even the Iron Road could reach, and it had to be clear, on occasions such as this, that he had given up much more than his braids and blanket when he walked through the school gates the autumn before to watchfully enter the House of Pratt. Perhaps if he had stood up and sung a brave song, he would have showed them what a Lakota man really was.

But a boy did not do that at Carlisle.

The Indian school was housed in an almost-deserted barracks founded before the Revolutionary War in the prosperous burg of Carlisle, a former munitions depot in the heart of the Cumberland Valley in south central Pennsylvania. Bounded by Letort Creek on one side and Garrison Lane on the other, the school grounds had a military appearance, perhaps reminiscent of Clarence's old home at Red Cloud. While martial in aspect, however, this new abode was as shabby as a medieval ruin. The old barracks were crumbling. Buildings with no roofs had been exposed to the elements for the better part of a decade. It was only with the labor of scores of Indian students and their mentors that Pratt set about rehabilitating the grounds that first year. They rebuilt the roofs, cut down weeds, painted buildings, erected a seven-foot-high picket fence around the campus to discourage would-be runaways and keep curious gawkers at a distance. The new students sawed and patched and nailed and hammered away in their first taste of vocational education, an object lesson in how the labors of mind and body could be merged in a school with a captive and hungry clientele far from home and family.[2]

Carlisle would be the training ground for the first cohort of Indian children in a grand Victorian-era experiment: the off-reservation boarding school. Boarding schools had existed before on Indian reservations and agencies; there was also a long tradition of missionary schools administered by religious authorities and colleges like Harvard and Dartmouth that provided residential Indian education. But Carlisle was different, and it spawned dozens of imitators in a movement that dominated Indian education for more than half a century and that still exists, in altered form, today. The school was federally funded, located far from the home reservations of most students, and operated according to a military regimen that educated Native students in both basic literacy and vocational skills. It only grew more crowded and powerful with time: By 1888, only a few years after Clarence left, Carlisle had enrolled over five hundred students and had a budget of $81,000, more than $2 million in current value.[3]

The Carlisle Training School was segregated from the rest of town, ironic given its mission to assimilate Indian children into the broader American populace. The campus gradually expanded from twenty-seven acres to an expansive three hundred. There were separate dormitories for boys and girls, teachers' quarters, a superintendent's house, a guardhouse that dated to the Revolution, various outbuildings and old stables, and a prominent bandstand on the main quad, a favorite haunt of Pratt's from which to observe his Native children at work and drill. The school had its own private cemetery, also separate from town, which would come to harbor the coffins of dozens of Indian children from across the country. Bells and bugle calls sounded the time of day. Boys and girls were organized into military companies where they marched and drilled like cadets. Every morning they went to services in the wooden chapel—also raised by student hands—and on the Sabbath filed off to Carlisle Sunday schools for spiritual guidance.[4]

The dorms were built on an open plan, without doors, so that students could be easily monitored. Pratt later came to favor small rooms that allowed for more privacy, and after a few years girls slept three or four to a room. The boys were divided into two buildings, one for children under twelve, the other for their elders; the small boys' rooms housed maybe a half dozen residents. They used oil lamps to light the buildings, and steam heating replaced coal-burning stoves after the first year. Inspections were a daily part of dorm life—hair combed, clothes cleaned, shoes shined, beds properly made. Each child was issued a chair, an enameled bed, and a wooden trunk for personal items, the frosty landscape of what would come to be the aristocratic poster child for Indian boarding schools.[5]

The clock ran as true as a heartbeat. First bell rang for the girls at 6:15 a.m. (earlier for waitresses). They observed a moment of silence, roll was called, daily chores were assigned, and only then did they file into the dining room for breakfast. For two hours they engaged in general housekeeping of quarters until nine o'clock, when classes began. At eleven thirty those waitressing for dinner were excused, and the meal was served at midday. The girls trooped off to class again at half past one until four o'clock. Supper was served at six, and the evening hours that followed were filled with study and amusements, including jump rope, dolls, and roller skates. At quarter after eight a whistle blew, and roll was called again in the sitting room. They read Bible verses, the girls recited the Lord's Prayer, and lights were out at nine o'clock sharp. "If anyone is inclined to the belief that the Indian is sluggish or inert," the school paper boasted, "let them spend a day among us, and they will soon be converted from the error of their thoughts." Such was the routine that young Jennie Dubray, the future mother of Clarence's children, would find when she entered Carlisle the year before he left.[6]

The boys, many of them Lakotas that first year, had the look of raw recruits. Their first clothing issue consisted of cheap woolen togs and funny-looking suspenders. Their new boots squeaked when they walked, and their pants had the curious novelty of pockets where you could stow your hands if it was cold. The clothes were too big for many of the younger ones, but they wore them to bed anyway out of sheer excitement. They wore paper collars around their necks, socks on their feet, and smart derby hats for show. Gone were the painted faces many had worn when they arrived, and the bracelets, breast plates, rings, and pendants, too, their old blankets burned or hauled off in the rubbish. The red flannel underwear was scratchy and uncomfortable, and their nightshirts looked to them like something that girls or women would have worn.[7]

Gone, too, was their hair. Having their long hair shorn to a nub would have been a shock to Lakota boys. Their people believed that hair embodied the human spirit of its owner. Young people might wear their hair in ways that signaled marital status or the onset of puberty. A lock of hair might be taken from a newly deceased relative and preserved for a year as a way of "keeping the ghost" before the spirit could return to the place where it was born. Lakota leaders, or "shirt wearers," wore ceremonial buckskin shirts fringed with hair locks, whether taken from enemies or given by their own followers. In fact, Lakotas regarded cutting their hair as an act of bereavement, not as a gesture of conformity and submission, as Carlisle would have it. Laura Pratt, the Captain's wife, would find this out when, one day in her husband's absence, she tried to force a young boy to have his hair cut by a barber. The boy refused her order and did the deed himself with a knife, only to spend the whole night wailing on the parade ground, along with many of his peers, since as he explained, it was what his people did after chopping off their hair. Clarence had his hair cut short soon after arriving at the school, and never, so far as we know, went back to the old way. Some of the new habits would stick with the boys for life.[8]

Imagine, then, after months of training, how the boys strutted and swaggered by day, their bearing like would-be warriors without guns. They formed into companies with corporals and sergeants. They policed and guarded their dorms and grounds, checking for fire and suspicious doings. Students who misbehaved were court martialed, judged by cadet officers who heard witnesses, decided on guilt, and recommended punishment—pending, of course, Captain Pratt's approval. Sentences included lockup and withdrawal of privileges and rations of bread and water. Corporal punishment was practiced for serious offenses, though the school publicly maintained that whipping was forbidden.[9]

They marched to their meals by the hands of the clock. They ate in the dining hall—one hundred feet long at first, a later fifty-foot extension increasing capacity to three hundred. There were nine tables at the outset, eighteen children seated at each, served by one of the girls. The plates of food were waiting on the tables when the children, many of whom scrambled to find the biggest helping, came in. They bowed their heads in thanks to the Lord before the first fork was raised. By that first spring, nearly two hundred Indian youths sat side by side, many from tribes that had been deadly enemies, English the only way they could converse. Boys and girls were segregated, as were older and younger students. They ate potatoes, onions, cabbage, soup, meat, and white bread. Clarence and many others were already used to agency grub, but the portions at Carlisle were rarely enough: "We never had to be called twice!" recalled one of Clarence's friends.[10]

But the school was there to do more than just feed and drill them.

Those first days they sat in the classroom as though struck dumb by a miracle. (The miracle of education, they were told.) The novelty of their condition outstripped their understanding. The teacher held up a book called *First Lessons for the Deaf and Dumb*. They couldn't grasp a word she said. When they tried to talk, their tongues went limp. They could hear and speak just fine, but they didn't know the right words, couldn't always make the right sounds. They had never been in a school before. The chairs they sat in made them squirm. Clarence was fifteen years old, some of his classmates older still, and the idea of reading and reciting like little ones embarrassed them.[11]

They read the lines on the blackboard with painful effort:

> Mr. Keep ran.
> Willie Ely ran.
> Joseph Page ran.[12]
>
> Throw a ball.
> Throw a newspaper.
> Throw a pencil.[13]

They built longer sentences as the weather got colder:

> There is an apple on your desk.
> There is a book in your chair. . . .
> There is a horse in the street. . . .
> There are many stars in the sky.[14]

They could hear that the words had a voice. The voice was there when they said the words aloud, but the sounds they made ran through the room like a rushing stream of water they couldn't control when they read from the page. That was how the world began to feel to them. That voice, it lingered clearer and sharper over time, different than anything they had ever been told. When they went to look for it again, to turn back the page of a book an hour later, it was still there. And *it would still be there tomorrow*. There was magic in that, and something to be afraid of too. The black words cried out like a murder of crows perched along each lined and cryptic branch of the page.

With time the children grew more confident, more careful. As the snow melted and buds came out in spring, they wrote down so many promises:

> We must study our lessons.
> We must obey our teacher.
> We must learn our lessons.
> We must wash our hands and faces every morning.[15]

They recited and wrote and listened. No matter how much they tried, though, some things in the book they didn't understand:

> We can not hear.
> We can not speak.
> We can learn.[16]

But they could speak. They could hear.

> Can you lift an elephant?
> What can you lift?
> Can four men lift an elephant?[17]

Clarence had never seen an elephant, and there was no picture of one. He would have to know more to tell if four men could lift an elephant, but it seemed doubtful if it was anything like a horse.

Every week the teacher made them write a letter home. The book gave them a path to follow:

> My Dear Mother, I wish very much to see you. I love you. I study my lessons. I write on my small slate and on my large slate in the school-room. Mr. _____ teaches me. . . . Mr. _____ is the principal. I like to stay in the Asylum. I wish to become wise. . . . I am very well. I send my love to all my friends. Your affectionate _________, _________.

It was more like copying than writing. It would take time before they could write in their own thoughts and words, but the act of writing, they came to see, was proof to their parents they were still alive.[18]

The new words were hard to remember, still harder to say. They were told not to speak in Lakota and punished if they did. Everything they knew how to say was suddenly wrong—that was what Carlisle taught them. But if the teacher had known their language, it would have been so much easier to teach them hers. They learned you said the adjective before the noun, not after, which seemed all backward. The words for older brother and younger brother were the same, which seemed disrespectful. The force the Lakota knew as Wakan Tanka was what the white people called God, and they even had pictures of his son. They called a horse a *horse*, not a "holy dog," as his people did. Men and women said things exactly the same way, which jumbled them together too much. And another thing: their book, written for deaf people, called the school an *asylum*. They didn't know what an asylum was, exactly, only that it meant something like a prison where they put people who were *witko* (crazy) and had no way to escape from their teachers.

His name was now *Clarence Three Stars*. The *Three Stars* part was easy—he could draw three blazing lights on the skin of his erasable slate. But what did a *Clarence* look like? He learned soon enough that he could write out both his names by scratching on his slate with the lank, curly letters they forced him to learn. And if they could write down a word, the children came to see, they could tell people far away how they felt about something. Writing was like an arrow with a string of words tied like feathers to a shaft. You pointed it at someone and fired. A message flew through the air. The pencil and chalk were useful tools, it seemed, but wobbly, harder to grip than a bow or knife and slippery as buffalo fat. Captain Pratt said the script they wrote would free them and make them good men and women if they worked hard.

They read maps that told them about places they had been—and others they would never visit. Some of his friends studied their geography carefully because one day it might help them find their way home. The native races of Africa were barbarous, they read. Most of Europe was ruled by kings (they had no idea what a king was). Their families lived in a territory called Dakota, which seemed only right because it sounded like what their own people called themselves, though the small green patch on the map that showed their home looked pitiful in a big book. An island, a peninsula, an isthmus, an ocean—the world was too big to comprehend in a few months. But there was nothing in the books about the things they knew—the feathers that marked a man's courage, or the way to boil meat in a buffalo bladder, the plants they picked to cure cramps and fever, even how to know the place where the bears emerged in spring. Still, they were impressed by what it took to make a book about the world. They had been told at home that the earth was spread out flat with four corners. But the teacher told them the globe was round and always moving. They doubted this at first, thinking they would end up standing on their heads as it turned. One day a Ponca boy said while looking at a map, "Where did that man stand when he took the picture of the world?" In time they came to understand how to read the maps and know mysterious things, like the day an astronomer came and predicted an eclipse that happened just as he said it would. And yes, there it was, on page 78 of *Swinton's Geography*: a picture of an elephant, with floppy ears and four legs and a long, furrowed nose. And no, they decided, it was impossible that four men could ever lift it.[19]

The world was stranger than any of them could have imagined. One day a group of the older boys and girls was invited to nearby Dickinson College. There they got a lecture and demonstration on the subject of lightning, a topic Lakota children would have known much about given the role of the thunderbirds (*wakinyan*), who hurled flashes of light across the sky. After the students linked hands together, the professor cranked an apparatus to send out an electric current that gently jolted them amid peals of laughter. He shot another charge that shattered a miniature house into pieces, the girls squealing in delight. They had never seen lightning, even a little bit of it, inside a room before.[20]

They drilled by day, dreamt by night. Some of their dreams were as strange as the maps they found in the geography book. Away from all the fuss and commotion, the mind lured the sleeping soul into reverie. Some of them hoped that after they fell asleep they would wake up in the morning able to speak English like white people, or that if they could only sleep in a white man's house, just once, they would magically have the right words and sentences on their lips and no need to copy from the books or recite the childish poems anymore.[21]

The next morning, though, the dreams would seem small and feeble. They would go back to their work, reading and writing and ciphering numbers. They studied music, too, and drilled in choral singing and learned to sing and pray every morning at chapel. Their families were sent monthly reports about their progress. But the place they came from was so small and far away that they couldn't even find a picture of it in *Swinton's*. They were captives of a sort, even if they had come willingly, at least by the will of their parents.[22]

Not one of them, of course, would have ever dared refuse what their elders asked.

Reading and writing were for morning hours. The rest of the day, for many boys, was devoted to farming. In nearby fields they planted potatoes, onions, cabbages, radishes, parsnips, lettuce, and sweet corn, a farm-to-table operation run out of a military barracks. Others volunteered to learn a trade. They made wagons, harnesses, shoes, clothing, tinware, and ironware; others trained as carpenters, painters, printers, and bakers. Once the operation was up and running, Carlisle was a veritable factory. In 1881 the school shipped over $6,000 worth of merchandise to Indian agencies. In 1883 the tailor shop alone made 410 coats, 770 pairs of pants, and 343 vests. By the next year between four thousand and five thousand pieces of laundry were washed and ironed by the girls every week. They learned what the pattern of life would be like as adults: girls performed the domestic trades, while apprentice boys and girls earned a variable rate of pay, sometimes as much as 16⅔ cents per diem, each of them given a bank book to deposit earnings that couldn't be spent without Captain Pratt's approval.[23]

Clarence chose the labor, modest but exacting, of working cloth. The patient shuttle of scissors, needle, and thread filled his afternoons. In the tailor shop they cut patterns from bolts of cloth, treadled the sewing machine, sliced buttonholes, and pressed the hot iron. They made clusters of scarlet braid and traced curves in colored stitching. There was a certain architecture in the trade, working as they did from fashion plates that hung like blueprints around the workshop. Clarence was good with hand and eye—the school paper praised him for sewing a pair of trousers with sergeant stripes in less than four hours, and he was entrusted with running the shop while the master was on leave. The boys stitched their clothes from homespun, while the girls sewed their own garments—along with the boys' underwear, of course, which wasn't considered a manly pursuit for a tailor. By Clarence's second year every boy and young man was garbed in a blue coat, vest, and pants with red stripes that buttoned up the front. "We aim to produce good marketable work and allow as little waste of materials as possible," boasted the shop, as good a workingman's credo as could be found anywhere in the great Commonwealth of Pennsylvania.[24]

By his third year at Carlisle, Clarence could write his own letter. "My Dear Three Stars," he began a missive to his cousin, "I want to write to you again and I have cheerfully to work all the time and to learn everything. I have accomplish a pair pants and coats too, every day because I can build the pants and coats too. I have work in 13 months in tailor trade, and I never become tired. We are perputual cheerfully attending school every day We are trying long suffering and hard think. Now I can able write letter this time that is all to say, write soon. From your cousin. Clarence Sioux—that is me."[25]

On February 8, 1880, a group of thirty-four Indian boys and girls was baptized in the town center, only a few months after stepping off the train in Carlisle. St. John's church was as imposing an edifice as any they had visited, built of hewed stone, plastered with stucco, and crowned by a bell tower 150 feet high that was visible from miles away on a clear day. The church front had massive wooden doors that opened onto the entryway. Looking into the sanctuary, the Indian youths could see the carved pine Norman arch that straddled the chancel, while in the back were three large stained-glass windows—the lamb, the cross, the chalice—through which the light poured from the east, illuminating the cross on the marble altar.[26]

They filed slowly down the aisle between the rows of wooden pews, while the white people watched them from their seats, just as they watched everywhere the children visited in Carlisle. The boys could see that the cross was at the end of their steps, to the east with the morning light behind it, the direction their own people considered as the source and beginning of all.

The Reverend William Cole Leverett did the honors. The boy heard his own name called, the very first of all the names they uttered, but it was almost hard to recognize because everything was in English now. "Packs Dog," they called him. Sunga Gnise, as his mother said it. The teachers muttered the name at school the first few days like it was something worn and shabby.

Packs the Dog stepped up to the large bowl before the altar. The reverend started speaking, though the words made little sense.

The people watching from the seats chanted with the reverend:

"Dost thou renounce the devil and all his works, the vain pomp and glory of the world . . . ?"

"*I renounce them all.*"

"Dost thou believe all the Articles of the Christian Faith, as contained in the Apostles' Creed?"

"*I do.*"

"Wilt thou be baptized in this Faith?"

"*That is my desire.*"

"Wilt thou then obediently keep God's holy will and commandments, and walk in the same all the days of thy life ?"

"*I will; by God's help.*"

Those were the words he had memorized.

The reverend took him by the right hand. "I baptize thee In the Name of the Father and of the Son and of the Holy Ghost. Amen." He daubed him with water and made the sign of the cross. "His name shall be Clarence," the reverend said. The name they gave him at school now was holy.[27]

Then they knelt and prayed. It wasn't like the formal salutes they did at school. This was on his knees, something helpless and submissive.

And so it was that Cloud Shield, Cut Ears, Spotted Tail, Talks With Bear, Bugler, and Little Scout were sprinkled with the holy water, and it washed away all their sin—as hard as it was for them to conceive what *sin* meant—and from that day forward they would join Clarence as Roger and Robert and William and Max and Oliver and Pollock.[28]

This is what church was. Everyone was watching, but no one danced. They were alone with their new names, and they knew something sacred and powerful had happened.

But the boys struggled to understand so much that was strange. What was the secret that made the *wasicu* so strong, like the power of the Iron Road and the busy hum of the workshop and the men who marched them on the grounds and the women who gave them lessons? That power was there in the church. The reverend made no hesitation, showed no sign of delay, not like the way Clarence's people would extend a sacred pipe three times—each time rejected—before it could be accepted on the fourth offering.[29]

Now they were here to worship the three forms of God. But why did the white people stop at three? The Lakota holy numbers four and seven had no power in Carlisle—the four directions, four seasons, four virtues, the four days of the Sun Dance. And where were the seven council fires of the Oceti Sakowin, the branches of the Sioux people? The numbers mattered. The boys were in a world now where everything was counted, from the trousers they wore to the letters they wrote home and the forks set out at dinner. The white people even tallied time. Some of the children struggled to understand what a week was (at least it had seven days!), when neither the sun nor moon could give them a clue. And why should they carve up every day into so many hours?

The young man was of the church now; he would be called Clarence in the eyes of the Lord. Two years later he was confirmed as an Episcopalian with fourteen other boys and girls. Then, on Easter Sunday 1882, he took his first communion, along with Luther Standing Bear and Edgar Fire Thunder, friends who would be with him the better part of a lifetime. Packs the Dog was the name that only the elders at home would call him anymore.[30]

He went to Sunday school and heard of the big flood and the son who spurned his father but came back and how the fish and the loaves were divided, of the dead man who sat up and walked again and the man swallowed by a fish for three days. They met in the damp, gloomy basement of the church to hear the stories. There was no end to the lessons he was supposed to learn, whether it was primer or scripture that instilled them. But there were doubts and muttering along the way. Why did they have to cut their hair if Jesus Christ's was so long? How did he know he would dwell in the house of the Lord forever?[31]

Reverend Leverett would baptize scores of Carlisle students. No one spoke much of the funerals he did for ten Indian children, however. The church was like Pratt's school in that way, quietly discreet about the losses. There was a final reckoning to the reverend's figures that only the big bound ledgers could reveal.[32]

Clarence arrived at Carlisle with his cousin Makes Himself Run (Kaiciyanke), subsequently known as Paul Black Bear. Paul was a prankster, it was said, always late and out of breath and given to breaking rules and pulling practical jokes. He was a confirmed cigarette smoker and once had to be doused with water after he fainted from inhaling too fast. He was known to unfasten the catches that bound the legs of dorm beds; the beds would collapse when a comrade sat on one and fell to the floor with a nasty bruise for his trouble. Having a relative close at hand, even a mischievous one, must have been a comfort so far from home, but the school was more about the new family Clarence would make than the one he left behind. At least a third of Carlisle students were either orphaned or had only one surviving parent, as Clarence was when he lost his own father. The lack of strong parental ties made children easier to recruit for school and probably more submissive once they got there.[33]

Clarence made friendships at Carlisle that would last a lifetime, among them a young man called Edgar Fire Thunder. Unlike most of the Indian children sent east in 1879, Edgar was a "mixed-blood." His father was an army trooper, and his Lakota mother, Bear Woman, gave birth to him in 1860, a boy with a visibly pale complexion compared to most Lakotas. His father left his family to go off and fight in the Civil War and was never heard from again. Bear Woman went on to marry Fire Thunder, a leading man in Red Cloud's band, who adopted Edgar. (Later it would be said that Clarence himself became an adopted son of Fire Thunder). Edgar, one source alleges, rode with Crazy Horse when he was a youth, though by the time he got to Carlisle he was recorded as a member of the Loafer band, which showed deference to the army and consisted of, as the name suggests, a rather sluggish agenda. His translated Lakota name was "Whiteman" (*wasicu*). And if not for an early photo, we wouldn't know that he entered Carlisle wearing two long braids and a choker, carrying a striped blanket draped over his arm and looking defiantly confident of his place in the world. When he arrived at school he was almost twenty years old and possessed of his own mischievous streak, known for ringing the school dinner bell well in advance of mealtime. He also had a gift for drawing, and one of his sketches from the 1880s remains today as a prime example of early Indian school art.[34]

Another school friend who would figure large in Clarence's life was Luther Standing Bear. The son of Chief Standing Bear from Rosebud agency, Luther, by his own account, was younger than Clarence by several years and distantly related to him. He was probably a "mixed-blood," like Edgar, and more inclined to assimilate than was Clarence, whose parents were "full-blood" Lakotas. As such, Luther was, in many ways, one of Pratt's favorite sons. He played cornet in the school band and gave the bugle call, day and night. He traveled to Rosebud to interpret for a Carlisle recruiter and advocated eloquently for the school. He accompanied Pratt to Washington to interpret for his own father before the Commissioner of Indian Affairs, and he led the school band on a trip to New York to celebrate the opening of the Brooklyn Bridge. When retailer

John Wanamaker asked Pratt for two of his best Indian boys to work in his famous Philadelphia department store in the spring of 1884, Pratt didn't hesitate to choose young Luther. He would be, in many ways, Clarence's cultural twin—and alter ego—for the rest of their lives.[35]

Luther developed his writing skills quickly, and his letters were often published in the school papers. "Dear father I am always fond of Carlisle," he wrote warmly at the end of his second year. "Because I am be glad I try to get knowledge, and Capt. Pratt what he says I listen, and I do it. And my teachers too." But he went further than merely singing Carlisle's praises. In 1883 he had grown bold enough to upbraid his own father for pagan religious practices after the death of one of his Carlisle peers: "You think we felt sorry cried and walked around and killed horses and gave them away the things which we have? or cut ourselves and crying for him every day because we love him? . . . You know it is not right to do that way. If we are truly civilized . . . I want you must give up the Indian ways, you must turn to the good way and try to walk in it, the way of which is God love." Barely in his midteens, Luther was instructing his father on the proper protocol of grief.[36]

When the famous chief Red Cloud came to campus, Luther took part in a competition to translate one of his speeches into English. His rendition, however, doesn't exactly make Red Cloud an orator of great distinction: "I went pass through the shops and saw what you can be done. . . . Also the girls can washing clothes and sewing. . . . Now you must not home-sick any; but you must try to be good and happier." The warrior's homily comes out in a dialect resembling something like Plains Indian pidgin, but Luther, doing the best he could, won a three-dollar prize for his rendering. Even when he struggled, Standing Bear was a Carlisle star.[37]

The school wasn't all homesickness and hard work. There was roller skating in the gymnasium (the floor laid by students, of course). Diversions like board games and marbles were common. Sometimes country outings were permitted, as when, in the summer, Pratt took Clarence, Luther, and a few others to the mountains near Pine Grove. They sported straw hats like local farmers, made (and sold) bows and arrows, and picked wild strawberries and plums. Since they weren't fed quite enough, as usual, Clarence and Luther did double turns in the chow line to make sure they had their fill. One day Clarence caught an eel two and a half feet long while fishing in a local stream, mistook it for a snake, and threw it in the bushes, only to have it resurrected by a companion and roasted for dinner.[38]

Study, work, sleep, drill, play—it was all there at Carlisle, and there were some who thrived under the Captain's vigilant eye. As one looked out across the quad on a December morning to see students lining up in formation after a newly fallen snow, they might have almost seemed like a tribe unto themselves, a white man's tribe that wore soldier uniforms and spoke English and ate potatoes with knives and forks. And for a few intense years, they were just that. But then they would be torn away from the place and forced to take their own road, in some ways even more alone than when they had come. Pratt had reckoned to destroy their tribal past and shape them as individuals. There was something he didn't figure on, though: in order to standardize the children he had to unify them; in order to tear them away from their tribes, he had to make them part of something bigger; in order to rob them of their former identity, he had to give them a new one. They came from one tribe and became, as students, veterans, and alumni, members of another. "One time a girl asked me what tribe I belong to," mused one early student. "I stood still and thought what to say, then I said I belong to Carlisle tribe and I'll soon be America."[39]

If ever there was a figure who embodied an entire institution in his personal beliefs and bearing, that would be Carlisle founder Richard Henry Pratt. Pratt wasn't the first leader of an Indian boarding school, and he wouldn't be the last when, in 1904, he was summarily removed from his post for insubordination, an ironic fate for a career military man and fierce disciplinarian. Indian boarding schools still exist today, if in a far different form than what came to be known as the Carlisle Industrial School. But he remains the best known of any Indian school superintendent, a dubious distinction in the sometimes infamous annals of Native education.

Pratt's experience wasn't as an Indian educator but an Indian fighter. He rode against Cheyennes and Comanches on the southern plains, noting the prowess and tracking abilities of the Tonkawa scouts he commanded at Fort Griffin and Fort Sill. He marveled at how scouts could see things on the horizon with the unaided eye that he couldn't make out with a pair of field binoculars. And he was impressed by the deliberate, if ruthless, way they could round up and break wild horses in the course of a single day. He saw how the mustangs could be tamed with shrewdness, diligence, and muscle and set his sights on corralling the Indian riders themselves if the opportunity ever presented itself.[40]

Before very long, it did. In 1875 he was posted to St. Augustine, Florida, to oversee a group of Indian prisoners—Apache, Comanche, Kiowa, and Cheyenne—at the old Spanish bastion of San Marcos, renamed Fort Marion. Pratt decided that rather than merely confine the prisoners, his stewardship would teach them skills they could use when their sentences were up. They learned to read and write, to sing hymns, to say the Lord's Prayer. He had them dress in military uniforms and even posted some of them as guards. He gave them meaningful work in crafts and trades—cutting shingles, baking bread, selling drawings, making bows and arrows for the tourist trade. After three years he accompanied several of the men to Hampton Institute in Virginia, an experimental school for African Americans that would be the bridge to his own idea for educating Indians at Carlisle.[41]

Most white people were calling for the punishment—or annihilation—of Indians in the aftermath of the Custer battle. Not so with Pratt, who, practically alone, was planning a way to educate them instead. In 1879 he regaled Carl Schurz, U.S. secretary of the interior, with an unlikely boast: "Give me 300 young Indians and a place in one of our best communities and let me prove it is easy to give Indian youth the English language, education, and industries that it is imperative they have in preparation for citizenship." But army officers were susceptible to empty boasting about Indians. Captain William Fetterman allegedly promised that, with a mere eighty soldiers, "he could ride through the entire Sioux nation"—before his command was wiped out in 1866. Lieutenant J. L. Grattan had said that with only thirty men he could whip all the Indians on the prairie—until, given those men, he led them to a violent doom in pursuit of High Forehead. But Pratt's brag was of a different order. He didn't vow to slay the fathers, only to educate the daughters and sons, even if that promise sounds patronizing more than a century later.[42]

Pratt was a pragmatist, and a shrewd one. He lectured Lakota parents about why a school was their only road to salvation: "Cannot you see that [your children] will be of great value to you if after a few years they come back from school with the ability to read and write letters for you, interpret for you, and help look after your business affairs in Washington?" Indians, it seemed, would need interpreters to keep from being robbed by people who looked and dressed exactly like Pratt. He knew that for Lakotas, language was the most important tool—or weapon—in the struggle to keep their homeland. "If you had been educated," he implored, "you might be helping to make the laws that take care of us in these United States." But the laws were another thing altogether, and lawyers were not what Carlisle would make of Indian students—they would become blacksmiths and tailors, farmers and tinsmiths, cooks and seamstresses, if they could even find work to begin with. Beyond learning the times table and patriotic poems, their status, even if the Captain hoped otherwise, would be second rate.[43]

Pratt knew all, observed all, and determined all from his perch overlooking the main quad at Carlisle. He and his wife, Anna Laura, lived in the spacious, porticoed superintendent's quarters, built in the early nineteenth century and renovated later, on the east side of campus. Though abandoned for some years, their Carlisle lodgings were a sight more respectable than the frontier quarters they had known in the army. At Carlisle they raised a son and three daughters (one of the girls named Richenda, for her father), a crew that would eventually bring twenty-one grandchildren into the family fold. Anna Laura would sometimes accompany her husband in his forays to find new students; she had even helped teach Indian prisoners how to read at Fort Marion in the days before Carlisle. Captain Pratt was only a short stroll away from the frame gazebo on the quad, his preferred observation post for surveilling his Native scholars; the superintendent was warily referred to in the school papers as "the man in the bandstand."[44]

The Captain was a man of two minds: a racist in his complete faith in the superiority of white, Christian culture but a vigorous advocate of the assimilation and equality of his Native charges. He was a military officer, a product of rank and hierarchy, who settled on a subversive, egalitarian idea that he waved in the face of the public with all the confidence of a man wielding a Colt Peacemaker: the people he had warred against on the frontier could, in time, be made the match of any American, at least any average one. If "Kill the Indian in him and save the man" is the infamous motto we remember him by, the unspoken corollary is no less important: if the man was indeed saved, the children of Red Cloud could improve the lot of their people and stand as relative equals with their white brethren.[45]

Pratt was a mercurial man—scolding one minute, cheerleading the next. He approved of humiliating Clarence before a classroom of peers, only to later choose him for an important mission to Philadelphia. He once asked young Edgar Fire Thunder, an apprentice blacksmith, to make a welcoming speech to a group of several dozen congressional dignitaries. Edgar launched into the story of how he came to the school, recounting his long journey, when suddenly he became tongue-tied before his audience, stammered badly, and came to a crashing halt in front of them all, the victim of a severe case of stage fright in a language he hadn't yet mastered. Pratt, who had been listening, stepped in and suggested that Edgar put on his apron and meet them in the blacksmith shop, where he would show them how to weld an axle. A delegation member later noted how gracefully he rescued the boy and gave him a chance to show his mettle by means of his own two hands—which he subsequently did—using the eloquent vernacular of hammer and anvil.[46]

Others didn't earn the same sympathy. Asa Daklugie, a Mescalero Apache, was the son of Juh, chief of what was, by many accounts, the most recalcitrant group of Apaches the U.S. cavalry encountered in their years of search and destroy warfare. Asa wasn't the kind of man-child who took to personal intimidation, even from the commandant. A nephew of Geronimo, he rode with the famous medicine man before surrendering to the army in 1886. Shipped eastward to Florida in the forced exile of the defeated Apaches, he was, as a young prisoner of war, rerouted to Carlisle, where he arrived in December of 1886, ostensibly all of twelve years old. Since Carlisle assigned ages to children who appeared to have no precise idea when they were born, he was probably several years older than that. Daklugie was only four feet eight and ninety-three pounds when he got to Pratt's school, his home for the next nine years. They cut his hair, which hung down to his knees. He was taught household chores, including how to make a bed. He was given a name he hated—Asa, a moniker he altered to Ace later in life. He liked the regimen of sports and military discipline the school offered, but it was hardly a strain for a boy who knew what it was to plunge into an icy stream to take a cold-water bath and then be forced to do it over again—or be hit with a switch by his uncle Geronimo. He preferred dueling with knives to the boxing matches at Carlisle, which seemed, from his training, slow and ineffective.[47]

One day Asa was sent to Pratt's office as punishment for disobeying a teacher. After the door was closed behind him, the Captain locked it, grabbed a whip, and approached the student. Ever the defiant warrior, Daklugie grabbed the whip and tossed it away. When Pratt shook him by the collar, the boy picked the Captain up and dangled him in the air like a flimsy scarecrow, only setting him down after a thorough shaking. "I could break your neck with my bare hands," the Apache boy warned him. Pratt's manner changed immediately. He addressed Asa politely and even laughed at their predicament. After Daklugie agreed to treat the teacher with respect, the two parted on amicable terms, and Asa was never reprimanded again. He must have been a lot taller by then than the four feet eight he arrived at, but such incidents with Pratt were telling—the superintendent was a bullying martinet possessed of a strong paternal streak but capable of both belligerence and compassion.[48]

Though Daklugie arrived two years after Clarence departed Carlisle, his tour overlapped with that of the future Mrs. Three Stars, Jennie Dubray. By the time the young Apache left in 1895, the school had almost eight hundred students. He became an Indian scout at Fort Sill, where he made thirty dollars a month and wrote, years later, "I am doing well and supporting my family and using the Carlisle's education." Asa's sudden and fierce rebellion softened over time. He would develop a grudging respect for the father of Carlisle and later request to have his two daughters educated there.[49]

God was the Father. The President of the United States was the Great Father. And Captain Pratt was the father they all knew—beloved and feared, admired and resented, obeyed and resisted—the "man in the bandstand" who could see and hear everything that happened, even, perhaps, when they were asleep and dreaming.

The summer of 1882 found Clarence doing stoop labor in the wheat fields of nearby York. "I get sore hands but I get well, and getting hard and rough, so just like farm mans hands," he wrote in a letter to school. He recounted working in the fields until he was attacked by a swarm of bees and had to frantically fight them off. Published in one of the school papers, the letter reads like a story from a primer that Carlisle students would have copied from: "That bee wants to bit me but cannot do it. I make fun with that bee. That bee bit a dog. That dog was running away." He was flexing a small muscle that would one day prove strong, testing his English in the world outside the seven-foot picket fence of Carlisle.[50]

Clarence was an early participant in the "outing" program that was Pratt's pride and joy in his mission to integrate Indian youth into the larger world. The idea of "outing" Indian students didn't originate with Pratt—in the English colonies it dated as far back as the Puritans—but he experimented with the practice before Carlisle even opened. His experience managing Indian prisoners at Fort Marion taught him that supervised labor could mold character and create incentive better than strict confinement could ever hope to. Prisoners who picked oranges, rowed tourists, sawed lumber, and dug up palmetto roots at the old fort convinced the Captain that daily work could be the bridge from a segregated education to integration and triumph in the world beyond. Some of the prisoners followed him to the Hampton Institute in Virginia and later to Carlisle as "trusty" monitors and disciplinarians.[51]

The outing philosophy, crystallized in the first years of Carlisle, was called "the planting out" in official parlance. The practice amounted to a modestly paid summer apprenticeship, usually in a nearby rural community, and only recommended for more advanced students. Though it took a while for the practice to become widespread, over one hundred of the best students had undertaken the outing on local farms during the first two years. A primary aim was to improve English skills in a natural setting far removed from the classroom; as students were sent out alone or in pairs, they encountered a level of language immersion that couldn't be enforced in the dorms. A two- or three-month sojourn also encouraged independence of spirit and self-reliance, important traits, it was thought, in breaking tribal bonds. Students were paid from one to fifteen dollars per month, half the money put in their hands, half deposited in a bank account and not redeemable until they left school. As Pratt put it, the outing would "give lessons in economy and thrift" that would last a lifetime, not to mention that it cut school costs since the employers paid expenses and wages. Finally, the practice served to keep students in the orbit of school for the summer months rather than returning them to family and home, where they were prone to take up bad habits like attending tribal dances or speaking their native tongues.[52]

The ritual, as indeed ritual it became, was a calculated risk. Many students came back frustrated after a few days or weeks, though Pratt claimed the practice a success from the outset. Patrons were carefully screened—given questionnaires, interviewed, and monitored—and later supervised, as far as was possible, almost as closely as participating students. Many employers were older couples who maintained a strong relationship with students long after their time together was over. But while Pratt touted the outing as a model experience, there were disasters, too: violence against students, alcohol abuse, compromised health, even pregnancy.[53]

The outing was voluntary, at least in principle, but the rules that governed it hardened with time. By century's end, Carlisle boys who applied for the experience were required to sign a paper itemizing a raft of prohibitions that would have made the Ten Commandments seem relaxed—in essence, a labor contract for adolescents. Correspondence with Indian girls was prohibited. Pupils had to attend church, if available. Tobacco and liquor were taboo. Bathing was required twice a week. The outing period could only be shortened with Pratt's consent, and changing jobs was forbidden without his approval. Pupils were expected to save up to three quarters of their wages, remitted to the Captain by mail. It was a rigid inventory of rules that made Pratt superintendent, chief bursar, and father confessor all at once. "Failure to carry out these requirements will be cause for ending our relations," he warned his cadets. He was a man for whom fallen virtue called up visions of exile and rank dishonor.[54]

The field experience often wasn't related to one's school trade, and so Clarence, who apprenticed as a tailor, did his outing on a farm and machine shop the summer of 1882. His employer was Michael Schall, a gentleman farmer who not only employed young Three Stars but leant him money. The next year the Captain remitted to Schall the tidy sum of $5.89 for a debt Clarence incurred the previous summer. The boy had worked off the debt in the tailor shop, Pratt offered, continuing, "The lesson [for him] has been valuable and will last during life." Perhaps he was right, because balancing books and tending store were both vocations in Clarence's future. But little in the outing could be taken for granted. Pratt was irked that the summer with Schall wasn't well spent since Clarence couldn't improve his English after spending so much time with what turned out to be a German-speaking family: "It is quite an objection if the parties speak other than the English language," the Captain griped. Such a lapse would never have been allowed at school, but life beyond Garrison Lane was full of surprises.[55]

We don't know how eagerly Clarence set off for Carlisle; we do know that he elected to stay there when given the chance to leave. Once their initial three-year tour of duty was complete, "scholars," as they were called, could choose to remain an additional two, which Pratt encouraged as a way to advance the school mission. While most Lakota children from the initial "class" of 1879 chose to return home after three years, many eventually came back. And five of the original students stayed on without any break at all, including Clarence, Luther, and (probably) Edgar. They had, after all, taken their first holy communion together, Episcopalians all. Standing Bear acknowledged that his father's advice that he learn as much as he could about the white man's ways figured in his decision. Luther, in fact, was the only one not to follow the departing group as far as Harrisburg to bid them goodbye, and for a few hours he regarded himself as the only Lakota student at Carlisle. This was probably the first significant decision any of them had ever made on their own.[56]

Pratt informed Uncle Three Stars about Clarence's decision to stay, but only after-the-fact: "It was arranged with the consent of his friends and at his own desire that Clarence should stay two or three years longer and perfect his education," he wrote him. In fact, the Captain neither wanted nor needed permission for Clarence to stay. "There seems to be no good reason why a change should be made and he return this year.

He is getting on so well that it would be a great pity to have him forfeit his opportunity." Though Pratt signed the letter "your friend," his tenor was more condescending than comforting. Clarence was almost nineteen years old by this time and capable of thinking for himself. But the break with Pine Ridge was clear, and the boy who had left the agency with his hair in braids and wrapped in a blanket was now a sophisticated man of the world, or at least of the Cumberland Valley.[57]

The schoolroom was, at first, an alien place for Clarence and his kind. Just as his grandfather High Forehead and many like him refused to be jailed or confined, sometimes dying in defiance, many Indian children of later generations regarded the boarding school, and even day schools, as places of detention and dishonor. Some Indian parents, like Geronimo and the Comanche war leader Quanah Parker, wanted their children to go to school. But that didn't mean they went willfully. Not all students ran away from school, either—some even tried to escape *to* it to gain status and material comfort. In some cases, boarding schools became an alternative to the extended family where children could be sent because they would be fed, clothed, housed, and free of family traumas.[58]

Eventually, families didn't have much of a choice. Compulsory school attendance for Indian children was enacted in 1891, and at some agencies it was practiced even earlier. Of course, attendance was required at public schools across the country, but Indian parents were under extreme pressure to comply. They knew all too well that withholding children might instigate a brusque visit from the agency police in search of truants or, even more alarming, an end of rations for the entire family. Some parents hid their children, others offered up orphans in their place, and a few surrendered a weaker or less capable child that wasn't as promising as the others in their attempt to foil officials while seeming to cooperate. Only in 1893 was parental consent required for sending children off reservation.[59]

Clarence's cohort, the first at Carlisle, was an ambitious trial run for the thousands of children who followed in their wake. Even now the memory of boarding schools is a bitter one in Native communities, a system that wasn't seriously reformed until the 1970s. Students were often hectored by teachers, bullied by peers, struck or beaten for minor transgressions, and even sexually abused by authorities; they were also often desperately homesick. Short of overt rebellion, resistance took milder forms like complaining, indulging in mischief, maintaining silence, or taking unexcused leave when school days weren't exactly something to write home about. Boys formed gangs for purposes of self-defense. Some showed defiance by running away (even multiple times, known as "incorrigibles" or "chronic runners") or committing arson, like the two unhappy Carlisle girls who attempted to torch their dormitory in 1897.[60]

Over its thirty-nine-year history, some 1,800 students went AWOL from Carlisle, the vast majority male and a third of them successfully. The first desertion was in 1883, during Clarence's tenure, but only seventeen were counted during the first decade. The numbers steadily increased from there, until, by the early twentieth century, about one hundred might decamp in any given year. Some left, never to be heard from again, even by their families. Some ran away in groups. Many were caught and returned to school to be punished and disenrolled. As an added disincentive, the school billed families for costs incurred retrieving their sons and daughters, and students who deserted even forfeited the money they had in their bank accounts. There was no typical runaway. Some went back to their families, had a change of heart, and grew nostalgic about Carlisle as the years went on, and like Asa Daklugie, they sought to send their own children there. But Carlisle could be dark and unbending too. The advertisements for later runaways sound like wanted posters for fugitive slaves: "Thomas is a full blood Indian with straight black hair and dark eyes, short and stocky with a full round face," noted a special school bulletin. "His age is 18 years . . . Thomas likes Wild West shows and it is our supposition that he may have joined a show. I enclose a franked envelope which you can use if you have any information."[61]

Still, it would be a mistake to think that Carlisle and schools like it were universally hated. Many students, far from opposing the school routine, accommodated themselves and embraced the new order. Luther Standing Bear became an eager convert, recruiting and interpreting for Pratt, leading the school band on out-of-town forays, playing taps on his bugle every night, becoming a walking advertisement for boarding school success. Others took a more pragmatic approach and devoted themselves to learning what they could for the sake of self-improvement or even tribal gain, taking Pratt's advice that a good education was the best hedge against incompetent or malevolent officials.[62]

Many were those who both resented the Carlisle Way and welcomed it, a paradox students might carry with them for a lifetime. Some abandoned the school but regretted their decision later. Others pined bitterly for home during their tour—but ended up sending away their own children to be educated, a decision that played out in boarding schools across the country and would one day bear on Clarence himself. Indian students may have chafed at the tenor of military discipline, but many were those who valued a system that gave competitive honors. And others would find that becoming literate was, however punishing and laborious, a useful tool for transcribing and preserving oral beliefs, legends, and tribal traditions. Clarence Three Stars was exactly this kind of accommodationist—careful but curious, respectful of tradition but determined to enhance it.[63]

What Carlisle had given him of value was invisible, perhaps, but invisible in just the way blood is.

On January 16, 1880, Abraham Lincoln died. It happened right there on Carlisle campus. No bullet through the brain had felled him. No assassin with a pistol burst through the door and onto the balcony box. No one hurled himself from the box and fled on foot, no funeral cortege bore the body into the heartland to be wept over by thousands of grieving mourners. No, the descent into death was silent and gradual, a case of pneumonia followed by spinal meningitis. Abe, as he was known—sixteen years old and son of Cheyenne chief Antelope, no. 89 on the official Carlisle roster—was buried in the school cemetery.[64]

The next December two Lakota children, Ernest White Thunder and Maud Swift Bear, passed away. Measles and scarlet fever caused several more deaths during the winter of 1881. In 1884 six children perished from, in Pratt's words, "disease of long standing," and thirty-six more were sent home for failing health, some never to recover. In 1887 it was seven deaths from tuberculosis. The next year Pratt reported twenty-one more, most of them Apache disciplinarians who had followed him from Fort Marion, and all from consumption, though he offered in his official report, as he often did to parents, that many were already weak when they arrived at Carlisle. "Other than that," he beamed, "the health of the school has never been better."[65]

Indian boarding schools were breeding grounds for infectious disease. Inadequate diet, overcrowding, lack of professional medical care, and absence of quarantine procedure doomed many children, already disoriented and homesick, to an early death. Carlisle seems to have offered a healthier environment than most, but financial imperatives could be counterproductive. Since budgets only increased with enrollment, schools like Carlisle had an extra incentive to recruit even more students, sometimes stretching capacity and increasing the likelihood of spreading infection. Pratt's domain was far from the only one. Haskell Institute, in Kansas, for example, counted one hundred deaths in fewer than thirty years. And many students were afflicted by diseases that, if they didn't kill outright, hobbled their victims for a lifetime, not least of them trachoma, a widespread infection that could lead to loss of sight.[66]

Since rumors of death tarnished Carlisle's reputation, dozens of children were sent home after falling sick (if they were not too ill to travel in the first place), diminishing the school mortality rate. Even then, Pratt could be stubborn about sending them home, so determined was he to shape their future. He told Chief Big Bull of his son, who had survived a case of whooping cough, "We do not want him to die here any more than you do . . . but he has recovered from that now and I should not like to recommend that he be sent home, without there was some good reason for it." Young John Bull was something of a success story, it turned out, when he was discharged for ill health three years later and became an Indian chief of police in Oklahoma.[67]

For others, fate wasn't so obliging. In the early years, Pratt kept a vigorous correspondence with families who lost children at Carlisle. To Chief White Thunder he described the funeral of his son Ernest, dressed in shirt, collar, and necktie, surrounded with flowers and borne to the school chapel in a coffin by six of his best Lakota friends. They sang hymns and listened as the pastor told Ernest's peers that one day they would have to die too.

The four-page letter is exhaustive and heartfelt, though Pratt couldn't stop from proselytizing even then: "I want you to learn about the good book and what it says . . . because it is that book which makes the white people know so much as they do." He deflected any blame by telling the grieving father that Ernest was sick before he came to Carlisle and that "he was not a wise boy and did not try to take care of his health. I only say these things to help you see it in what I think is the right way."[68]

In December of 1883 he wrote to inform Road Traveller at Cheyenne/Arapaho agency that his daughter Leah had died. When she came to school "her whole body was filled with malarial poison," Pratt recounts, and she was too sick to send home. She died, after a temporary recovery, of uremic poisoning. The Captain reports they put a stone on her grave with her name on it, "the same as we do with our own children." There is the obligatory reference to the Great Spirit and the comfort that Leah was "relieved from all the sin and hardness of this world," which should make her father's sorrow very short. The missives are a strange brew, at once earnest and self-serving, Victorian form letters that mingle deep compassion with exculpatory excuses and religious badgering.[69]

By the time Clarence left Carlisle, over thirty of his fellow students had died. Official records show that when the school closed in 1918 some fifty Apache youth had perished, twenty-four Sioux, and seventeen Cheyenne—a lengthy roll call that included the children of approximately fifty tribes. Of some eight thousand boys and girls who would enter through the gates on Garrison Lane, over two hundred would never leave the school alive, some reburied today at the edge of the old campus after the original cemetery was moved.[70]

When he walked out of the school gates for his annual outing in March of 1884, Clarence was a survivor. He was twenty years old and had done five years at Carlisle. He had the equivalent of a fourth- or fifth-grade education. He was on his way to the big city, another trip on the magical Iron Road. Though he couldn't have known it, he wouldn't be coming back to Carlisle any time soon.

4

Philadelphia

Clarence Three Stars and Luther Standing Bear's arrival in Philadelphia one day in early spring may have fetched no mention in the local newspapers, but two young Indian men from the Dakota Territory emerging from beneath the Gothic spires of Broad Street Station would have been almost as unlikely a sighting as a white elephant. The day the young men alighted from the train, March 18, 1884, was cloudy and breezy, a Tuesday it so happened, the temperature reaching a balmy fifty-six degrees. Saint Patrick's Day had come and gone the day before, culminating in the Hibernian Society's grand dinner at Horticultural Hall. That morning, the papers reported, the secretary of the Episcopal Church Temperance Association spoke to six hundred machinists of the Philadelphia and Reading Railroad about reducing liquor licenses. The police department complained of choked gutters and a large hole in front of the Colonnade Hotel. George Trenwith, arraigned for murder, appeared in court and "seemed perfectly cool, and even smiled once or twice." While riding a streetcar on Eighth Street, the unfortunate Michael Mack was robbed of a pocketbook containing $1,340, the *Inquirer* reported. And so it turned out, a white elephant was indeed soon to be exhibited at the Forepaugh three-ring circus downtown, later called a fraud by no less an authority on that subject than P. T. Barnum. It was life as usual in the City of Brotherly Love. Only two months earlier the new hall of the Improved Order of Red Men opened on Race Street, an exclusive fraternity using "Indian" rituals where neither Clarence nor Luther would have been allowed to step through the front door because they didn't have the good fortune of being Caucasian.[1]

They had come from school to city on a kind of gamble. Only days before, Captain Pratt had approached Luther with a plum job offer: the chance to work in the Philadelphia department store of John Wanamaker, arguably the most famous commercial emporium in America. Wanamaker, ever on the outlook to make a philanthropic gesture, requested two Indian boys to work in the store, an offer his friend Pratt was eager to accept. To date, the Carlisle outing had been largely confined to rural environs, but this was a chance to give it an urban, cosmopolitan cast more befitting the Gilded Age. Pratt chose Standing Bear and gave him permission to choose a companion. But the stakes would be high, he warned: "My boy, you are going away from us to work for this school, in fact, for your whole race," he told Luther. "If you are a failure, then we might as well close up this school. . . . Go, my boy, and do your best. Die there if necessary, but do not fail." The Captain laid a burden on the boy so weighty that Standing Bear almost burst into tears.[2]

Luther had to search his heart to settle on a worthy chum, but it didn't take very long. He went to Pratt and told him, in no uncertain terms, "I want Clarence Three Stars." A fellow Lakota and distant family relation, the boy told him, Clarence had known difficulty at Carlisle but was trying hard to do his best. It wasn't long after that Luther and Clarence set off on the eastbound train from Carlisle accompanied by a doctor and a Sunday school teacher as chaperones.[3]

They disembarked that March day in Philadelphia, a place far removed from the city William Penn founded—far removed even from the one Benjamin Franklin settled in after fleeing his indenture as a Boston printer. It was another magnitude of change for Clarence, a city of close to a million souls that would have made Carlisle seem like a trifling burg in just the way Carlisle had made Red Cloud Agency seem little more than a fortified prairie ranch. It was a city of great wealth—home of yachts, private trains, and castles—but also one where close to one in ten people was on outdoor relief and four thousand more were boarded in the city almshouse on any given day. The city had dozens of bustling public markets and modern conveniences like drinking fountains and professional sports teams, like the Philadelphia Phillies, who still play there today. The city was in transition from its Quaker founding and revolutionary glory to a world filled with modern ambitions marked by a thick coat of soot, grease, grit, and grime. The towering monument of City Hall, crafted in ornate Second Empire style, had already been started a dozen years before Clarence arrived and wouldn't be finished until a decade after he left. He and Luther walked through the looming colossus that first day.[4]

The Workshop of the World, as Philadelphia came to be known, had become an industrial Goliath—sprawling railroad yards, coal depots, shipyards that ran for miles along the Delaware River, a crossroads of commerce and manufacture. It was a Dickensian sort of place, with the wild scramble of lives—rich and poor jostled together on the ordered north-south grid laid out by Penn between the Delaware and Schuylkill Rivers—overlaid with the rough-and-tumble expansion of an Iron Age city flexing its muscle. By the time Clarence arrived, Chestnut Street already had electric lighting. The city would soon be shipping 35 percent of U.S. petroleum exports. It led the nation in the manufacture of train locomotives, and its horse-drawn street cars led all American cities by 1880, carrying 117 million passengers in a single year by the middle of the decade. Clarence would take a streetcar to work at Wanamaker's, one of thousands of city dwellers who could sleep in the suburbs and still make good time to the city center before the coming of the automobile.[5]

The Gilded Age Quaker city had once been no stranger to Native people. The Lenni-Lenape settled the area centuries before and had extended a friendly hand to Penn. During its decade as the federal capital, the city hosted eastern tribal delegations, and even after the capital migrated south in 1800, tribal visitors would often stop on their way to Washington. The Quaker fathers and mothers had allied themselves to Indian causes, and the Indian Rights Association, a humanitarian organization dedicated to making citizens of Native people, was founded in town in 1882. Even so, a pair of dark-skinned Indian laborers like Three Stars and Standing Bear would have stuck out in a city dotted with English, German, Irish, and Balkan enclaves. Race prejudice was widespread. African Americans, who made up the city's most visible minority, were banned from joining trade unions and limited to domestic jobs and unskilled labor. It was only in 1884, the year Clarence arrived, that a Black man was appointed to the police force amid considerable controversy.[6]

Carlisle had hardly been a healthy sanctuary, and Penn's city would prove no better. The nineteenth century saw epidemics of typhus, dysentery, smallpox, and yellow fever sweep the city. The week before Clarence arrived, seventy-seven people died of consumption and twenty-one more of typhoid fever, the typhoid rate exceeding that of all American cities. Sanitation was sketchy. The cobbled streets, five hundred miles of them, were hard to clean. People of means preferred not to drink the city water and bought spring water when they could. About 15 percent of buildings had water closets, while the rest were equipped with outside "privies," and night soil was a common fertilizer. Smallpox victims had to give their consent before they could be quarantined. The city would only remove small animal carcasses from the street, while the removal of dead horses, often left to rot, was entrusted to the whim of private citizens. Given the prominence of epidemics, the board of health decreed that corpses had to be buried at least eight feet underground in city cemeteries. And as one might expect, quack home remedies were all the rage. Cod liver oil and lime were considered a fitting tonic for consumption. Radway's Ready Relief Pills were said to cure malaria, diarrhea (in "fifteen or twenty minutes"), pleurisy, typhoid fever, lumbago, neuralgia, and sleeplessness—but the promise was often an idle one, and at twenty-five cents a box.[7]

Almost greater than the dread of silent killers was the fear of fire, a frequent fate for buildings with timbered interiors and wooden floors where an old rag or stray match could set the night ablaze. In 1884 alone flames ravaged the flour warehouse of E. Lathbury; the hosiery mill of J. R. Bridges; the chemical works of Powers and Weightman; the Falls of Schuylkill brewery; the malt house of Frederick Fischer; the biscuit bakery of George Jones; and Carr and Crawley's hardware. The fire call boxes on city streets were scarce and ineffective, so much so that the "telegraph" alarm system often proved faulty, making the prospect of billowing flames and the tardy city engine company a common sight. The Crew Levick Oil Company, the Clark Brothers furniture factory, and George Miller and Son confectioners all burned to cinders that year too. And that's not to mention the old Chestnut Street skating rink, used by John Wanamaker for storage, that went up in flames, alongside Phelan's lumber yard, on August 1 with losses estimated at $160,000.[8]

This was the city they came to, Clarence and Luther, youthful ambassadors for Pratt and his dream of racial integration. For all that must have been marvelous about the city, nothing could have been more spellbinding than the glory of Wanamaker's itself, where they would work for the foreseeable future. The main store was just east of City Hall, and there they were greeted that first day by William Wanamaker, John's brother. Three Stars had been to Wrightstown and York for previous outings, but the Philadelphia assignment was special. If Carlisle was an experiment in disciplined education, so Wanamaker's would be a workingman's trial by fire, a test of two young men abruptly dumped into the cauldron of city life without family or tribal ties. In many ways their experience would anticipate, by more than half a century, the Indian Relocation Act, which moved reservation Indians to urban areas after the Second World War. Brother Wanamaker dispatched Luther to the invoice department and Clarence to shipping.[9]

Alas, they were menial jobs. Clarence's work as a tailor would have stood him in good stead for something better—if better was the word for those who plied his trade in the city. Philadelphia led the nation in cloth production; the industry would soon employ 35 percent of workers citywide. But cloth workers toiled in creaky attics and grimy sweatshops for sixty hours a week—it would take another two decades to get their work week shortened—earning just a dollar a day. Child laborers numbered in the thousands, a practice that wouldn't have surprised a young man once described by Pratt as the "best tailor" at Carlisle, a calling he undertook at school before he reached his majority. The movement for compulsory schooling in America, in fact, was partly an attempt to break the grip of child labor, which Carlisle and other boarding schools exploited to great advantage. Three Stars, who started cutting cloth at sixteen, knew only too well that labor and learning went hand in hand in the land of Wanamaker and Pratt.[10]

Schooled as they were in the virtues of military restraint, Clarence and Luther had to accustom themselves to a strange new world. The Carlisle school physician arranged for them to board and study at the Boys' Educational Home, an extension of a school known as the Lincoln Institute that offered a primary education for Indian boys on the far side of the Schuylkill, at Forty-Ninth and Greenway. At first they rode a wagon with other students to their jobs across the river, but they switched to the streetcar line when they heard, in Luther's words, "the rough, profane language which these boys used on their way to work." The decorum of Carlisle had been strict and unforgiving—but the conditions they would soon find at the boarding house and school would be enough to make most boys nostalgic for the parade ground and early morning roll calls in the meticulous house that Pratt built.[11]

Few names in the history of American commerce have the resonance of John Wanamaker, founder and owner of one of the great American stores that would revolutionize the way consumers shopped across the country. The department store, where middle-class men and women could find goods shipped from around the world at a standard price in a convenient urban setting, would change the way retail business was done in the Gilded Age and long after. Given his special role as Carlisle envoy, Clarence surely met Wanamaker during his stay. Working at the store was a formative experience for a young Lakota—a scenario he never could have imagined as a boy growing up near the White River—as he grappled with the crowded and confusing and sometimes frightening streets of a big city. His employer, Mr. Wanamaker, was to nineteenth-century Philadelphia what Ben Franklin had been to eighteenth-century Philadelphia—a civic father renowned for charity, an aptitude for the bottom line, and an unshakable belief in the triumph of technology.

Born in 1838 in Philadelphia, the store founder worked his way up in the retail clothing industry while organizing the Bethany Sunday school and becoming a salaried secretary of the Young Men's Christian Association (YMCA) at age twenty. His frail health prevented him from serving in the army during the Civil War, and in 1861 he opened his first clothing store, in the heart of the city. In the 1860s and '70s he pioneered or developed many of the concepts that modern shoppers would come to take for granted—fixed prices, full cash refunds with the return of goods, copyrighted newspaper advertising, restaurant space in a retail house, summer vacations for employees, a mail-order bureau, foreign buyers—and the list doesn't end there. Only a few years after young Clarence would leave, elevators were installed. Though Wanamaker had eminent American rivals like Marshall Field in Chicago and Rowland Macy in New York, he developed and standardized many of the conveniences that shoppers still expect 150 years later.[12]

In 1876 Wanamaker opened the Grand Depot, the store where Clarence and Luther went to work, at Thirteenth and Market Streets on the site of the old Pennsylvania Railroad Freight Depot. As many as seventy thousand people were said to have attended the official opening. According to local lore, General Ulysses S. Grant was said to have remarked, "It takes as much generalship to organize a business like this as to organize an army." In 1878 the Grand Depot became the first store to be lit by electricity through the use of twenty-eight arc lamps and eight dynamos; the next year the Bell telephone was introduced in the store; and in 1880 pneumatic tubes were employed to transfer cash, yet another business first. By the time Clarence started work in 1884, the store had close to two thousand employees, the workforce of an institution that must have made Carlisle's inner workings seem quaint. The nephew of old Three Stars had to have been staggered by the wealth and opulence so casually displayed in a store that covered more than four acres.[13]

And what a store it was! The facade was a stylish blend of Scheherazade and urban warehouse, with Moorish arches and crenellated towers fronting the old edifice. On the ground floor the railroad freight house had been transformed by Wanamaker into a department store worthy of a mad geometer, with a hub at the center and broad aisles for pedestrian shoppers that radiated outward like the spokes of a giant wheel. Each aisle that moved outward from the center was lined with counters strewn with merchandise and organized into departments with names like "Linen Sheeting," "Laces," "Gloves," "Ribbons," and "Silks." The counters were lined with stools where shoppers could sit and handle merchandise. It was a vast indoor marketplace that matched the ambitions of the Industrial Age, tolerating nothing of the lazy patchwork of stalls in traditional markets. The chatter of buying and selling echoed throughout the high-ceilinged structure, sounds that were like nothing the Lakota boys had ever heard, from the thunder of a summer prairie storm to the thumping drum of an Omaha dance. All aisles met at the central hub, much the way, in fact, that the panopticon in the middle of the main quad was the observation center of Carlisle life. The design of the first floor, with an almost cosmological clarity, radiated from toilet soaps and valises to calicoes, plain cottons, and cashmeres. The farther one walked from the heart of the store, the more ample the stock and impressive the view. The depot at the corner of Thirteenth and Market was a buyer's paradise run by a mogul who wanted to please everyone he could, most certainly including God, and to carry away a healthy reward in the doing.[14]

The store sold books, razors, and bath robes; muslins and musical instruments; fine wool plaids, ginghams, and gold jewelry; macintoshes and slippers and notions and feathers and toys and china; not to mention silverware, clocks, and carpets; perfumes and powders and face creams. It was Wanamaker who had offered monetary prizes for an employee essay contest on the subject "What Is the Best Way to Wait on a Customer?" The prizewinner insisted the employee owed true loyalty to both her employer and her customer, a dictum that implored those waiting on the public to ceaselessly practice the Golden Rule, whether in dispensing ladies' accessories or directing a panicky soul to the Lost and Found department. Wanamaker had infused a large organization with a utilitarian (and profitable) credo of public service, all of it wrapped in a philosophy that emanated Christian benevolence. The store down the street from City Hall was, with all due apologies to church history, a kind of civil and commercial monastery.[15]

Brother Wanamaker was the abbot in charge. "The store must be a pleasant resort, not a trap," he advised. "The advertising must be carefully prepared news; visitors must be secure from importunity; employes must be trained in the new system, and in the law of courtesy; and mail orders must be filled by shoppers instructed to think only of the customer's wishes." The man who was practically the darling of Philadelphia believed that fixed prices on hats and shoes and the returnability of goods resembled an immutable physical law "as sure as that which impels the apple to the earth or the needle to the Pole." The sale of books, paintings, and musical instruments had expanded the reach of the arts until "every home ha[d] been put in closer touch with civilization," he exhorted, while boasting, just in case people didn't fully get it, that the Wanamaker system had gallantly liberated women from "the drudgery of the needle."[16]

Clarence toiled in the Wanamaker system as he had at Carlisle. He'd given up his tailor's scissors and was now delivering goods in the shipping department, spending occasional days at Oak Hall, a sister store that specialized in men's clothing. What could he compare to these days of wonder? The tiny sutler's store at Red Cloud where he might have seen a dusty pile or two of gingham and calico? The lively horse trading his people did when they gathered for the Sun Dance every summer? The depot on Market Street was almost bigger than the sky, as loud and splendid as the largest herd of ponies he'd ever set eyes on. Wanamaker's was to offer him a lesson in commercial ethics, too, one that would inform his professional career for years to come. One price for all. Full refunds for returns. Debit balances to be paid monthly, echoing Pratt's fixation with settling accounts. And the customer was (almost) always right. Given the Wanamaker ethic, it's no surprise that Three Stars would later deplore such Indian agency practices as skimping on rations, fudging numbers, tipping scales, and the shoddy practices that shadowed much of the commodity trade on the reservation. In this year of his education, he was learning at the feet of a master. Wanamaker said of Clarence and Luther that they were "as industrious and as faithful as any employe in his service."[17]

And so John Wanamaker became one of the father figures that Clarence, fatherless from childhood, would come to admire. Wanamaker was a man as impressive as Pratt in both fortitude and achievement, and more ambitious still, devoted as he was to the divergent callings of commerce and of Christ. In fact, it turns out that the two men had many ties. Wanamaker's had issued the first suits and pants worn by Clarence's Carlisle cohort in 1879. More than thirty years later, the genial merchant wrote Pratt to wish him well on a fishing trip to Canada, predicting, on his return, "We shall all be so happy to see you back again in your old haunt, and no one more so than your old friend, John Wanamaker."[18]

Pratt was a steel-toed pragmatist; Wanamaker, a cagey romantic. The Captain ran his school like a military business with a sharp-edged bottom line; Wanamaker, for his part, orchestrated a bustling urban campus whose mission was to teach employees *and* customers how to live, work, and trade in a modern world. Both sat as the head of paternal institutions whose core mission was a kind of levelling equality where everyone merited the same treatment. Both were teachers in a larger sense, too, even missionaries—Pratt of racial equality and Indian citizenship, Wanamaker of virtuous profits and uniform consumer rights. They were founders of institutions emblematic of late nineteenth-century mass culture—and both embodied the hopes, and anxieties, of an age.

Years later, Pratt would boast of Clarence and Luther that "the short period they each spent under the influence of the push of Mr. Wanamaker's hive of industry did more to fit them for usefulness than ten years in the best Indian school that could be devised," a claim that offered grudging acknowledgment of Carlisle's own limitations. Keen to underline his ultimate goal, the Captain explained that such an experience would allow the boys to "hold their own among white men, which is, after all, to become the final lot of all Indians if the Government is ever to be freed from the care of them." The outing was an education all its own, sometimes in ways that even Pratt couldn't foresee.[19]

Mr. Wanamaker may have been the toast of Market Street, but one of his Indian apprentices was miserable. Clarence's charge was to visit sales departments and collect items destined for home delivery. But the job didn't take. He felt slighted when the clerks called him "Indian," a name that made him both resentful and homesick. After six months at the dreary task, he determined to write Pratt and ask for permission to leave.[20]

The Boys' Educational Home where he lived was a branch of the Lincoln Institute, founded as a refuge for orphaned children after the Civil War. By the 1880s the number of war orphans had diminished, and the benefactors of the home, including some of the wealthiest women in Philadelphia, settled on the noble cause of educating the American Indian. It was Pratt himself who inspired their decision when he brought a group of Carlisle boys to celebrate the Philadelphia bicentennial in 1882. The boys, who boarded at the Lincoln, so impressed the ladies that the mission of the institution took a sharp turn. The school opened to fifty Indian girls in 1883, many transferring from Carlisle, and the next year one hundred boys were admitted to the Educational Home, located on a ten-acre plot in west Philadelphia. As he had been at Carlisle, Clarence was among the first recruits.[21]

But the place where he now took his meals and studied in his spare time was anything but a home. A city inspector wrote, the very month Clarence left Philadelphia, that "the house was dirty and disorderly, the children rough and untrained, and the care-takers severe in manner and rude in speech. The slatternly servants and the extremely dirty kitchen were a disgrace to a low-wharf hotel." Even worse, the instruction was judged as inferior and the boys spent much of their time fighting. Further, scolded the inspector, there wasn't even a Bible in the large third-floor dormitory where most of the students slept. The only thing he was willing to recommend was the food, cold comfort for a place intended to civilize the poor Indian. It was a place that a young David Copperfield, perhaps even Oliver Twist, would have readily recognized.[22]

There was more. "The teaching is a feeble copy of public-school instruction," lamented the inspector. "These Indian boys, many of whom are grown men, strong and hearty, would learn to speak English more rapidly, and learn trades more quickly, if out on farms and mingling with the world." But Clarence had tried that two years before, only to be assigned to a German-speaking farmer who couldn't, or wouldn't, speak English. The Boys' Educational Home evaluator wondered, out of exasperation, why the children were there at all. "Poor teaching in the school-room," he concluded, "a sham of industrial training, and most of them getting a training in pauperism by this semi-idle life." Clarence was anything but idle at Wanamaker's, but this was the environment he returned to every evening.[23]

The boarding school resembled a vision of Carlisle gone bad—or, as some might say, Carlisle gone even worse. The report recommended the board "thoroughly test the pretensions of this Institution," but it was allowed to soldier on for years. Before the turn of the century, the Indian Rights Association reported the flogging, chaining, and beatings of students along with enforced silence at mealtimes and punitive isolation. One student attested that the Boys' Educational Home would promote the schoolwork of children who had been there for years as being the product of newer arrivals, or "show scholars," to boost the school's reputation. The discipline and training that enhanced Pratt's dominion, at least in some eyes, had been turned entirely to punitive ends. Congress finally cut off funding for the school in 1900, and students were transferred to Carlisle. The Institute had "educated" over a thousand Indian children, including Clarence, in the meantime. Three Stars would give different accounts of how long he boarded and "studied" there, once claiming a tenure of two years. He would later declare himself a graduate of the school, a somewhat dubious distinction but a status he had never achieved at Carlisle.[24]

Adrift and alone, Clarence wrote Pratt that he wanted to leave Philadelphia and return to Pine Ridge. He gave no explanation, but he was finished with school and work. Pratt first advised him to stay put and then thought better of it and agreed, reluctantly, that he could leave his job, but he asked him to stop at Carlisle on his way west. Clarence quietly refused the offer, informing him of his departure only after he had returned to Dakota Territory. It must have been a disappointment to the Captain, who hoped to have the young man direct the Carlisle tailors as head cutter. "Clarence's return was influenced by unrequited affection," he mysteriously wrote the Pine Ridge agent in 1884. But it's not clear who was unrequited—or why. "He was determined to quit, regardless of the reputation of the school or the race we belonged to," Standing Bear later grumbled. "I worked all the harder, just to let them know that not all Indians are quitters." Three Stars, then twenty years old, returned home as a boarding school walkaway, if not a runaway. He and Pratt had done a delicate dance of snub and salute, their familial bond frayed but not broken. From the Captain the young man had learned a sense of order, hope, and purpose, even if they came wrapped in a frigid parcel.

He had survived his foray into the white world but wanted out.[25]

He was finished with Carlisle. He was finished with Philadelphia. He was finished with education.

But he would come back, sooner or later, to all of them.

5

Coming Home

The same year young Three Stars stole back to Pine Ridge, 1884, the pedestal cornerstone for the Statue of Liberty was laid. Grover Cleveland was elected president. The Washington Monument was given a capstone, a landmark young Three Stars would see for himself in due time. The Panic of 1884 started a bank run on Wall Street, shuttering thousands of businesses nationwide. The Indian Census Act mandated that Indians on most reservations be counted and their names submitted by the local agent on an annual basis; Clarence would soon be enumerated as "#1735" on the Pine Ridge roll. The Supreme Court decided in *Elk v. Wilkins* that even Indians who claimed birthright citizenship and paid taxes were denied the right to vote. And in England, Mark Twain, whose very name the Lakota children unwittingly hollered when steaming down the Missouri on their way to Carlisle, published *Huckleberry Finn*, the tale of a boy who was soon to light out for the territory, headed in the same direction as Clarence, though the Carlisle walkaway was coming home a good deal better educated than Twain's restless fictional urchin from St. Petersburg, Missouri.[1]

The truth was that Three Stars had been proselytized by his years at Carlisle, even at the Lincoln Institute, but had proven an unfinished convert. He would take what was valuable from his education—some of it earned willingly, some of it not—and leave the rest for the sentiment of old school spirit. The most famous of Indian boarding schools, in fact, couldn't contain the grandson of High Forehead for long. Was English useful? He needed it to find a job. What about math? Wanamaker's taught him that a head for numbers would take him far in the world of work and money.

Without Pratt's direction, the course of his adult life was unimaginable. But he would go through life as a veteran of Carlisle, not a disciple.

The Pine Ridge he returned to was a raw place. Guns were common, and drunken rows led the agent to require all firearms be left at his office. A fence surrounded agency buildings and separated the village from the world outside. The paths that led to the small Episcopal Church were unpaved, and a small log schoolhouse stood nearby. Conveniences were just beginning to appear: a seventeen-thousand-gallon water tank was pumped by a wind engine into a well and distributed to administrative buildings via water mains. Perhaps most auspicious, the winter before Clarence returned, the new boarding school opened on a treeless, grassy plain within sight of the agency, a place that would figure large in the education of this ambivalent Carlisle recruit.[2]

With his long hair shorn, Clarence didn't look like many of his peers. It would be said years later that he returned "at a time when it was considered a disgrace for an Indian to wear a hat, trousers and shoes of the white man." It was only by "disregarding the taunts of his tribesmen," the observer continued, that he could pursue the path Carlisle prepared for him, even if he did so on his own terms. He knew how to read a book. He knew how to write a letter. He even knew what an elephant looked like. And he knew what it was to survive a journey to a different world and come home to tell of it—that is, if anyone would listen.[3]

Five years in the east had changed everything. He looked people in the eye now when he spoke to them. He knocked on a door before he opened it. When he pointed at something, he used his finger, not a lifted chin and pursed lips like the old people did. The Omaha dances he found shabby. He expected girls who had been to school to act in a Christian way. He talked more about history than fables and legends. His old name he put away like a wool blanket in summer. He didn't wear moccasins, talked a lot about the weather, and was inclined to heed the counsel of doctors. The things he owned clung fast to him, obdurate as a shadow, while the things he didn't were a nudge to work harder and make something better of his life, as Carlisle had gone to great pains to teach him.

His family—Uncle Three Stars, his mother, and grandmother (listed in the census as Smoke or Tobacco Smoke)—would have soon noted the changes in a boy who left home by steamer five years before. He was wearing shirts and pants. His Lakota was rough. He looked at camp food with a wary eye. He had left as an adolescent but returned as a man, and it was hard to know the details of exactly how it had happened. Packs the Dog was lost to them, perhaps forever. Clarence had come home in his stead. He lodged with his mother in a camp close to Three Stars, but the place wouldn't contain him for long. Pratt referred him to Agent McGillycuddy as a "competent boy," adding that "he has many good qualities and I trust you will be able to make use of him." But making use of him wouldn't be as easy as it sounded.[4]

The fact was that Clarence had logged more time brandishing a tailor's shears than a hunting bow. Even so, his long hours in the workshop hardly prepared him for the knowledge he would need to run a farm or store on Pine Ridge. Most returned male students searched in vain for reservation jobs that matched the skills they learned in boarding school. The need for tailors was negligible since the government already supplied Lakotas with factory-made shirts and blankets; the girls who returned, having also learned to sew, took to commodity bolts of cloth with easy expertise. What other jobs were there? Clerking positions, which required basic literacy, were already filled by whites.

Clarence probably considered himself lucky when, soon after his return in October, and probably with McGillycuddy's help, he was appointed Indian teaching assistant, a minor position not even noted in the annual report of the new Oglala Boarding School the next year, and a post that didn't augur well for intellectual growth.[5]

Opened in late 1883, the school was assembled from lumber hauled more than a hundred miles from the nearest rail line in Nebraska. The campus consisted of two three-story dorms where boys and girls were segregated, the buildings connected by a short wing containing work rooms and a kitchen. The premises were lit with kerosene lamps—or tallow candles when supplies ran short. Windows were closed and locked at night to keep boys and girls apart, which made infectious diseases like tuberculosis all the more common. Rooms were heated with red-hot Franklin stoves, which burned at a fever pitch during a typical Dakota winter. There were no fire escapes, however—a glaring absence considering that the building would go up in flames, apparently with no casualties, a decade later.[6]

The fixtures would have been familiar to any Carlisle boy. Clarence's room was probably as spartan as the one he had had as a student: an iron bed, a dresser, and a table and chairs. But he was a world removed from Wanamaker's, where he could touch the linens and hats and scarves and shoes from the marketplaces of the world, even if he couldn't afford to buy them. Clarence would have recognized the induction ceremony, too, if ceremony it was. The younger ones were taken in hand by the bigger children. They were led into the bathing room and doused in a mixture of hot water and kerosene, scrubbed with soap and brush by their elders to remove prairie vermin, and made to watch helplessly as their clothes were burned to a heap of ash. The school uniforms they wore included brogans that pinched their feet and made it hard to walk, and that was exactly the point. Trying to run away from school in them would have been torture.[7]

Proper grooming was mandatory. Girls submitted to having their hair done up in a single braid, while boys had their locks cut as they did at Carlisle. That first year, a popular story goes, the boys were taken inside to have their hair cropped, while a large crowd of parents gathered in the yard outside to celebrate the opening of school. The teachers sheared the boys in the bathroom, the drawn shades allowing them to work in peace—until, that is, a breeze lifted one of the shades and exposed their scandalous labor. The gawkers outside looked in with amazement. "They are cutting the hair!" someone yelled, and the parents stormed in to seize their sons and scrambled off in a panic until the schoolyard was deserted. Only gradually were they convinced to come back in the coming weeks. A haircut was an anticipated hazard in Pennsylvania; on Pine Ridge, it felt like a personal attack. Like so much else, the authorities reasoned, Indian people would get used to it.[8]

The school mission resembled Carlisle's: provide a primary school education and instill in children an appreciation for mandatory, and sometimes grueling, physical labor—a system used to feed and clothe the institution cost-free. The boys did farm chores, while the girls mastered the nuances of home economics—sewing, cleaning, washing—and did so, on advice of the agent, without recompense. Shortly after Clarence left, the school had 129 acres in cultivation and more than 400 in pasture, where swine and milk cows were herded long before anyone had heard of lactose intolerance in Native Americans, a condition that makes it difficult to digest milk after infancy. Full board was provided. The children were "carniverous," the agent noted, but time and hunger would make them more eager to eat beans, flour, and vegetables, he predicted. Little was wasted, not even the discarded flour sacks that were sewn into makeshift nightgowns for the girls.[9]

Those same girls, forbidden to wear traditional double braids or even pluck their eyebrows, found distractions where they could. They made "camp" in the school playground when they had a few moments of free time, using boxes and spools for wagons, pieces of muslin for tipis, and strands of their own hair and sticks with brown cloth to make dolls with tiny belts and moccasins. It was like a diorama to show a life that their parents had known but that was swiftly changing before their eyes. Men would gather on a rise of ground and remember days gone by as they watched the girls play. To see real Lakota tipis pitched nearby, within view of the school, was to witness the clash of two worlds, the wooden dorms with bell towers looking like the masts of a large, cumbersome ship mysteriously moored on the buffalo grass by an inscrutable hand of fate at the edge of White Clay Creek.[10]

It took two years for Clarence to be promoted to disciplinarian. As a school enforcer, he would implement many of the same rules he had learned, if reluctantly, in the dorms and quadrangle of Pratt's dominion. He had learned how to stand at attention in good weather or bad, how to march to class in an orderly manner, how to file into the dining commons and not shovel his food. Clarence had returned with knowledge useful to the tribe, at least for children whose parents had settled them in school hoping that the white man's way was best. He had scaled the next rung of the boarding school ladder, entrusted with duties more about taking wayward students to task than taking up an arithmetic or history lesson.

He did the job into his midtwenties, shepherding students, some barely younger than himself, through a world of supervised sports, drilling squads, and work details. There was the ringing of bells; the confirming that clothing was in good repair; the checking that everyone bathed and went to bed on time; the making sure that absentees were duly recorded. It was a kind of master-sergeant role working below the matron, the boss of the dorms who gave marching orders to her young officers. It was never a job that agreed with his temperament. Years later he would evince no desire to take up the cudgels of the disciplinarian ever again.[11]

The "new" Clarence often alienated his own kind. A Lakota woman grabbed him by the collar one day in a crowded trader's store and demanded to know why he'd almost starved her boy to death. It seems her son had run away from school, been found and returned, and then punished with a diet of bread and water. Clarence assured her he was only following orders, not issuing them, which subdued her for the time being. Another occasion found him on a recruiting mission at Orphan's Camp, near Wounded Knee, when he was accosted by an old man who accused him of stealing Lakota children for the boarding school. He waved a fist in Clarence's face and advised him he better shed his white man's clothes for Lakota garb because "educated Indians are no account." Clarence was hardly ruffled. He proudly recounted the incidents in a published letter to Pratt, fondly signing it, "Your Grandson, C. T. Stars."[12]

A proper Lakota upbringing and a Carlisle apprenticeship had developed in Clarence a well-honed moral sense. In 1889 he lodged a formal complaint against an agency official who liked to lurk in the vicinity of the Episcopal church "to catch girls," in Clarence's disgruntled view, "not to catch God's words." More disturbing, Three Stars contended that the same man, when serving as superintendent of the Oglala Boarding School, "secretly took one of the big girls in his room," a rare, if oblique, accusation of sexual abuse for the time. No less than Charles Gallagher, son of the reservation agent, also earned Clarence's ire. He called him a "worthless . . . demoralizing teacher" who made a habit of harassing Lakota girls. Three Stars developed a keen dislike of "worthless white men" who loitered on the reservation in hopes of finding a Lakota wife so they could pasture their horses and cattle on tribal land—and perhaps, one day, claim an allotment. "Squaw men" he called them, with equal parts vulgarity and derision.[13]

The school harbored less visible—but more lasting—dangers too. Clarence had seen the ravages of measles, scarlet fever, and tuberculosis at Carlisle. But another, more lingering, enemy was trachoma. Three Stars later reported being partly blind in his right eye, likely the end result of an early bout with the affliction at Carlisle, in Philadelphia, or at the Oglala school.

The trachoma germ was passed as discharge in the form of tears or pus through rubbing the eyes or wiping hands on a towel that was shared with others. The germs could be spread by eye secretions even as one slept. Lack of ventilation in small one-room cabins, as well as common bedding, scarcity of water, and shared clothing, made "sore eyes" a disease that struck whole families on the reservation. The contagion flourished in the close quarters of boarding schools, where everything from bathwater and washbasins to books and pencils were shared. The active part of the disease often began in childhood, but scarring of the cornea and subsequent blindness might occur only decades later.[14]

The cures were often worse than the affliction. Reservation doctors had children use bits of cloth or paper to wipe away the germs, and then burn the infected materials or douse them in boiling water. Other disinfectants were cumbersome and potentially noxious: formaldehyde gas, chloride of lime, burning sulfur, or a solution of carbolic acid. Among the most difficult therapies was grattage, in which the follicles of the inner eyelids were scraped and treated with mercury bichloride. Especially disturbing was the tarsectomy, in which a tarsal plate of the eyelid was removed. The surgery was approved by the Indian Bureau in the 1920s and practiced on many Native patients who either didn't need it or didn't have trachoma in the first place, and the practice wasn't discontinued until years after Clarence had left the teaching ranks.[15]

Eventually the sickness reached epidemic proportions. A 1912 survey by the Public Health Service found almost 30 percent of Indian boarding school students were afflicted with trachoma; a more general study of reservations found an infection rate of 23 percent, figures that dwarfed contagion rates from elsewhere. Before long almost half of boarding school students were infected with trachoma, and even nonresidential Indian day schools, where Three Stars would spend years of his career, were so stricken. Getting—or even giving—an education in Indian country qualified for hazardous duty.[16]

Whatever perils it may have sheltered, the Oglala Boarding School was popular. By 1890 there wasn't enough room to hold all the children whose parents wanted them there. But high enrollment couldn't hide the ambivalence they felt at giving over their sons and daughters to a big school on the prairie. Since children were provided room and board, not to mention a fresh suit of clothes every year, parents were, in some respects, bribed to enroll them. The question for many parents was whether they could afford *not* to send their children to school. Some families simply refused, and the police were instructed to encourage their enrollment, even if "care should be exercised not to provoke the Indians to open hostilities," advised the Indian commissioner.[17]

Agency police, directed by Major George Sword, a formidable Lakota figure on Pine Ridge and a future colleague of Clarence, monitored the campus. A member of Sword's police visited the school daily and rang the bell at the top of each hour. Attendance was compulsory, and officers chased down absentees. Failure to attend school had severe repercussions: federal law permitted withholding rations from families whose children were truant. Still, authorities were at a loss to understand why students would even want to elude them. In 1892 six runaways at Oglala were reported, five of them girls "stolen away by their people" and a "morose" boy who walked away a few days before the "jollification of closing day," when each child was required to shake hands with teachers, matron, superintendent, and other staff in a symbolic, if forced, act of good will. "These schools were just boxes filled with homesick children," complained John Lame Deer, a boarding school veteran who became a well-known medicine man on Pine Ridge. "When we enter the school we at least know that we are Indians. We come out half red and half white, not knowing what we are."[18]

He could have been describing Clarence. Three Stars began as "Indian assistant," moved to disciplinarian, and directed his own classroom his last year at the school, an evolution that did Pratt proud. But the prospects for Indian teachers were bleak. "To date I have failed to find an educated Indian or half breed possessing the requisite degree of backbone, discipline and judgment in his composition to fit him to fill successfully the position of teacher in charge of a day-school remote from the agency," the agent wrote. "And I have tried several of them. These Indian graduates do well in subordinate positions in boarding schools, in shops, and in outdoor industrial work instructing their people." In 1888 all day school teachers on Pine Ridge were white. By the next year Clarence had been appointed as temporary teacher at the boarding school, and it wouldn't take long for him to prove Agent McGillycuddy wrong about the intelligence and independence of Indian hires.[19]

Whichever side of a teacher's desk a Lakota person sat on, assimilation was imperative. The purpose was to teach students, in Pratt's words, "that it is more honorable to be an American citizen than to remain a Comanche or a Sioux." As he and others had argued, it was cheaper to educate the tribes than to fight them. Concerning how they would go about it, "No school will be permitted on the reservation in which the English language is not exclusively taught," the Indian Office intoned. "This language, which is good enough for a white man and a black man, ought to be good enough for the red man." Three Stars had learned English the hard way—conscripted, confined, and immersed in the tongue a thousand miles from home and family. Perhaps this is why he would never fully abide by the Indian Bureau's language decree, even as he proudly reported back to Pratt that he was improving his English by teaching it to his students.[20]

The 1880s saw Clarence's life ebb and flow—from buckskin to braided uniform to a suit of civvies; from west to east and back again; from agency boy to promising scholar to master of his own classroom and soon of his own schoolhouse. Carlisle, Wanamaker's, the Lincoln Institute, Oglala Boarding School—together they were the turning point in his education, though far from the end of it.

6

A Dubious Deal and Wounded Knee

On a spring day in 1883 a band of fathers rode their horses over the rough prairie grass to the little schoolhouse by the water. Their sons were waiting to be collected by them there in the small log house on Wounded Knee Creek. Their teacher, the missionary Amos Ross, could do nothing to stop what was about to happen. Perhaps, he might have reasoned, this was a chance for the boys to put their education to work, sitting there in this same house where they had been learning how to read and write. It was time to mark their names on a piece of government paper.

The men picked up their sons from the schoolhouse and rode over to the Two Lance place. More than a dozen boys assembled there, as they did at other sites across the land served by Pine Ridge Agency. There was Tasimke Wanbli, all of four years old. Nanpa Glinaji was five. Wipasica, who was ten, towered over both of them. Cagu was sixteen, and poor little Tiyo Wicaktila was barely three, perhaps the youngest of the lot. With them was a man named Samuel Hinman, a reverend who spoke fluent Lakota and would translate for the boys because their English was poor. George Sword, the agency police chief, was drawing up a list. He wore a metal star on his breast and was said to have been a fierce warrior in his youth, having many times killed a Crow baby during a raid by cracking its head on a tree before it could cry out to betray him. The boys may not have known the story, but many white men did.[1]

First, the fathers signed their names on the paper, which is to say they scratched out an X or held the pen while their name was written for them. Then they pushed the boys forward. They had been told by Hinman that because the children would be there forever, longer than their fathers anyway, they should have a say in the matter too. The boys stepped out, one by one, and "touched" the pen as officials across the agency scribbled down their names. Almost 150 of them signed.[2]

For the boys of Pine Ridge, it was their first taste of an American referendum.

The paper they signed gave the government permission to carve up the Great Sioux Reservation into smaller reserves and sell the "surplus" land at fifty cents an acre. So many of the Lakota men were against it that the government was hard pressed to get the assent of three-quarters of adult male signatures, a stipulation of the 1868 treaty. Hinman later told Congress that the ritual with the boys was just for census purposes. Agent McGillycuddy, of similar mind, categorically denied that any children's names were included in the final tally. Even so, they admitted, in Lakota thinking the son of a widow was considered head of family and listed on the census as such whatever his age, which may have explained the confusion. Besides, they contended, parents may have wanted the children to sign so the little ones would be able to claim the honor later in life. The white men were desperate to get every vote they could find.[3]

Whether Hinman and McGillycuddy were truthful is hard to know, but fixing elections was common sport in Gilded Age America. A suitcase packed with $10,000 in small bills that traveled south to win a Florida recount helped Rutherford B. Hayes secure the 1876 presidential election. People sold their votes by the thousands on election day. Before 1888 voting by secret ballot was, in fact, virtually unknown. Voters were required to cut out their ballots, coded by party and color, and bring them to the polls at the risk of suffering bodily harm before casting them in full sight of everyone, including their opponents. The Pine Ridge referendum didn't have much of a sterling example to build on.[4]

So it was that Lakotas were introduced to American democracy. Their initiation wasn't in the form of an election per se, since most Lakotas weren't U.S. citizens who could cast ballots for actual candidates. Instead they would vote in a series of up or down referenda that would decide the fate of the tribe forever; it was, in symbolic terms, their legacy to the legendary seventh generation, the Lakota future of hope and healing. Imagine a ballot issue so significant and so irreversible being debated by a body politic so inexperienced and so disheartened, and that is what happened in a string of visits by renowned public figures tasked by the Great Father with acquiring much of the land granted to the tribe by the ur-document of modern Lakota history, the treaty of 1868.[5]

In 1883 Clarence was off at Carlisle learning how to read and write. But his uncle Three Stars was at the agency for the initial parley the year before, when he signed with an *X* the document tendered by what was called the Edmunds Commission, after Newton Edmunds, former governor of Dakota Territory. Since there was widespread misunderstanding of whether the agreement would force Lakotas to give up ownership of land or merely lease it to the government, what men like Three Stars thought they were signing, as with so many Indian agreements, is open to question. The press stirred up accusations of fraud. Chief Red Cloud, who signed the initial agreement, retracted his assent when he learned it intended to cede millions of acres of Lakota land to the government. With the threat of a Senate investigation pending, the commissioners aborted their plan. Edmunds and his associates went back to Washington empty-handed but undeterred.[6]

In 1888 a second commission, this one led by the redoubtable Richard Henry Pratt of Carlisle, landed in Lakota country. The Pratt Commission was tasked with getting the same three-fourths majority of adult males to approve opening much of the Great Sioux Reservation for white settlement. This time they came prepared, handing out printed certificates showing white and red men shaking hands in front of a country schoolhouse—an 1880s version of an "I Voted" sticker. They brought printed ballots, too, some colored red and others black, a way to force Lakotas to declare their vote publicly. Each adult male would show his preference when presenting the colored ballot of his choice—and so become a marked man. But the ballot design was hapless. Red ballots signified a "No" vote for the land cession, while black ones signified "Yes"—a strategy that made no sense for Washington since traditional Lakota belief heralded the "red road" as the righteous way and the black road as corrupt. Many Lakota men must have been baffled, if not incredulous, that the government seemed to be urging them to take the wrong path.[7]

Clarence, working as disciplinarian at the boarding school, surely knew of Pratt's tour by way of the Carlisle grapevine. The first time he set eyes on Pratt had been nearly ten years earlier, when he stumped at Pine Ridge to find students for his Carlisle school project, promising parents that their children could be trained as interpreters so they wouldn't be cheated on treaties anymore. But even for this junket the translation services were dubious; at Standing Rock Agency, the first stop for the commission, one "mixed-blood" interpreter had to be removed because he didn't speak English sufficiently well, a reminder that the art of translation hadn't improved much since the days of the Grattan disaster.[8]

Pratt and his colleagues never even made it to Pine Ridge. After sizing up sentiment in the first few Lakota agencies, they realized their mission was a bust. "Although a canvass of all the agencies would, undoubtedly, have enabled us to secure two or three times as many votes as we did," the commissioners crowed, "it was conclusively demonstrated that it was not possible for us to obtain the three-fourths vote required by the treaty." The Lakotas were sufficiently opposed to carving up their reservation into a bundle of smaller, diminished ones. If they weren't going to win the ballot issue, the commission finally reasoned, why bother to finish it at all?[9]

Pratt and his partners may have promised not to employ any threats during the campaign, but their final recommendation was sobering: "Rations, annuities, and all benefits under former treaties should be firmly withheld from those who willfully refuse to comply with these requirements," they wrote. "These requirements" included allotment of the reservation, sale of surplus lands, and mandatory school attendance. Nearly ten years after his stirring recruitment speech for Carlisle, Pratt was saying it didn't matter what the Lakotas wanted anymore—sooner or later, they had no choice but to succumb.[10]

In 1889 came yet another junket, the ultimate chorus in a broken American folk tale—another rap on the door, a third wish from a genie, a final warning from the dire wolf. This one was named the Crook Commission, led by George "Three Stars" Crook, famed Indian fighter; Charles Foster, former governor of Ohio; and William Warner, governor of Missouri. And this delegation was not going to be defied. They hired white men and "mixed-bloods" to lobby their cause at the Lakota agencies. They paid for feasting. They made Lakotas who came to the parleys stay put until they acquiesced, knowing full well they were worried their crops needed tending at home. They pressured Red Cloud and the reluctant Little Wound to remove themselves to another agency so their followers would be more pliant. They extended the term of voting to continue after the commission left, to catch any latecomers. They did everything short of bringing a cannon to the party, as Grattan fatefully had done. The strategy succeeded at all the agencies in acquiring the votes of three-quarters of adult males—all of the agencies, that is, except Pine Ridge. The 1868 treaty, in fact, had stressed the importance of obtaining such a majority from each agency band, not just the tribal whole.[11]

It wasn't the way Lakotas would have decided an important matter, at least not before the *wasicu* came. There would have been speeches, yes, and much deliberation, some of it long and seemingly endless, just as with Crook. But the end result of hearing many voices and views, some of them bitterly opposed, would have been a consensus, however fragile, on the best way to move forward. What did it mean to vote in the white man's way? Did old Three Stars really tally numbers from among his band? Counting heads in a literal sense, however, wasn't the point. The voice in the Lakota way was communal. Consent was assumed if you belonged to the band and stayed with it. If you didn't like what the leaders decided, you could pick up and go. But how did one leave the United States of America? From what Lakotas had heard, it would take many days just to get to the end of it.[12]

It wasn't so much a referendum as a fire sale. The commission dispensed with the color-coded ballots this time. Those who assented signed a form that amounted to a quitclaim and that was considered a deed by the U.S. government. Dissenters were required to sign a separate sheet—a list of incorrigibles, they were warned, that the commissioners would take back to Washington to show the president. The Lakotas were told the government was tired of providing them rations and annuities while they developed lazy habits. "There is no white man who is so poor that he has to get money from the Indian to live," chided Crook, a rather naive surmise when one considered the lack of Indian names in all but the most rudimentary positions on reservation employment rolls. Earnest students like Clarence Three Stars were lucky to find a job at all.[13]

American Horse, a tribal moderate, gave his assent, but he saw what would happen once the lands were allotted and taxed as the agreement proposed: "As soon as we take our lands in severalty that the Government will have them all in a string, as it were, like ropes leading from one to the other, and when we have these established the Government will be pulling at each one of our strings and pulling the money to him." Charging Shield was even more blunt: "The Great Father owns us. We are considered nothing more than beasts. Here are some rations here, and if they were taken away our children would be crying for it."[14]

The honorific of Great Father, as Charging Shield put it, was itself an inexact translation. Lakotas spoke of "*tunkasila*," or grandfather, in their speeches but not "Great Father." When a Lakota man called a commissioner *tunkasila* it was a sign of respect, not childish submission, although the *wasicu* were anxious to see kowtowing even where it didn't exist. Oglalas were less in awe of the commissioners than English-speaking listeners might have thought, and the use of "Great Father" by the scribes was a subtle way to depict the tribe as abject and even childlike.[15]

In the end, Chief Standing Bear, Luther's father, signed the agreement at nearby Rosebud, even as some Lakotas threatened to kill him. His son, proud veteran of Carlisle and Wanamaker's, signed as well. And number 439 of those who "touched the pen" at Pine Ridge was young Clarence Three Stars. The final collective tally at the agencies exceeded the three-fourths hurdle, if barely, and only then with late votes making the difference. The third time was the charm, Washington might have said of its commissions, notwithstanding the Lakota belief that a matter of importance should be tendered four times before approval. A fourth commission bearing more gifts and promises never came, though many Lakotas would one day wish that they had waited—or simply refused—before selling nine million of the twenty-two-million-acre Great Sioux Reservation. What had been a vast expanse of land was now reduced to a passel of smaller reservations—Standing Rock, Cheyenne River, Lower Brule, Crow Creek, Rosebud, and Pine Ridge.[16]

Clarence, class troublemaker at Carlisle and walkaway at Wanamaker's, was now an upright citizen at the Oglala Boarding School, even if he wasn't really a citizen at all, only voting to push his people into the world of schoolhouses, churches, mortgages, and tax liens. His education had only begun. After concluding the commission's business, Governor Warner, resentful of the resistance they had encountered, warned the Oglalas of "professional Indians." He said, "I fear many of you are attempting to follow [their advice]. These men live by pandering to your prejudices and not upon your prosperity."[17]

A professional Indian, in fact, is what Clarence was soon to become.

In 1890 Three Stars gave up his job at the boarding school, though it's not clear he had anything to replace it. That was the year Lakotas heard news of a Ghost Dance religion led by an Indian Messiah who would restore their lives to their former glory before the arrival of white people. For most boarding-school students, the appeal would have been unpersuasive. But hundreds of Lakotas earnestly took up a dance that promised release from government control and a return to times when the buffalo were plentiful and the ancestors would come back to life. Rumors of an Indian revolt, inflated if not invented outright by local newspapers, drove the village of Pine Ridge into a panic. By November troops of the Ninth Cavalry had arrived to protect the agency from a supposed attack. In mid-December Sitting Bull was killed by Indian police after he resisted arrest at Standing Rock Agency, preventing him from going to Pine Ridge in support of the dancers. With rumors of a fight imminent and the death of Sitting Bull confirmed, the village prepared for the worst. The soldiers wrapped a spool of barbed wire around the boarding school, stationed armed guards on the perimeter, and locked the doors day and night, as much to hold the children hostage as to keep them out of the line of fire.[18]

On December 29 the massacre of hundreds of Lakota men, women, and children at Wounded Knee Creek, some twenty miles distant, put Pine Ridge on red alert. As the wounded limped and staggered back to the agency, the authorities converted the Episcopalian Holy Cross Church from a place of Christmas celebration to a makeshift emergency ward

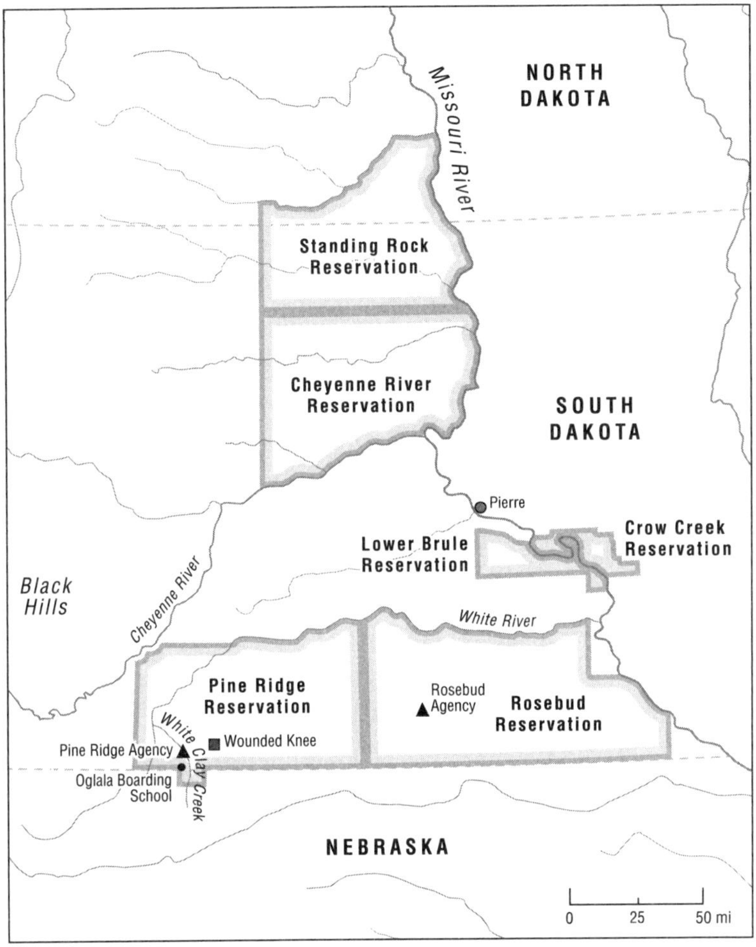

Map2. The Lakota World, 1890. Erin Greb Cartography.

for survivors. Meanwhile, the children were confined at school with their teachers, doors and windows barricaded. For days they were stranded, the occasional stray bullet winging a building in the tense aftermath of the tragedy. Though Clarence had left the school, he was deeply touched by the conflict: he had catechized in the very chapel where the wounded suffered; he acted as a go-between to bring the recalcitrant Little Wound back to the agency after the debacle; his friend Edgar Fire Thunder had signed up to scout for the army; and the massacre brought to his attention an acquaintance who would soon become a prominent Indian advocate and family friend.[19]

That man was Charles Eastman, a Santee Sioux raised in a traditional Dakota camp in Minnesota. After attending a mission school, young Eastman boarded a train in 1876, three years before Clarence departed for Carlisle, to make his own epic journey to the east. He attended Beloit College (Wisconsin), Knox College (Illinois), Dartmouth College (New Hampshire), and Boston University, where he received a medical degree in 1890, the same year that he was posted as agency physician to Pine Ridge, where he would make the acquaintance of Three Stars and his kin.

Eastman's first assignment in South Dakota was nothing short of dreadful: tending to the halt and lame of Wounded Knee. Only days after the disaster he led an expedition to search for more wounded—and more difficult still, to collect and bury the dead. Such was the dramatic launch of a distinguished career as a medical doctor and Native advocate. Eastman went on to represent the Santee Sioux tribe in claims against the government; revised thousands of Sioux names for the federal allotment rolls; became a renowned writer and lecturer; represented Native people at the First Universal Races Congress in 1911; was a leader in the Boy Scouts of America in the greater outdoors movement; and was one of the founders of what would become the Society of American Indians, where he served as president in 1918. A harsh critic of the reservation bureaucracy, he even argued for the abolition of the Indian Office, which he blamed for "all the ills of our Indian civilization.'"[20]

Ohiyesa, as Eastman was known, became a friend of Clarence's uncle, Three Stars. When the old band leader brought his wife to the doctor with a dislocated shoulder one day, Eastman gave her a dose of chloroform and smartly snapped the arm back in place, a seeming miracle to onlookers, especially when she woke up laughing. In the future he was often asked by Oglalas, "Give me some of that stuff you gave to Three Stars's wife." It had been an act that cemented his reputation as an effective healer, although he left the agency in 1893 after his complaints against agency corruption were rebuffed.[21]

In the meantime, Clarence cast about for a new career. Like other returned students his future was dubious, even if Pratt was loath to admit it. Only months after Wounded Knee, Carlisle returnees on Pine Ridge had met a dizzying array of fates. Bennet Whirling Bear was likely dead; Guy American Horse definitely was. So, too, had Alfred Lone Eagle, Thomas Brown, and William Black Eagle been laid to rest. Baldwin Blue Horse rode with an Indian rodeo show, but he was "mentally deficient." Edgar Fire Thunder lost twenty-five head of cattle to the warring Lakotas, called "hostiles" by the government, as did Amos Lone Hill and Maggie Stands Looking. Dana Long Wolf was in the penitentiary. Robert American Horse, who had once mocked Clarence in front of class, had become an Episcopalian catechist and was said to be a good influence on everyone. Newton Big Road was a policeman. Clayton Brave became a government scout after getting shot in the leg during the campaign. George Fire Thunder was doing middling well but was something of a disappointment, and Emma Hand had done well "in so far as she could." Lizzie Dubray, Clarence's future sister-in-law, was a good wife but had lost $300 worth of furniture in the war; Alice Lone Bear and Millie Bisnett wore pretty dresses and looked civilized, while Edward Yankton couldn't find a stitch of work even though he donned white man's clothes trying to get it.

Some of them dressed in blankets, some wore uniforms as scouts, some worked at the agency, and some, like Isaac Kills Hard, even rode with the ghost dancers. Twelve were employed as scouts or police, while another four, feckless to a fault, were "doing nothing in particular." It was an uncommon crowd, those Carlisle boys and girls, and only a particularly big tent could hold them all. As for young Clarence Three Stars, he was "faithful, steady, efficient, an influence for good [and] quiet," Pratt happily noted. He was, at least on the surface, a sterling advertisement for the school—and the Captain never let him forget it.[22]

The aftermath of Wounded Knee required tact and diplomacy. Lakotas wanted a peace settlement and compensation for their losses; the government sought exoneration for a massacre and reestablishment of civil order. Two Lakota delegations were dispatched to Washington in the winter of 1891. The first, chosen by General Nelson Miles, was led by American Horse, Little Wound, and several who had fought at Little Bighorn, their objective to highlight dreadful reservation conditions in the wake of

Wounded Knee, a fiasco barely two months old. The second group came in early February and shared the same boarding house. This group was meant to show the educated and progressive elements of the tribe, called "friendlies" in the parlance of the day. Clarence Three Stars arrived with them as the first "full-blood" Sioux interpreter to ever visit the capital, a reminder of the disadvantages "full-blood" tribal members faced in any negotiation. Chief of police George Sword, who had a knack for getting a front-row seat at every spectacle, accompanied them in full police attire.[23]

They were the latest in a long line of Indian missions to the capital. The pilgrimage to Washington was a practiced rite of passage for Native headmen, and some, like Red Cloud, had visited close to a dozen times. Tribes sent delegations to negotiate treaties, to ask for extended aid, to proclaim their sovereignty, or to mediate tribal claims. At the same time, they exposed themselves to elaborate spectacles of propaganda and power that showed the immensity and grandeur of the white world. They went to see the Capitol Dome and the congressional galleries and the Marine Barracks replete with a military parade; they might have even taken a trip to Mt. Vernon to see where the first Great Father of the country was buried. While the splendors of Washington were a powerful way to teach the lesson of white dominion, a century of delegations had transformed Indian visitors from guileless onlookers to shrewd and seasoned political lobbyists.[24]

Lakota visitors to the city worked hard, watched closely, and made the best of their visit. An 1870 delegation suspected that they saw large numbers of white people in New York, Philadelphia, and Washington because the government was moving the crowds around with them as they travelled. Some lived it up—the Red Cloud and Spotted Tail delegation of 1872 ran up a hotel bill of $5,000 ($105,000 in current value). Others grumbled at their reception, as in 1875, when Little Wound was offended that the delegation had received nothing in the way of rifles and horses: "If we go home without anything of this kind," Little Wound said, "when we arrive there, the people will all laugh at us." Many returned laden with presents. Luther Standing Bear's father came back from Washington decked out in a silk top hat, a starched shirt with cuffs, and cowboy boots that were so tight his wife could only pull them off by dragging him around their tipi. His children, it turned out, ended up using the hat as a water bucket. Very few, in the end, were like Crazy Horse, who resisted the offer to visit the Great Father's seat of power because he feared the trip would compromise his negotiating position.[25]

Most tribal leaders of the day spoke a brand of English that was halting, at best. But the men they chose for interpreters—they were rarely, if ever, women—were a motley crew. Many—like John Richard, who served on one Red Cloud delegation after killing a soldier in a drunken brawl only months before he decamped in the capital—were barely literate "mixed-bloods" with shady reputations. Red Cloud tried to use his own brother-in-law to interpret in 1875, but Todd Randall's Lakota proved so inept that the famous warrior was visibly puzzled by the exchanges. Indian visitors came to prefer having at least one interpreter from home and a second, perhaps trained by the Indian Office, as a way of confirming that words were being correctly parsed. One Red Cloud delegation brought a half dozen "mixed-blood" interpreters who spent more time boozing and carousing in bordellos than engaging in diplomatic doings—and who then demanded payment for service, an ultimatum that was roundly refused. Local Carlisle students might be hired to translate, but the professionalization of the interpreting corps didn't happen until the turn of the twentieth century.[26]

The 1891 Lakota tour of Washington, then, teetered on a shaky tradition. The day the delegation met Secretary of the Interior John Noble, "not a blanket or a feather or a blotch of paint was to be seen." American Horse cited Three Stars and his old tormentor at Carlisle, Robert American Horse, as two Carlisle veterans who hadn't found positions on Pine Ridge commensurate with their education; Clarence, in fact, after leaving the boarding school, was working as an agency clerk. Government bigwigs tried to explain why rations for Pine Ridge, contrary to earlier promises, had been inadvertently reduced the year before. And just in case anyone didn't get it, the secretary went on to warn his visitors "never to let their young men dream that they could ever get anything by force from the United States." When American Horse, known for his grand oratorical flights, rose to speak again, he was cut short and the audience abruptly ended.[27]

The delegation moved on to Philadelphia, a homecoming of sorts for Clarence. The group made a beeline for Wanamaker's, where the police kept curious onlookers at arm's length, and the Indian mission marveled at a demonstration of the large coal furnaces. They visited the Lincoln Institute, too, which the *Baltimore Sun* hailed as Clarence's alma mater. At a service sponsored by the International Peace Society at Christ Reformed Church, Indian commissioner Thomas Jefferson Morgan, a Baptist minister, regaled the crowd with the honesty of the Indian agents in caring for a conquered people, some of whom he said were "lower than the lowest animal." Indian advocate Herbert Welsh, co-founder of the Indian Rights Association, rose in indignant defense to condemn the agents' cowardice and corruption, which led to the massacre at Wounded Knee: "In Dakota the blood of 500 people has been shed to enlighten the minds of the savages," he said dourly. "The difficulties all come about through the officials—the positions are political spoils. . . . Choose fit and honest men, and do not dismiss them. That is the crisis of the hour."[28]

The following week, "the dark skinned sons of the forest," as the press called Clarence and colleagues, were feted at City Hall and police headquarters. That evening they were entertained by a hundred students from Carlisle and the Lincoln Institute, who serenaded them with "My Country 'tis of Thee," "Auld Lang Syne," and Stephen Foster's "Old Folks at Home" ("Swanee River"). The junket was almost over. The group returned west by train via Carlisle, probably a bittersweet trip for Clarence in the shadow of the journey he made seven years before when he abandoned his job in the Quaker City. With Washington far in their wake, Young Man Afraid of His Horses was asked in Chicago what they had gained from the trip. "We had some promises, but they are like all the other promises of the Great Father," he said. "We are not fooled and we go home with heavy hearts. . . . We shall tell our people that we have got more promises. Then they will laugh at us and call us old men."[29]

They had complained and flattered, marveled and wheedled, offended and listened, and laughed and dazzled and were still, as they crossed back over onto the prairie, riddled with doubts. The papers recorded that "all the graduates of [the Lincoln Institute] remained faithful to the government during the recent uprising," a compliment that included

Three Stars in his first official visit to the city that George Washington had built, or perhaps just planned, or at least imagined from his nearby perch on the Potomac. But it confused them that what seemed true in the East never seemed just so on the prairie. It was as though the heart of the world changed when one moved across the land. Some said it was two different worlds, but it was really only one, a single world squeezed between the dream of what was pledged to the tribe and the disappointment, even wreckage, of the legacy of their confinement. The monuments and crowds of the East were imposing and impressive, while their own country, wide and broken and hilly, was the home of flour sacks and one-room houses and blizzards where a man could wander away and lose himself in a snowdrift and not be found again until spring. If there had really been two worlds, they could have taken refuge in one of them and built it all over with their own hands; they could have gone on living in their own way and in their own time and never come out again. But Clarence was beginning to grasp the truth before he was even thirty: the world was a shared one, and their piece of it would always be in peril.[30]

7

Family and Tribe

The year after he returned from Washington, 1892, Clarence married Jennie Dubray, a fellow Carlisle student whose acquaintance he likely made during the year they shared on campus. Jennie was the daughter of Antoine Dubray, born as Antoine DuBreuil in 1822. Antoine was one of the crusty French trappers who worked out of Saint Louis and roamed the Mountain West in the decades before the Civil War. An employee of the American Fur Company, he seems to have had a trading post on the Missouri River and lived for a time with the Arapaho tribe. Antoine worked as a guide, interpreter, butcher, and herder, and it's said that he married four different Indian women—most at different times—three of whom were "mixed-blood" daughters of French trappers, a common cohort in the Mountain West. Jennie's mother was, as best as one can untangle her family tree, Julia Moran, a Rosebud Sioux who died in or around 1878—although Jennie's death certificate names Sallie Robinson as her mother, and her probate records, alas, list Laura DuBray. Carlisle records describe Jennie as a "half-blood," in the parlance of the day, but she's listed as "one-quarter-blood" in Indian Office records, so the racial background of her mother is uncertain.[1]

Antoine's legacy, in human terms, was almost biblical. He's said to have fathered as many as twenty-seven children over a period of almost four decades. Estimates for his great-great-grandchildren, as the family has it, run as high as 2,400 (not entirely implausible if one does the math). The Lakotas called him Pehin Sica (Bad Hair), for the wild shock of red hair he sported. It was said that Antoine, also known as Chat, was fluent in English, French, Arapaho, and Lakota. He was a landowner in

Denver, for a time, before moving north to live with the Sicangu Lakota on the Rosebud Reservation, where he fathered Jennie. Family sources say he fought with an Arapaho raiding party in a skirmish near Denver after the Sand Creek Massacre in 1864, but the trail of his adult exploits runs cold for much of his later life.[2]

The boisterous DuBray was a wild drinker and practical joker of considerable renown. Acting as interpreter in 1859 for the Southern Arapaho chief Little Raven, he was so drunk he fell out of his seat and brought negotiations, at least for that day, to a premature close. He died in 1901, family lore has it, when he fell off his wagon, perhaps because of a heart attack, on his way home after acting as butcher at a government beef issue. His daughter Jennie inherited a share of his estate that amounted to 90/2025, which gives an idea of what a fractionated estate, divided among heirs by rigid Indian Office rules, could look like in Indian country, even as far back as more than a century ago.[3]

Jennie was, by her own account, thirteen when she entered Carlisle in 1883, late in Clarence's tenure. Their eventual union is no surprise given the strong bonds that connected many Carlisle scholars, especially the social occasions organized for returned students. She was in the seventh grade and some twenty-one years old when she was discharged from the school in 1892. Only two months later, on August 7, 1892, she married Clarence in a Rosebud church. "Neither are graduates," noted the Carlisle school paper, "but both have such a store of wholesome common sense, and are so endowed with the true spirit, that we predict for this much-loved couple, a fair, prosperous and happy future." When she died many years later, Clarence would testify that she had been seven years younger than records showed, which would have made her only fourteen or fifteen on their wedding day, no doubt a lapse in the memory of a grieving husband.[4]

Typical of Carlisle girls, Jennie's vocational trades were listed as sewing and laundry, but she was accomplished in her schoolwork as well. She was an honor roll student in 1886. In 1890 she gave a debate speech in favor of land allotment, saying, "I for one shall be glad when we shall have no more talk about wards of the Government. This bill makes us 'come of age.'" She recited John Greenleaf Whittier's poem "The Common Question" with uncommon aplomb at a public assembly. She enrolled in the Normal Department, was a pupil teacher, and generally appears to have been a model student. Education was the morning star by which Clarence and Jennie would steer their lives together.[5]

In courting Jennie, whose father was a Frenchman, Clarence planted one foot in the "mixed-blood," assimilated world that was spreading on Pine Ridge and nearby Rosebud. "Mixed-bloods" tended to be better educated by white standards, which was true of Jennie, who had spent nine years at Carlisle. Usually their English skills were more advanced, and they were reputed to have knowledge better adapted to the world of markets and missionaries that white settlers brought with them. "Full-bloods," on the other hand, were fluent Lakota speakers, tightly bound to the *tiyospaye* (extended family group) they grew up in, practiced Lakota religious and social traditions, and were much less likely to sell their land once it was allotted to them.

The two were married the year Clarence received his first real teaching commission. Acting agent Captain G. L. Brown observed how the young man handled a provisional teaching assignment at Yellow Bear's Camp in 1892: "He is unquestionably the best example of Christian civilized full-blooded Indian on this reservation," Brown gushed, "and in every way deserving of the high esteem and regard in which he is held by his own people and by the Whites as well." Pratt, for his part, vowed that he "would trust him implicitly and recommend him most highly." The Captain even offered to send articles of clothing for Clarence's students and signed an affectionate missive that ended with "loving remembrances" from himself and his wife. A temporary appointment at Day School No. 11 soon yielded a full-time job at Day School No. 19 in Medicine Root District in the fall. Before the academic year was out, Clarence and Jennie were tending the schoolhouse like old hands, ordering new fenceposts and a windmill for a two-hundred-foot well that would have required the grit of Hercules to winch a bucket of water up to the rim. By 1895 they'd been selected to make a special display from their school for the Cotton States and International Exposition in Atlanta.[6]

Clarence's school journey ran against all the prevailing winds. The intent of Native instruction was to propel children outward into the world: they would learn basic English in the nearby nonresidential day schools, transfer to a reservation boarding school after the third or fourth grade, and culminate their journey by learning a trade or vocation at a faraway off-reservation school like Carlisle. "The plan educates the child away from his home more than towards it," one agent explained. But Clarence began his schooling in the East, returned to the roots of the land he left, then moved ever deeper into the rural pockets of Pine Ridge in the decades to follow, a reverse migration that was indicative of a man ill-suited to following the conventional itinerary the Indian Office envisioned. He was original, backward, and contrary all at once.[7]

And before long he was a father. In 1893 Clarence and Jennie's eldest child, Sophia, was born, and the following year Jennie gave birth to their first son, Paul. As fast as they could move forward with their lives, however, part of Clarence's own past was disappearing. In 1894 the Oglala Boarding School burned to the ground. The blaze was considered something of a mixed blessing since the building, barely ten years old, had already become decrepit, but records don't reveal whether the fire was accidental or deliberate. The Indian Office, appalled by the prospect of large wooden "matchboxes" stuffed with hundreds of students going up in flames, was swift to punish any suggestion of arson. A pair of girls convicted of trying to torch a Carlisle dormitory in 1897 were fined $2,000 and sentenced to eighteen months in prison. Three Haskell students who doused a sewing room with kerosene, apprehended before they could burn down the whole building with a box of matches, were sentenced to a reformatory. A Menominee girl was given life imprisonment at Fort Leavenworth for gutting her reservation school. Hazards everywhere abounded for Indian teachers and students alike.[8]

More troubles were in store for the young couple. In 1896 Agent W. H. Clapp notified Clarence of his transfer to a day school on the Colville Reservation in Washington state. Reassignment was a common fate for Indian service teachers, so Clarence readily agreed, asking only for a delay of some months so he could save money for expenses. But the matter became contentious when Three Stars requested the reason for his transfer and received no answer. Sensing that something unseemly was afoot, he tendered his resignation, under protest, until his complaint could be investigated.

Soon enough the motive for the transfer came to light. Washington had decided it would no longer permit Native people to teach on their home reservations, a policy meant to limit fraternization between teacher and student. Clarence stiffened. "I want to teach among my own people where I am known," he wrote the commissioner. The transfer, Clarence believed, disguised a malignant intent: to discourage Indian teachers with hardship assignments and thereby run them out of the service altogether. Given the previous agent's support, Three Stars regarded himself as "removed without cause," a key step in his evolution as self-appointed Oglala gadfly. Pratt commiserated with Clarence about being a "victim" of Clapp, an army man who had long denigrated Carlisle, and advised his former charge that he was better off as an independent man than in government service.[9]

Agent Clapp struck back: "He feels himself much aggrieved at not being retained in day school work here," he noted of Clarence, "says he regrets ever having gone to school, and uses his influence in and about the school where he was formerly employed, to make trouble for the teacher, and foment discontent among pupils and patrons." Though he didn't clarify what the troubles were, Clapp was a military man who didn't take kindly to what he considered insubordination. Clarence was getting a reputation for being an outspoken Indian, perhaps even a subversive one.[10]

Now that he had a family to feed, the business of doing business was never far from his mind. Through much of the 1890s he ran a trader's store in Corn Creek, near Allen, putting to work the retail know-how he had absorbed in Philadelphia. "His mastery of arithmetic was remarkable," Pratt would later enthuse. It was a skill that must have come in handy as he threw himself into the task of buying and trading everything from horse feed and thimbles to starched collars and sheer muslin. In fact, Pratt had leaned on the Indian commissioner to appoint his former student as official trader in 1891. For that matter, Charles Eastman leveraged his reputation to ask the commissioner that he revoke the license of a nearby white trader so that the competing Three Stars store could flourish. Being a small shopkeeper made him master of his own house, not a small cog in a big city emporium, and now he would get a close look at the underbelly of big money and political influence as it played out in the land of Crazy Horse and Red Cloud.[11]

A trading post like Clarence's, a veritable prairie oasis, had a treasure for everyone. Saddles and lariats and ropes and cinches for the serious cowboy, stacked on the floor and suspended from the rafters. Bolts of calico for the women, pairs of overalls for the men. For crafters, a glass case full of beads. For the hungry, tins of tomatoes and beans and carrots; for cooks, sugar and salt and baking powder and tubs of butter. There was green coffee too, beans unroasted. Stick candy for children. Jerricans of kerosene for seekers of light. Maybe a ten-foot galvanized-steel Acme windmill and pump jack. Or a double-barreled, ten-gauge shotgun with checkered grip and automatic shell ejector with a thirty-two-inch barrel. It was well nigh a hallowed place, often ordered with reckless abandon, things piled, stowed, and shelved by the eccentric fancy of the owner that neither compass, logic, nor strictures of common sense could decipher. It had become the Three Stars store when the previous trader was run out of town on charges of graft and corrupting an Indian servant girl.[12]

At about the same time he was running his own shop, Clarence began clerking for the powerful businessman Henry Dawson, owner of a general merchandise store in Allen who may have simply co-opted the Three Stars business. H. A. Dawson, as he was called—another mentor to Clarence—was known in the press as the "big cattle king" of Pine Ridge Reservation. A vice president, and later president, of the Western South Dakota Stock Growers Association during the early twentieth century, his wealth was unimaginable by Oglala standards. In 1901 Dawson paid $160,000 to purchase five thousand head of cattle from a fellow rancher, an amount greater than the entire appropriation for Carlisle Industrial School that year. Nor did he tolerate thieving in the neighborhood, at least in certain guises. In 1902 he joined a group of ranchers to offer a $500 reward for information leading to the arrest of cattle rustlers, almost as much money as Clarence could earn at day-school teaching in an entire year. But in matters of the law Dawson could ride either side of the fence, as when his own cattle were impounded by the Indian Office for trespass on the reservation shortly before the turn of the century.[13]

Dawson's Indian Office ties were cozy: Henry and his wife, Fannie, were good friends of later Pine Ridge agent J. R. Brennan, who was known to host the couple in Rapid City when they visited from out of town—no surprise, since Brennan sat with Dawson on the Growers Association executive committee. Brennan's successor as superintendent, H. R. Tidwell, happened to be one of Dawson's debtors, another strand in the complex web of cattle, power, and money on Pine Ridge. An astute operator, Dawson received the government contract after Wounded Knee to bury the massacred dead in a mass grave—for the not inconsiderable sum of $1,250. The newspaper ads for his mercantile crowed that the Maryland-born entrepreneur was a "dealer in everything," and while he may not have sold imported silks and shawls, he was a shrewd prairie Wanamaker with an eye for making a dollar in good times or bad.[14]

Clarence had to improvise to survive; in fact, he had done so for years. He and Jennie ranched on acreage they occupied before the allotment surveys, their sole landed stake in the world. They had a herd of cattle and their own brand—C3S—emblazoned on the left side of cattle, CTS on the left hip of horses. No matter what the boss farmers said, planting was hard and harvests were slight—the land was only good for grazing and not much more. They made do with what they had gained back east, which happened to be a good working knowledge of spoken and written English; a rudimentary understanding of retail; a commitment to the Episcopalian faith; and a vision of something greater that existed beyond the confines of what school and church had prepared them for, an opportunity that would take some time to appear.[15]

With Wounded Knee a memory, the Oglalas moved forward in their subsistence economy, achieving some success in small-scale ranching and farming. Slowly, the festering wound of the massacre began to heal. But in every corner of Pine Ridge, Lakotas could see the telling signs of waste and graft. In the spring of 1897 the Oglala council chose four men—Red Cloud, Patrick High Star, American Horse, and Clarence Three Stars—for an important mission to Washington financed by the tribe. Their spokesmen would press tribal treaty claims, select a lawyer to represent them in the courts, and testify about rampant government corruption, all before the chairman of the Senate Committee on Indian Affairs, Richard F. Pettigrew, senior senator from South Dakota. Clarence would also share with Charles Eastman the task of translating the powerful words of the daunting Lakota leader Red Cloud. Before they left the capital, the delegation would even have occasion to meet with President William McKinley.[16]

When Three Stars appeared with Red Cloud before Senator Pettigrew, he was standing next to one of the great Native American warriors of the nineteenth century. The year they went to Washington, the old man was seventy-six years old and going blind, deaf, and lame. Red Cloud was a magisterial man even in his dotage—plucky, clever, stubborn, brave, determined—and a warrior who had overseen such battles as the Fetterman Fight and the Wagon Box Fight, in a campaign that achieved decisive defeat of the U.S. Army on the Powder River after the Civil War.

America likes to name its wars after Indian tribes (Seminole, Modoc) or warriors (King Philip, Pontiac, Black Hawk). A man with a war named for him, after all, sounds like a troublemaker. Red Cloud, in fact, is the only warrior who can lay claim to having been victorious against the United States in a campaign that remembers him by name. Red Cloud's War, finished by 1867, forced the army to abandon its forts along the Powder River and led to the Fort Laramie Treaty of the following year. The leader of that war was said to have counted coup, or to have struck an enemy warrior, eighty times in eighty battles, a convenient symmetry that almost sounds like a trope from the oral tradition but probably wasn't an exaggeration at all—this claim was modest compared to newspaper accounts that alleged he had taken part in over two hundred fights during his lifetime.[17]

He was born in 1821 on Bluewater Creek near the place where General William S. Harney punished the Lakotas in a brutal campaign the year after the Grattan incident with High Forehead. Red Cloud had been present for most of the great encounters, both peaceful and violent, between Lakotas and white people for a span of fifty years—the 1851 treaty (probably), the 1868 treaty (which he signed belatedly), the Black Hills agreement of 1876, the Fetterman Fight and Grattan Fight, numerous visits to Washington, and a slew of visiting commissions that over the decades had stripped away Lakota land where his ancestors had camped and hunted for generations.[18]

Red Cloud's life was full of blood and thunder on the battlefield—and the stuff of quiet tragedy that happened at some remove. His father, Lone Man, was a victim of the liquor trade and died an alcoholic. When Red Cloud married his wife Pretty Owl, another woman he loved, Pine Leaf, who he hoped might become his second wife, hanged herself on the couple's wedding night within full view of the newlyweds' lodge, an act said to have caused the young man to take a lifetime vow of monogamy. When Red Cloud was barely twenty, by his own account he shot and killed Bull Bear, leader of a rival Oglala band, to end a drunken skirmish over a kidnapping, an act that gained him renown in some circles and lasting enmity in others. Bull Bear, it turned out, had earlier killed Red Cloud's uncle White Hawk in a long-lasting feud, and Red Cloud's own cousin (or brother) Yellow Lodge bit the dust in this latest skirmish. The skein unwound from there, trailing from trespass to revenge to violent retribution in a cycle that followed Red Cloud like a stubborn shadow. He had come to Washington the first time in 1870 as a great warrior, pursuant to his victory in the Powder River conflict, heralded by the *New York Times* as "the most celebrated warrior . . . living on the American Continent." But 1897 was the last time he would visit the city, shuffling along the corridors of the Capitol with interpreters Eastman and Three Stars, younger men now acting as his eyes, ears, and tongue, even though this time he had come with the gait of a simple beggar, if a proud and distinguished one.[19]

He had a reputation for cruelty. Pine Ridge physician James Walker relayed secondhand tales that Red Cloud had, for example, held up the Union Pacific Railroad once and threw the fireman into the coal furnace. Another time he was said to have tied a railroad man to a telegraph pole and drilled him full of arrows. But Walker, like most others, had an acute opinion of the old man, whether for good or ill. With Red Cloud's position came responsibilities, too, like the one that called on him to be ritually upbraided by his people on occasion for being like a weak and cowardly woman and whipped by a crowd with leather quirts, all to prove that he could withstand any reproach with dignity and restraint, a story confirmed by Three Stars himself.[20]

The old man sat to give testimony that April day, and his eyes, sensitive to the light, were covered with a pair of black goggles. Red Cloud stood up and stepped forward to shake the chairman's hand. Though the old warrior appeared to be the supplicant, he let Pettigrew know very quickly how he viewed their relationship: "My friend, you are my debtor, I am a creditor. I have got my goods all with me in words of promise."[21]

Over the next two days the Lakota envoys unveiled a spectrum of abuse that included everything from the proposed policy of allotment to shoddy clothing rations and overgrazing; from fraudulent beef issues and "mixed-blood" marriages to the lack of farming tools and the dishonest taking of the Black Hills. The other three delegates spoke at length before Clarence's turn came. And Three Stars came out fighting, arguing that the Black Hills accord (1876) was never ratified by the necessary approval of three-fourths of adult Lakota males. He was representing an Oglala council on treaty violations, and his critique is one of the earliest demands on record for reparations regarding Paha Sapa, as Lakotas called the Black Hills. "We have been looking for a lawyer" he told Pettigrew. More to the point he vowed, "We have the power to select a man." It was the beginning of a legal crusade that would crawl through the labyrinth of official Washington at something of a slug's pace, only considerably slower.[22]

Are there any other legal matters, the senator asked? The door opened a little wider. We might talk about intermarriage between white people and Lakotas, Three Stars countered. For a long time white men intermarried into the tribe and were adopted as equals, he explained. But too many of them were looking for tribal benefits now like land allotments and rations, so "the woman is the one making a living for him, instead of the man making a living for the woman." He argued, as did Red Cloud before him, for closer enforcement of an 1888 law that said subsequent intermarriage with Indian women would not give so-called "squaw men" tribal privileges.[23]

Pettigrew turned to the question of land. Three Stars had eighty-five head of cattle, he told the senator, but was opposed to the idea of allotting land—not yet begun on Pine Ridge—as was almost everyone in the tribe. "None of them want to do it?" Pettigrew asked. "None of them want to do it," Three Stars echoed. If he were individually allotted, he explained, he would have less land to work and be forced to cut back his herd, a loss that would make a pauper of him. And planting was out of the question. The farming and mowing tools were low grade, and the boss farmer didn't even bother to show Indians how to use them. Besides, wheat and other big crops just wouldn't grow, not even for white farmers. "I have seen Indians try to plow and plant corn and turnips and other things," said Clarence. "Just as these old men said, it sprouts, it looks nice when it comes up in the springtime, but in the middle of the summer it is scorched away."[24]

Once they settled on the subject of cattle, Pettigrew's ears might have burned from the sheer sleaze of it. The beef ration was far short of what was promised, the Lakotas said. When officials weighed the cattle, they did it en masse and used crude estimates of their weight. The cattle were wintered on barren ground, and so they lost much of their heft before slaughter; many died from disease or weakness on their way to the distribution center but were butchered anyway. Once the cows were slaughtered, the scales were tipped by the heavy hand of agency personnel, and inspections were cursory. Three Stars said the beef left over was so poor he typically fed it to his pigs.[25]

However bad the inefficiency and corruption, the arrogance was worse. Clarence told of his uncle Three Stars, who once complained that the agency was issuing bulls instead of cows and one day took a "stone" (testicle) to the agent to prove it. The agent dismissed the complaint and simply advised that Three Stars "throw it away." American Horse said one official peed on the butchered beef before issue just to taunt his patrons—and threatened anyone who talked about it. The authorities salted the hay so that cattle would drink more water and increase their body mass before weighing. People like H. A. Dawson bought yearling calves from Indians and then left them on the reservation to fatten up. The poorest of cattle were left for Indian issue, while the fattest ones were shipped to Omaha. "We are people the same as any other race," declared Three Stars, his frustration mounting. "We consider ourselves human beings. We made a treaty with the Government and they promised to give us none but good things, woolen clothing and good beef, which they never fulfilled."[26]

Next, they moved on from livestock to apparel, a threadbare and dingy tale. None of the annuities Three Stars had received since 1884—shoes, coats, pants, vests—had been fit to wear. He would give the clothes away to acquaintances and later see them for sale in a store over the Nebraska border. "An Indian loses the money which he received under the treaty on that, and the white man makes a pile of money out of it," noted a Carlisle tailor who knew what a decent pair of trousers felt like. And like Red Cloud, he claimed his people would do better with money than cheap annuities: "I am entitled to receive the benefits coming to me from the treaty and laws," Clarence declaimed, "and I have never received a cent." Since he apprenticed at Wanamaker's, where quality was top-notch and refunds were standard policy, the rot of the government system must have appalled him.[27]

Pettigrew pushed the man from Carlisle to talk about education too. By that time Clarence had experience with both the boarding and day schools, and he deferred to the former. "In a day school it is impossible to make them talk English," he said. "I have taught little children to speak English the best I know how. The only place I can force them to talk English is right there in the schoolroom, right there before my eyes, but outside of that I have no power." His philosophy about the day schools was soon to change.[28]

The senator heard them out, but little relief would materialize. The Black Hills legislation gathered dust. Allotment would soon create myriad problems for the tribe. The controversial use of leasing and grazing contracts devolved into a pathetic game of finger-pointing on Capitol Hill. A full generation later, Red Cloud's grandson James would go to Washington to complain about forced leasing, taxation of trust land, and nonpayment of lease money, since so many of the underlying problems had never been fixed.[29]

After the delegation left Washington, it was another dozen years before the legendary Red Cloud passed away. The old warrior didn't go down in violence like many Lakota leaders had. Unlike Crazy Horse, he wasn't stabbed with a bayonet. Unlike Sitting Bull, he didn't die in a hail of gunfire. Unlike Bull Bear, allegedly his own victim, Red Cloud's end in 1909 was quiet. It is the first part of his life, fiery and violent, that people most remember, not the second, which lasted almost four decades. During this time, the son of Lone Man was an isolated and controversial leader, a man shunned by parts of his own tribe for the killing of Bull

Bear, who lived in the only two-story house afforded an Indian on all of Pine Ridge. He may have lived by the sword, but he would die by a slow accrual of maladies: the piling up of years and the dulling of senses and the nagging of insults, like the time he was jailed for hunting game the way his ancestors had freely done for centuries and then forced to pay a fine of two horses before he could walk out a free man.[30]

Red Cloud's world had gradually pulled inward. After beating the army on the Powder River, he devoted the balance of his life to helping his people retain the land promised them by treaty. He refused to sign the 1889 land agreement that diminished the Great Sioux Reservation. But by that time he had already offended the more radical Lakota leaders, like Crazy Horse and Sitting Bull, when he declined to take up arms during the Little Bighorn campaign. He worked to moderate, not inflame, the Ghost Dance movement of 1890 and even filed a claim for damages when his house was looted by those who supported the dancers, making his position as leader even more suspect. The final years saw the quiet "rearguard" action of an aging leader, not like a war cry in the midst of raid or battle but through cautious counsel that attempted to salvage what could be had of negotiations and promises long past.[31]

Three Stars had listened to the old man regale him with the story of Grattan and High Forehead. In time the two became trusted acquaintances, if not friends, a reversal of a long tribal feud. No one had forgotten that Red Cloud killed Bull Bear, whose successor as leader was his son Little Wound, leader of the Kiyuksa band and the man who led Clarence's family to Red Cloud Agency in 1876. Over the years, the enmity between the Little Wound and Red Cloud bands may have simmered, but it seemed to have abated by century's end.[32]

The Lakota delegation returned to Pine Ridge in the spring of 1897, full of promises but empty-handed. Clarence went back to his ranch and his work as a trader. His career as a professional Indian was hardly over. But in another few years, as the prohibition against teaching on one's home reservation was relaxed, he was ready to return to the schoolroom, this time with a clearer vision of what he hoped to accomplish.

8

The Teaching Life

The children arrive after sunrise, on foot, piled in a buggy, several straddling a single horse. The school is nestled on a flat under the ridge of a rough stretch of badlands. There are two buildings: one a schoolhouse, the other an industrial workshop and residence for Clarence and his family; both are single-story frames with narrow windows and short chimneys. A barbed wire fence encloses a playground of swings, poles, bars, and a teeter-totter, homemade like the homespun clothes the children wear. The buildings have the spare dignity of New England, but New England is far away except for on a wall map in the schoolroom and in a story they once read about Paul Revere.[1]

Inside the schoolroom the girls sit in calico dresses, their hair carefully braided. There's Susie Star and Annie Chase-in-the-Morning, Lucy Dreaming Bear and Lizzie Flying-horse, Nellie Kills-Brave and Lucy's sister Charity. The boys, like Archie Tobacco, Fred Good Bear, and George Water, have their hair cut short and are dressed smartly in shirts and trousers. Ranging in age from six to fourteen, they number twenty in all. They study in the mornings from books and primers, the highest being the *Third Reader*. The wall is filled with maps and lessons and framed photos of presidents Theodore Roosevelt and Abraham Lincoln. Howard Water can say the Gettysburg Address by heart. Frank Calico can recite "When Johnnie Comes Home from the Boarding School." On Columbus Day they salute the flag, sing "America," and say the Lord's Prayer in unison with heads bowed and hearts all strung together.[2]

By turns they learn by rote and impulse, and the patience of the teacher makes them brave. First Mr. Three Stars says the English word. "Then he interprets every word he taught us into Indian language so we understand," remembers one of his students, Rose Catches. "Not once, not twice. He'd remember this and ask us what he told us, and some of us, we can't answer. Then he went through it again. He don't just go one way and let it go," she recalled almost seventy years later. "He's a teacher." Above all, he knows the elementary question of teaching deep in his bones: "What must it feel like not to know?"[3]

They point at and talk about things in the room. An older boy gestures at the picture of Abraham Lincoln and tells the class about splitting logs and walking a long way to return books and losing a mother so young you could cry. They talk about things outside too. The teacher explains what *wonderful* means. What is wonderful in the world? Why, the sun, Charity says. The sky and the land, says Archie. Someone else says *trees*. "Why are trees wonderful?" Clarence asks. Silence. Then someone blurts out, "Because no one can make them."[4]

He gives them a story from the book to read aloud. "The Boy and the River," it's called, a most peculiar tale. "A boy was sent to market with butter and cheese to sell," it begins. "What is a market?" the teacher asks. (They're quiet because most of them don't know.) The grandparents of Lizzie Flying Horse wouldn't have had a clue. The teacher himself wouldn't have known when he was a boy. What is a market? What is cheese? And what, by the way, is butter? Some of them know what that is—it gets their fingers all greasy, and they have to lick them clean when they spread too much of it on a piece of bread.[5]

Go back to the story, Mr. Three Stars nudges. They read that the boy going to market stood and watched the river go by and decided he couldn't get across. So he sat down and waited for the river to run by him. But it didn't stop running, because it couldn't, not the way a horse or a wagon or a man would stop. How silly, the children must have thought—it was a river! The boy just turned around and went home, butter and cheese under his arm, without ever crossing over and getting to market. What kind of boy would give up so easily? "Take off your shoes and hop across!" offers Fred Good Bear. Archie and George would never have thought a river would run on until it just became a trickle. Only a boy in a book would do that.

So the teacher asks, "How would *you* have gotten across? If there were two of you, what would you have done?" They ponder that for a minute, Annie and Nellie and Fred and the others. Maybe carry someone else on their shoulders, one of them says, keeping at least one of them dry. Good. The teacher was making them work outside the story now, getting them to think about the world beyond the page. "What work do rivers do?" the book asked at the end of the story, and it was a fine question—as far as it went. But Mr. Three Stars was getting them to solve a smaller problem first: How do I get to that market? How do I cross over and keep going? How do I do something when it looks like I can't? He might as well have put it another way: "This is a book. The answer is not in the book. The answer is inside you. The book can only help you get there."[6]

The boys and girls sit on different sides of the schoolroom. While Clarence speaks to the boys, the girls are busy drawing designs. When he's finished with them, he goes to the girls and asks them what the drawings mean. He collects their sketches and makes them into a book. It is *their* book, not like the ones they have to read in class. Not like *Baldwin's Third Reader*, where Paul Revere's horse leapt forward like an arrow from a bow, and the British soldiers destroyed whatever they could find. Not like Benjamin Franklin, who paid too much for a whistle once and wasn't able to go to school, but he read every good book he could find and became one of the smartest men in the world. Not like Pocahontas, they read, who told her father of John Smith, "You can not kill him without first killing me," changing the history of our country. And not like Israel Putnam, who was captured by Indians and almost burned alive, but they cut him loose and sent him home because he was so brave. ("Why did they make him a prisoner in the first place?" some of them might have wondered. "Was he a captive the way Crazy Horse was?")

So they read about history and geography and ancient peoples, patriots and myths and fables, and, of course, Indians too, though the Indians in these books didn't seem like real Indians at all. They learned why Persephone returns to the upper world in spring. How the rats followed the magic piper and filled the streets like water, but the children went away when their parents wouldn't pay him. And fables. The fox didn't want the grapes anyway. The grasshopper didn't save like the ant—so he ate his fields and danced through the summer. There were landscapes to learn, too, solemn and scary: "Land where my fathers died, Land of the Pilgrims' pride, from every mountain side, Let freedom ring!" (What *was* a Pilgrim, anyway? they surely wondered.) They even learned how to pray: "The Lord is my shepherd; I shall not want," one of the pages began. "He maketh me to lie down in green pastures. He leadeth me beside the still waters." They mumbled the words in unison, though not a single one had any idea where the valley of the shadow of death was, nor were any of them very curious to find out.[7]

Copy twenty words of one syllable. Find ten words which begin with m. *Write five more words which rhyme with* jump. That's how the hours passed at Day School No. 27. And when he sensed they were bored with books and writing, Three Stars would say something like, "Which is most useful, shoes or moccasins?" He would pick three boys and three girls and give each of them time to answer. They chattered back and forth like magpies. Shoes are stronger, but moccasins are quieter and softer. The answer wasn't as simple as it seemed. The younger ones watched and listened. They learned about words, how to say them right, how to hold up their head when they talked to others—and most important, what it means to have a choice and how to think your way through to the end of the game.[8]

The stories they heard at home were different than the ones they read at school. Their family tales had a moral, but they were dark and funny too. So Clarence gave them some of both. He told about the time Iktomi the spider, the Lakota trickster, came upon some ducks swimming in a pond. The ducks asked him what was in the sack he was carrying. "Oh, I have some songs in there," said Iktomi, "that I'm going to teach some people in a far off country." One of the ducks asked if he would teach them one. "Of course," he said, "but first you'll have to come out of the pond." They were curious enough to walk right out of the water. He lined them up and said, "Shut your eyes tight," and if any of them didn't do that, he warned, they would have red eyes for the rest of their life. He said, "Move!" and they started to dance round and round in a circle, eyes closed shut, and then Iktomi took each one by the neck and wrung it like a wet shirt before they could make a sound. Just before he got to the end of the line, the last duck opened his eyes and saw what had happened to his friends and flew away, feathers and nerves all aflutter. "I am wiser today than yesterday," it quacked from afar. And that is why the wood duck has red eyes, said Mr. Three Stars with a smile. The lesson, he advised, is to "be watchful."[9]

But the book lessons at school were all about hardship and failure. A crowd of thou-shalt-nots assembled at the bottom of every page. "She learned her lesson." "There's a lesson you won't forget." "Now that'll teach you!" Sometimes they just set aside the lessons and talked about other things. There were so many ways he could open their eyes. Teaching was showing how to put the bulb in the ground, how to cut a straight line with some scissors, the difference between a home and a home run, the way to sing a round in class and hold fast to your part when other voices joined the melody. Three Stars got them to wonder about the world so much that some days they would even ask him to learn. The reward was sitting back and watching as they talked their way through a riddle, listening all the while for the lively word, the surprising collaboration, the startling shout of wonder.

There were good days and bad, to be sure. Sometimes the class was all wind, and nothing could be caught, like a hunter leading home an empty horse. On others he was like a conductor who barely needed to move his hands, the children taking the cue and responding with good sense and cheer. Even so, after all these years his English was broken. He could hear it when students spoke and echoed his own way of making words. He was reminded, sometimes, that their struggle had once been his, far away, in a place where he didn't know how to read and where a map of the world was as strange as a crack of thunder in winter.[10]

At noon, the children got up from their desks and leaped into action. Boys and girls both prepared the hot lunch, perhaps the biggest incentive of school. For parents who struggled to plow and plant the land, not having to feed the children was one less worry. Susie and Annie were the cooks for Monday, preparing a lunch of potatoes and beans, bread and gravy, apple sauce and coffee. Jennie Three Stars oversaw the slicing and boiling, the pouring and ladling, the setting of the table and saying of grace.

Afternoons were outside if the weather was good. At recess they played rodeo, the little ones riding on the backs of their elders. They played baseball and rode the swings. Later, the boys lumbered about their farm chores. There was a small barn, a garden of several acres, fields with cows and horses. The girls cleared the table, meantime, and washed and mended clothes in the cottage. In the bathing room, everyone got a weekly scrub at three o'clock on Friday.[11]

At four o'clock the day was over. The books and slates and unripe questions were tucked away under the chairs.

Susie and Lizzie and Lucy and Archie and Fred would then start for home. They carried their learning with them, across the stream, over the fence, up the winding path, through the open door and yonder.

In 1901, after an interlude of several years, Three Stars returned to teaching in the day schools. The waiver of restrictions about teaching on a home reservation gave him new life. He seems to have craved something beyond the daily demands of running a small ranch and general store, and in so doing returned to what had begun as a job ten years before and would now become a career, perhaps even a calling. Over the next twelve years much of his teaching was done at Day School No. 27, a few miles northwest of the agency. Ranging in age from six to eighteen and continuing through the third or fourth grade, Three Stars's students were provided uniforms, books, farming and domestic tools, and a hot meal at noon. Jennie was the "housekeeper," or matron, wherever her husband taught; she also assisted with teaching duties, and together they made a decent living. Teaching paid more than a freighter's or day laborer's wage, the most common jobs held by reservation locals, but wages of husband and wife were hardly comparable, a fate Jennie was prepared for at Carlisle where she hadn't been remunerated for domestic work at all. Jennie earned $300 per annum as matron, and Clarence earned $600 as teacher, eventually earning $720. His salary in 1902 was above the average paid to South Dakota teachers, but it was far below that found in nearby Montana, Wyoming, and Colorado.[12]

Day school teachers and housekeepers were often married. Husband and wife were an ideal way to model for Indian neighbors a "modern" couple. The husband was leader and mentor; the wife directed domestic duties like sewing, baking, and cleaning. Together they were a kind of “object lesson” in family harmony, much like the lessons Clarence would teach his students on the classroom sand table, only more influential. Indian Office guidelines discouraged couples with children, but many, like the Three Starses, broke with the model. Between 1893 and 1911, by which time Clarence’s teaching career was almost over, Jennie would bear seven children: Sophia, Paul, Louisa, Clarence Jr., Guy, Thomas, and Mary. They enrolled, of course, in the schools where their father taught; Clarence often had several of them in his care at the same time. In fact, the Three Stars children had the unlikely privilege of being homeschooled by their parents in an actual schoolhouse—a little red schoolhouse, it turns out, after the Pine Ridge day schools were so painted in 1904 in honor of America’s legendary one-room institution.[13]

The day schools, thirty-one of them on Pine Ridge by 1901, were built near creeks and river bottoms, usually far removed from the agency. Clarence would teach at many of them during his career. Some older Lakotas, resentful of government interference, were tempted to keep their children out of the schools. “I find the best way to break up this practice is to shut off the parents’ rations for an issue or two” superintendent Brennan once observed. As at the boarding school, policemen were on hand to round up truants and carry them off to the nearest classroom. Reasons for absence were varied, though marriage (many students were in their late teens) and death were said to be acceptable excuses. Absentees might be mentally or physically incapacitated, too old to benefit from an education, or just too far away to get to the nearest little red schoolhouse.[14]

Buildings and grounds were modest. The typical school building consisted of one room for teaching and separate rooms for kitchen and bathing. Next door the school cottage had four rooms, three for the teacher’s living quarters and one for industrial arts. Both buildings were heated with stoves and lit with oil lamps. Day School No. 27, where Clarence taught for seven years, was built on White Clay Creek in 1898 on a parcel of forty acres, a humble spread that was to be hearth, home, office, and school for Clarence and Jennie’s growing family. While the Three Stars had oil lights and stove heat, there were no water or sewer connections. A barn, a woodshed, and two outhouses filled out the compound—with more than two thousand yards of fencing.[15]

In some ways the school was even better stocked than the old Three Stars trading post in Corn Creek. There were hay forks and manure forks; grubbing and garden hoes, iron rakes and an iron wheelbarrow; a scythe, a posthole digger, and a wire stretcher. They had a baseball bat, a catcher's mask and mitt, and a football pump for recess. They had shoes, overshoes, dresses, hosiery for boys and girls, aprons, and scarves. There were twenty-three wash basins, thirty bowls, thirty-three coffee cups, and twenty-seven saucers, thirty-three plates, twenty-three soup plates, and eighty-one spoons, not to mention assorted other crockery. There were towels, blankets, and comforters but only two beds—one single and one double. There were pans to bake with, fry in, and serve in, and there were tin measures, galvanized buckets, a shovel for fire coals, and a sieve for flour. And don't forget the seven washboards, nine dozen clothespins, ten whisk brooms, set of twenty-four forks and knives, and 150 feet of clothesline, all of which rolled off the tongue like a country verse of "The Twelve Days of Christmas." They had mirrors to look at and mop sticks to clean with, a washing "machine" and a sewing machine and a clothes wringer, and stuffed in the closet were well chains, a mortise lock, thirteen pounds of manila rope (very handy), and four well buckets. Remember, too, the fifty pounds of beans for emergency and twenty pounds of soap. For the boys there was an anvil, a bellows, a grindstone, tongs, claw hammers, butcher knives, auger bits, and paint brushes. And for the girls, agate buttons and sewing needles and scissors (buttonhole and common) and twenty thimbles and 120 spools of cotton thread. Day School No. 27 was better stocked than a fully laden frigate.

What about the proper business of school? There was an organ primer and thirty song books, a dictionary, twelve Bibles, 174 textbooks, and 135 library books, the serious ballast of Day School No. 27. They had penholders, inkwells, slates and pencils, a supply of ink, six blackboard erasers, more than two dozen school desks, tablets of unruled paper, and three stationary blackboards. No one could forget the two school bells and pair of American flags either, one flown from the pole in the yard every morning.[16]

This school had nothing to buy, only to borrow. It was a self-contained store of learning, a little Wanamaker's on the prairie where everything was put away at night only to be brought out again the next morning, and Three Stars had to account, as every teacher did, for every last dustpan and saltshaker and broken saucer at the end of the year or else be found in debt to the august and faraway behemoth in Washington known as the Department of Interior.[17]

Clarence's classroom methods were unconventional. He taught in both English and Lakota, a technique the Indian Office first discouraged, and later banned, in its mission to "civilize" children through the use of English only. He didn't force his charges to read from a primer at the outset, probably due to his own difficulty deciphering English at Carlisle. He would write words on the board and have students draw pictures of them on their slates. After they were finished, one child would act out the sequence: "horse—walk—trot—run—stop," then use a stick for the horse and make a starting point for a story. Or Three Stars would take the class outside to point out animals, buildings, and natural formations and say their names. He used a sand table in the classroom where everyday objects could be touched and handled. Known for his fine singing voice and a believer that songs were a key way to learn a language, Clarence kept an organ at school. "Study your pupils as you would study a book," he advised his colleagues. "Keep them busy with usable knowledge." By using drawing and storytelling, he relied on traditional Lakota teaching methods in a bicultural classroom more than a half century before such a concept was popular. "They like any lesson that is original," he advised, "it is more interesting than a fable." Students could speak of the assassination of President McKinley or the Rough Rider days of Teddy Roosevelt or just the everyday simple wonder of cottonwoods rustling in the breeze before the heat was broken by a crackling summer storm.[18]

His supervisors knew him as spirited and creative. "Many of the teachers have better education," noted superintendent Brennan, "but not better results. . . . He makes up for much of his lack of education, by energy and force in the schoolroom." Brennan commended Three Stars for "his native force and leadership among his people," while recognizing his "advantages over white teachers" who didn't understand "the difficulty in learning English" like Three Stars did. And this from a man who once admitted, "I am opposed to appointing native teachers in general." Said a visiting inspector, "I find him doing better than many white teachers who say that they have been to Normal School or College—who can discuss the great topics of the day, but who, quite often, cannot adjust themselves to the requirements of a little Day school." Three Stars learned to accommodate the values of white culture rather than simply surrender to them. He used English as a "technology" to help students survive in a world where English was necessary, but Lakota values and traditions prevailed.[19]

Even so, it was a long time before Indian teachers became common in Indian country. In 1895 the Indian Office allowed Native teachers to take noncompetitive exams instead of being certified through a civil service test. But a decade later, 450 of 500 teachers in the service were still white. Those like Clarence who were lucky enough to obtain a post found the rules of the profession difficult. Indian teachers, many raised in environments where child discipline was restrained if not rare, could be loath to mete out severe punishments. Indeed, Clarence had discovered as much during his stint as disciplinarian at the boarding school. The top-down hierarchy of the Indian Office was also at odds with the method of consensus building familiar to many tribes. And for those rare teachers like Clarence who taught on their home reservation, the presence of rival parties and competitive community politics complicated their lives, even though having extended family close at hand may have been a comfort. By 1912, near the end of his teaching career, the service once again explicitly discouraged the practice of assigning students to Indian teachers of their own tribe, even if the policy wasn't strictly enforced. That may have encouraged Clarence to change careers when he did, though he lasted longer than many teachers in the day schools, where social isolation, lack of advancement, and limited material comforts made turnover high.[20]

The irony of Indian schools wasn't lost on anyone who thought about it. The use of English-only instruction implied that white teachers, because they couldn't speak a Native tongue, would eventually be *less* intellectually flexible than their own students. It took Albert Kneale, a New York native who came to teach on Pine Ridge in 1899, two years to realize that the Lakota he tried to decipher among his students wouldn't help him at all with Cheyennes or Navajos, a jolt to him when he transferred to teach on other reservations. Learning English was just another step on the path of social evolution expected of Indian children, as basic as going to church or learning to eat with a knife and fork. But Native students were unique among second-language speakers of English in an important way: immigrant languages like German and Italian were eschewed in urban schools but tolerated in the communities where children lived. Native languages, by contrast, were not only banned in the classroom but targeted by official policy for eradication.[21]

Contrary to how Carlisle hoped to break down Indian communities by mixing students from many tribes, the day schools tried to strengthen those same communities, even if only in the interest of assimilation. Captain Pratt, in fact, disparaged the day schools as a futile attempt to delay integration into the white world. But there were those like Clarence who insisted on making of empathy a useful trait: "Mr. Three Stars knows his children as no white man could know them," one school visitor reported. "He understands their home life, for their home life was his before he went to Carlisle." Such a background was an advantage, but it also made the community politics of teaching more sensitive for a Pine Ridge homeboy than they would be for a tenderfoot like Kneale who hailed from upstate New York.[22]

Pedagogy had changed since Three Stars was a boy. Unlike rural schools of a previous age, the day schools of the early twentieth century were equipped with desks, books, pens, slates, and maps. The teacher was still the focus of attention, but regimentation had loosened. The focus on oral recitation was fading. Once the steady apprentice of Carlisle taskmasters, Clarence moved from the rote learning of his boyhood to coaxing his students to interpret and translate the world around them. While he may have drilled down on the finer points of intransitive verbs, Three Stars used the sand table to open up his schoolroom until it seemed the garden in the back and the enormous sky beyond were almost within reach. Orderliness and uniformity gave way to debate and wonder. His questions were less a catechism than a gentle prodding.[23]

Since the schools were built close to communities, teachers were expected to make regular home visits. While boarding school pupils tended to assimilate more quickly when apart from family, the day schools had a different advantage for the agency: they made it possible to proselytize parents. The teachers were bearers of an educational and cultural gospel, and matrons like Jennie visited homes to demonstrate domestic science and to "reach the hearts" of Indian mothers through their daughters. "Every instructor in these little [day] schools is expected to be a missionary bearing the light of morality, cleanliness, and knowledge to the very altars of the Indian's home," noted one official. Home visits required teacher and matron to make endless reports to appease the Indian Office's appetite for facts: which families eat on tables, how many cows do they milk, how many sleep on beds, which men wear long hair, which of them gamble—and that was only the start of it. One school inspector benignly called it a "sociological" study, but in fact the teachers were gathering intelligence for faraway Washington, even as they chatted about the lack of rain or the recent blight of grasshoppers.[24]

Beneath all the reading, writing, and 'rithmetic lurked an even more basic lesson. An Indian Office circular from 1911 advanced a framework for civic education that would teach students the ideals of self-government. So Three Stars developed an elaborate constitution for the "school city" that comprised the buildings and grounds of Day School No. 27. The fundamental precept, he advised, was that "one ought to love his neighbor as himself and do to others as he would have them do to him," a nod to his Episcopalian training. What's more, it said, "[Students] shall be taught to appreciate and utilize the benefits of education and the privileges of citizenship." But the rules of order went further than simple precepts. Students (called "citizens," in the constitution), were banned from swearing and bad conduct, forbidden from damaging property, encouraged to report untoward behavior, and urged "to check every tendency toward wrong thinking." Officers were elected for police, health, decoration, athletics, a "city council," a judiciary, and an attorney. Of fourteen pupils enrolled that year, four—Paul (16), Clarence Jr. (12), Guy (9), and Thomas (6)—were Three Stars's children. There were more posts to fill than there were students. Paul was president of the council, a member of the athletics committee, one of three judges in the judiciary, and the finance attorney—enough to keep busy even the most mischievous adolescent. The school on White Clay Creek set up its new order of business like a mini republic.

"There is an object of education," Three Stars wrote, "greater than merely learning the words and storing the mind with information." Even if their parents harbored doubts, Susie and Jennie Star and Samuel Little Soldier and Mary Flying Horse were being groomed to be good Americans.[25]

Outside the classroom, teachers had to be good with their hands. Three Stars could shoe a horse. He could shingle a house. He made benches and tables and boards for sidewalks. He could handle instruments, as he had done in the car shops at York during one of his school outings, and as an apprentice tailor working in a Carlisle shop with the Singer machine. As a small rancher he knew how to put in a garden. Mending garments, shoeing a mare, fixing a gate, planting potatoes—all were fit duties for his attention. Times had changed since the first classes at Carlisle, and Dakota job pickings were scarce. The trades that Clarence and Edgar learned were oversupplied on the reservation, made redundant by government annuities (like clothing) or obsolete by technological progress. Two-thirds of the day school population consisted of "full-bloods," most of whom would end up doing wage labor in harvest season, farming and ranching on a small scale, or working for the agency as freighters if they were lucky. The first day back to school after the summer break was even set back to October so parents and children could harvest potatoes for white farmers at three dollars a day in the Nebraska fields.[26]

To that end, the Indian school was always grounded in economics. By century's turn Native school attendance was compulsory, as it was coming to be at schools nationwide. Since appropriations were tied to enrollment, the policy of packing Indian boarding and day schools beyond capacity was an exercise in both high-minded strategy and transparent self-interest—more mouths meant more spending and more jobs. At boarding and day schools both, student labor provided essential maintenance as well as consumable fare ranging from sundry garden vegetables to dairy products to homespun pants, shirts, and dresses. Because of the split between educational and vocational learning, academic advancement was slow, and students could labor in the system for years. By 1910 about 12 percent of day school students were over fourteen, and the range of ages made teaching a constant challenge. By the 1920s the average Oglala was eighteen years old before finishing the eighth grade. Many were those who toiled in field and kitchen as older adolescents and adults in the orbit of the little red schoolhouse.[27]

Amenities ranged from adequate to meager. In school gardens they grew carrots, beans, beets, cabbage, turnips, pumpkins, peas, squash, potatoes, and watermelons. But produce was seasonal, and sometimes the hot lunch resembled a very thin gruel: a bean soup, as one Pine Ridge inspector put it, that consisted of "one bean and two soups." And though the children didn't pay to eat, there was no such thing as a free lunch: The cost of rations was "deducted from the Indians and sent to the schools," one agent noted, at the rate of $1.50 per pupil per week, presumably coming off the ledger for general appropriations. Clothing was little better. Boys were given two suits per year and the girls two dresses, but their garb was often ill-fitting. Shoes were frequently too small. There often wasn't enough material for the girls to replace their "objectionable shawls," as one official called them, a reminder that proper dress was an important part of their education. But Three Stars had long considered such "largesse" not only inadequate but misunderstood: these were not to be considered gifts, he insisted, but the fulfillment of treaty obligations.[28]

There were advantages to the way the Three Stars family lived. True, their children had to pick up and move with the regularity of military brats, since Clarence and Jennie worked at a half-dozen different day schools. And the family circumstances may have been modest—two beds for a family of six or seven! But in other ways they were richer than well-heeled city kin. The children had easy access to sporting gear and playground equipment. The kitchen cupboards were filled with enough dishware to feed seven families. They had a sewing machine, a washing machine, and more home and shop tools than a gentleman farmer could imagine. They even had a garden whose fruits they enjoyed with the help of a dozen obliging hands. And the children had access to a handsome library of over a hundred volumes, excluding textbooks, a rare bequest indeed in any Dakota homestead.

The day schools where Three Stars taught would eventually disappear. The sale of allotments to outsiders encouraged the growth of public schools, mostly for children of white ranchers. The new schools followed a similar curriculum, but most Indian children didn't know enough English to keep pace, and expenses like board and clothing forced many of them to stay in the government system. The public schools that catered to "mixed-blood" and white families soon expanded, however, and by 1930, given pressures to assimilate children and consolidate facilities, the majority of Indian students nationwide were enrolled in public institutions. It was an alternative that Three Stars himself would one day embrace when he founded a school that carried his own name.[29]

Other teachers, too, were pathfinders in the story of Lakota education. In 1891 Charles Eastman married Elaine Goodale, a New England writer who had gone west in 1885 after a teaching stint at Hampton Institute, Virginia, her goal to become a teacher among the Sioux. One couldn't imagine a more unlikely destiny for a precocious poet with a genteel upbringing. She taught at a day school at Lower Brule Agency for several years and, in 1890, was appointed supervisor of education in the Dakotas and visited Indian schools across the state. Goodale, in fact, might have been as good a day school teacher as Three Stars, and they shared many of the same beliefs, almost as kindred spirits. She taught her students the etiquette of knocking at a door before entering a dwelling. She dismissed Indian dances as encouraging vices like drinking. Like Three Stars she panned the poor quality of annuity clothing and argued for the payment of cash benefits instead. She saw the lack of employment faced by returned students. She, too, observed the futility of agriculture in Lakota country—neither deep tilling nor irrigation nor fallowing were practicable—and the difficulty of running cattle for a living if large tracts of land weren't held in common. Like Clarence she was bilingual, learning how to speak and write in Dakota, a close relative of Lakota. She even wore moccasins and traveled in a tipi when she did her rounds as supervisor of schools, making up for the lost time of a New England childhood.[30]

Even more startling is how much she resembled Three Stars as a teacher: both discouraged rote copying, encouraged conversational English rather than recitation, and dismissed out of hand the frequent complaint of white teachers that Native students weren't good at math or English. Both Three Stars and Eastman had figured out well before the end of the century what the Indian Office was still lacking forty years later: "Few, if any, of our teachers know how to begin to teach English to a non-English-speaking individual or group," Eastman said. Three Stars was the grandson of High Forehead, the boy raised in a canvas tipi at Red Cloud Agency, and Eastman, who grew up in a Dutch farmhouse in the Berkshires, was descended from Puritans; they had arrived by very different paths at much the same place by 1890, making eager learners of the fortunate children who came under their tutelage.[31]

Like hundreds, if not thousands, of others, the Eastmans had close ties to Richard Henry Pratt, a benefactor to many who fell under his spell. Several years after they met and married, the Eastmans worked for a spell at Carlisle. Though neither had attended the school, the pull of Pratt was irresistible, and in 1899 Charles began work as the school's outing agent. The job was a good fit for a man who was raised in an Indian camp and later graduated from medical school, capable of smoothing the way both for students and the white families who boarded them. He also traveled to reservations to recruit children and return east with those who would come under his supervision. Finally, he survived a near lethal bout of pneumonia and left the school to become government physician at Crow Creek Agency, but Pratt wasn't out of their lives yet.[32]

In 1911 Charles, feeling the economic burden of providing for a large family, confessed to the Captain in a desperate missive, "I have no money at all." Pratt, he hoped, would either put up some money for a lecture tour, finagle a salaried position for him, or offer an advance on a book he could write about American Indian history. "I am not asking a gratuity," he promised, "for I should work at it with all my might and I believe fairly earn the expenses of myself and family while engaged upon it." By this time the author of several books and a writer of national renown, Eastman was almost begging an old patron to pay his bills. He gently urged Pratt that even John Wanamaker might be solicited for the cause, but his search for a benefactor doesn't seem to have met with success.[33]

Elaine Eastman harbored doubts about Pratt's supreme confidence in boarding schools as the best place to erase the influence of the reservation. In 1890 she wrote to the Captain, "I differ fundamentally with you in regard to the best method of educating the Indians. I believe it is far wiser to educate the great majority of them in schools at their own homes."

Though professing grudging admiration for Carlisle, she concluded, "I am unequivocally opposed to your theory." In later years she had second thoughts, especially after she and Charles worked at Carlisle, where she edited the *Red Man* newspaper. By 1910 she would write to Pratt, who had by then been elevated to the brevet rank of general, "You owe it to the world to put your remarkable experiences and compelling ideas into permanent form." She later published an admiring biography, *Pratt, the Red Man's Moses*, very much in the Great Father tradition. She noted in its pages that his former student "Clarence Three Stars . . . was once reported as conducting the best day school in the service. Men like these," she continued, "rather than the highly educated product, afford perhaps the most convincing demonstration of the General's thesis."[34]

And yet Clarence's professional path could be used to justify almost any theory about teaching. After all, his success as a teacher was in the day schools, a system Pratt dismissed as "generally impracticable and a positive injury" to its patrons. The son of Yellow Knife was a star product of the boarding school system who was, at the same time, something of a determined sapper who would come to undermine the very premise of "civilizing" the Indian.[35]

During their decade and more in the day schools, a personal tragedy would leave a deep scar on Clarence and Jennie. Early in the new century they had sent their third child, Louisa, to be educated at the Pierre Indian Industrial School in the state capital. Pierre was more than one hundred miles to the northeast, and why they didn't want her closer to home at the local boarding school, or even at a day school on Pine Ridge, isn't clear. Her father appears to have believed for a time that the off-reservation schools were more effective, but he may have had a change of heart when, in 1907, the eleven-year-old Louisa fell ill at boarding school and returned to her family.

The Pierre facility was unexceptional as boarding schools went. The curriculum, split between academic and industrial activities, offered instruction through the eighth grade. Girls were tutored in piano, mandolin, and guitar—not so much for developing musical talent, one flyer admitted, as "for the purpose of breaking the monotony of the regular school routine." The school colors were navy blue and white; the school motto, “Step by Step,” was visualized as a series of ascending virtues—“Truth, Honesty, Industry, Reverence, and Courage”—that would mark the path to ultimate Success, a formula to which Captain Pratt would have heartily subscribed.[36]

Louisa’s routine would have been much like the one her mother knew at Carlisle. There was cooking and baking. There was cleaning and laundry. There was sewing, of course, a skill her father would have approved as an erstwhile tailor. And in the evening there were classes for the finer maneuvers of crocheting and knitting and embroidery. For recreation, there was a skating pond in winter. “While the sands of life are flowing,” hummed the school song, “while the days are going by, ever onward we are going, leaving school days with a sigh.” But high morale and a sound body didn’t always go hand in hand in residential school.[37]

The authorities sent Louisa home because she was infected with tuberculosis. Her father had encountered the illness at Carlisle, where TB accounted for most of the burials at the school cemetery in the early years. But she was returning to a place where the sickness was epidemic, its causes misunderstood. One Pine Ridge agent lamented that Indians died everywhere of TB and that they would continue to do so until intermarriage with whites bred out the bacillus. Some thought the consumption of tubercular beef issued by the government in the filthy slaughterhouses could spread the infection. But a prime cause was simply the change from living in tipis on the open land to crowding into small cabins that were badly ventilated, often dirty, and poorly drained. Even spitting was a common means of passing the bacterium, especially in close quarters, like the typical eighteen-by-twenty-four-foot log home where as many as twenty people might live. The warnings of doctors were sometimes ignored, and agency physician Dr. James R. Walker attributed part of the problem to the meddling of medicine men, who didn’t care much for the precepts of modern science.[38]

There simply weren’t enough physicians to stem the tide. In 1898, when Louisa was barely two, only a pair of doctors served an agency of 6,600 people; by 1906 there were still only two to care for 7,000. In 1899 Walker warned that half the population of Pine Ridge was afflicted with

TB, most of them children. Two years later, 68 of 130 deaths of those over age ten were caused by the bacillus. For a few years at the turn of the century Walker made some headway, and the mortality rate dropped, but not for long. The year Louisa returned home, TB killed over 300 people on the reservation. Walker noted that the death rate had overtaken births on Pine Ridge and reasoned that the Oglalas were "in a fair way to extermination" if something wasn't done about it. Tuberculosis was to Clarence's time what COVID-19 has been to our own.[39]

The first week of March 1908, after an extended stay with her family, Louisa Three Stars died of tuberculosis. She was twelve years old, and had been recently allotted land on Bear-in-the-Lodge Creek. The service at the Episcopal Church in Pine Ridge was conducted by Edward Black Bear and George Fire Thunder, brother of Clarence's friend Edgar. Louisa, who was even younger than her father had been when he first boarded the train for Carlisle and younger than her mother when she did the same, was dead. To imagine a life cut short before she had a chance to flower must have deeply grieved her parents, for whom education far from home had opened a new world. If Clarence and Jennie had hoped that Pine Ridge would be a safer haven for their daughter than Pierre, they were wrong—her homecoming was probably a preparation for what seemed foreordained.[40]

The blight of the epidemic wouldn't diminish any time soon. The Oglalas grimly joked of TB that a sick man ordering a new suit of clothes for the grave was almost dead before the material could be measured and cut. Lakota leader John Grass was said to have lost all seven of his sons to the sickness over a ten-year period. The Pine Ridge day schools gave prizes for the best essay in the annual Tuberculosis Contest. By 1915 the crisis was still growing, and the agent requested federal money for a sanatorium to isolate patients, an appeal eventually refused. In 1920, almost a third of Oglalas were thought to be afflicted, and close to half were stricken by 1922. The next year, 40 percent of deaths on Pine Ridge were caused by the "white plague," four times the national rate.[41]

Louisa was lost, buried now in the sprawling Episcopal cemetery in Pine Ridge village, another Indian casualty of yet another grim disease.

Soon after, Clarence penned and published a poem in her memory. It was an elegy for a child who had come back from the world beyond Pine Ridge, just as he had, irreversibly changed:

You and I seek for education,
In spite of old things,
Leaving Father and Mother,
Other relatives, friends,
And everything that seems
Endear to us, tho we went
(This is sacrificing) leaving
All for education, no matter
What comes in our way
We endure it all altho
We die; that is what we
Did, Louisa, I know it

You and I long for education,
A thing that is leading on
To, where? I asked. I answer,
Perhaps to a better land.
This is another definition
Of the word I give, but it seems,
It is pointing that way.
You and I see it, I know
For sure, because the Great Spirit
Seems to whisper it to my ears,
From time to time, day by day,
Giving us courage to continue
And endure it all, altho we
Die, and that is what we did,
Louisa, I know it.[42]

1. Little Wound (*left*), with wife and son, led a large Oglala band in the 1870s that included the Three Stars family and rivaled the following of Red Cloud. Library of Congress, LC-USZ-62-41716.

2. The first students at Carlisle Indian Industrial School, in 1879, were Lakota children from Rosebud and Pine Ridge. Clarence is in the front row, eleventh from right, under the window; Edgar Fire Thunder, back row, is eighth child from the left; Luther Standing Bear, hatless, is in the front row below the door. Cumberland County Historical Society, Carlisle, Pennsylvania.

3. By the time Clarence went to Philadelphia in 1884, Carlisle had established itself as the flagship off-reservation boarding school for Native boys and girls across the country. Cumberland County Historical Society, Carlisle, Pennsylvania.

4. For its first quarter century, Carlisle was governed by Superintendent Richard Henry Pratt, an army officer beloved and hated alike by Native students. He was eventually removed from his post for insubordination. Richard Henry Pratt Papers. Yale Collection of Western Americana. Beinecke Rare Book and Manuscript Library.

5. Luther Standing Bear accompanied Clarence to Philadelphia from Carlisle on a work assignment at Wanamaker's. Though the two became close friends and followed a similar career path early in life, they eventually had a falling out. Library of Congress, LC-USZ62-56421.

6. (*top*) The main Wanamaker store where Clarence and Luther worked was housed in an old railroad depot in downtown Philadelphia, fronted with an ornate facade. Library of Congress, LC-DIG-stereo-1s15062.

7. Wanamaker's Grand Depot emporium was at the cutting edge of the American department store in the late nineteenth century, offering merchandise from around the world at a standard price in an innovative and dynamic setting. Collection of the Historical Society of Pennsylvania.

8. John Wanamaker was as well known in Philadelphia as William Penn and Benjamin Franklin, a captain of commerce who introduced conventions that department-store shoppers take for granted even today. Library of Congress, LC-DIG-ggbain-04978.

9. (*opposite top*) Pine Ridge agent Valentine McGillycuddy (*seated at center*) doctored Crazy Horse during his final hours, ran his agency with an iron hand, and was a defiant foe of Red Cloud. Standing directly to his right, in uniform, is Captain of Police George Sword. Nebraska State Historical Society.

10. Three Stars worked as assistant, disciplinarian, and teacher at the Oglala Boarding School, built in 1883, which burned down a decade later. Library of Congress, LC-USZ62-17610.

11. (*above*) In 1890 the boarding school was posted with guards and rimmed with barbed wire during the unrest that led to the Wounded Knee massacre and its aftermath. Eastman-Goodale-Dayton Family Papers, Smith College Special Collections, 7956.

12. Charles Eastman began his career as a doctor tending to Wounded Knee victims at Pine Ridge. A renowned author and activist, he was a friend of the Three Stars family and colleague of Clarence's. Library of Congress, LC-USZ62-102275.

13. In 1891 Clarence traveled to Washington DC with a Lakota delegation seeking compensation for their losses after Wounded Knee. Reputed to be the first "full-blood" Sioux interpreter to visit the capital, Three Stars is in the third row from the bottom, second from the left. Library of Congress, LC-USZ62-4536.

14. Jennie Dubray married Clarence in 1892 and raised seven children. She studied at Carlisle, worked in the day schools and on the family ranch, and was allotted land that became the family homestead. Cumberland County Historical Society, Carlisle, Pennsylvania.

15. Red Cloud was a legend on the battlefield, a thorn in the side of reservation agents, and an influential Oglala political leader. He knew the Three Stars family well and traveled with Clarence as an envoy to Washington on an official mission in 1897. Library of Congress, LC-USZ62-104561.

16. Red Cloud was the only Oglala to have a house in the early days of Pine Ridge Reservation. Library of Congress, LC-USZ62-124293.

17. Richard Pettigrew, chairman of the Senate Committee on Indian Affairs, got an earful from Red Cloud and Three Stars about government corruption on Pine Ridge in 1897. Library of Congress, LC-USZ62-38927.

18. Clarence and Jennie taught at Day School No. 27, not far from Pine Ridge village, for the better part of a decade. The schoolroom is in the foreground and the teacher's cottage in the rear. The outlying grounds included a barn, a garden, and herds of cows and horses. From Phenix, *Southern Workman*, courtesy HathiTrust.

19. *(opposite)* This portrait of Three Stars shows him surrounded by school colleagues. From Ross, *Pine Ridge Reservation*, courtesy HathiTrust.

Day School Employees, Pine Ridge Reservation, South Dakota.

Edward Truman.

Mrs. Truman.

Clarence Three Stars.

George Simeral.

Mrs. Simeral.

20. (top) An innovative teacher, Three Stars went far beyond Indian Office norms to engage and educate his Oglala students. From Phenix, *Southern Workman*, courtesy HathiTrust.

21. Elaine Goodale Eastman, though less famous than her husband, Charles, was an effective day-school teacher, an accomplished writer, and a state supervisor of education. Eastman-Goodale-Dayton Family Papers, Smith College Special Collections, 1383.

22. Dr. James R. Walker combated a tuberculosis epidemic on Pine Ridge during his long residence on the reservation and worked tirelessly to record Lakota beliefs and lifeways. From Ross, *Pine Ridge Reservation*, courtesy HathiTrust.

23. George Sword (*center, in uniform*) was many things to many people: warrior, Episcopalian deacon, police captain, Sun Dancer, judge, and anthropological informant. Library of Congress, LC-USZ62-104571.

24. James McLaughlin, inspector for the Office of Indian Affairs, visited Pine Ridge as a government envoy in 1909 to soften up the Oglalas before Bennett County was opened to white settlement. State Historical Society of North Dakota, 00036-134.

MAIN BUILDING HIAWATHA INDIAN ASYLUM

25. (*opposite top*) For eleven years, the Hiawatha Indian Asylum was the home of Clarence and Jennie's daughter Sophia, diagnosed with a form of schizophrenia. She would spend over half her life institutionalized. South Dakota State Historical Society, South Dakota Digital Archives, 2009-07-02-012.

26. The Three Stars homestead, on Jennie's allotment near Bear-in-the-Lodge Creek, had sixty-five horses and thirteen acres under cultivation in 1925. The assessor who took this picture described Clarence (*standing, in overalls*) as an "agitator." National Archives and Records Administration, Washington DC.

27. (*above*) Clarence's allotment, which he patented and sold, is today a piece of rolling, high-grass prairie, dotted with thistle and hay in high summer. Photo by author.

28. Jennie Three Stars died in 1921, after an active life in school, community, church, and family, and is buried in Allen, South Dakota. Photo by author.

29. Clarence, buried in 1931, rests alongside Jennie in Inestimable Gift Cemetery. They are surrounded by several generations of their descendants. Photo by author.

9

A Place Called Pine Ridge

Clarence Three Stars lived most of his life on a broad expanse of mixed-grass prairie denoted on road atlases and topographical maps today as the Pine Ridge Indian Reservation. Established in 1889, the reservation was something of a cartographical oddity, being a rectangle made up of straight lines on three sides with a lazy, riverine border on much of the north side; the reservation was some three million acres, carved out of a country where the Lakotas, long inspired by the circle of life—the sun, the moon, the tipi, the round of seasons—were now boxed in by borders surveyed and drawn with an uncompromising straight edge. It was, in Lakota country, the equivalent of squaring a circle, the fence-post holes dug deep in the earth and running clear from Pine Ridge over to Oglala and up to Red Shirt, then back to Potato Creek and down to Allen and beyond, a forbidding jigsaw that crisscrossed the earth in the name of slicing it into surveyed sections that could be bought and sold like bolts of cloth, a pure-bred sire, or a fattened heifer on a tipsy agency scale.[1]

The village of Pine Ridge, established on White Clay Creek in 1878, was named for a ridge of pines that flanked the southern end of the reservation. Agent Valentine McGillycuddy noted the agency had moved eight or ten times before Pine Ridge: "The real responsibility [for lack of a permanent home] can be traced to bribery, fraud, and corruption on the part of some of the former representatives of the government, in the way of contractors, agents, & c." In other words, the tiny headquarters of Red Cloud and later, the Pine Ridge Agency, had migrated all over the map, nomadic in a way that only fickle government planners could have made it. In the early days Pine Ridge village was a crude domain, complete with privy vaults and cesspools that, even if covered, were a rank offense to the nostrils. Agent McGillycuddy worried that the wells were being infected and that Pine Ridge had become a hangout for renegades, especially Hunkpapa Lakotas who were said to steal rations and advise resistance. Slowly the settlement grew into something more respectable, as buildings were equipped with pipes for water and sewage, wooden plank sidewalks were replaced with concrete, and fruit trees were planted for shade, making the village a habitable place, if not exactly an administrative oasis. Turnover was high among the people who worked there, and most employees—agents, teachers, matrons, clerks—would come and go over the decades like field hands at harvest time, while most Lakotas dug in for the remainder of a lifetime, and the lifetimes of their children, and often even the course of generations to come.[2]

Pine Ridge became the home of the Oglalas, the people of Crazy Horse and Red Cloud, who while not force-marched hundreds of miles with large loss of life like the Navajos and Cherokees were nonetheless led on a dubious journey from one agency setting to the next, a cause for uncertainty and considerable anguish before they were finally settled. Their new home was part of an intricate system of reservations intended, ostensibly, to protect Indians from white encroachment—and to remove them from land that settlers, miners, and railroads desperately wanted. Many such reserves were instituted west of the Mississippi after the Civil War, not long before detention camps were being developed for suspect populations in places as far removed as Cuba and South Africa at the turn of the century. The reservations were an early draft in the story of modern mass detention, decades before such accommodations were called *concentration* or *internment* camps, far removed from the prying eyes of meddling judges, nosey politicians, or muckraking investigative journalists.[3]

A concentration camp? Impossible! Not in America! Given that Pine Ridge was the size of Delaware and Rhode Island combined, such a claim seems absurd on the face of it. But terms of confinement are subjective, and a windowless cell in a dark city lockup can, in another context, be no more confining than a rolling prairie opening to a long horizon. The Oglalas and the Cheyenne allies who settled with them met all the primary conditions of later subject populations. They were held, because of their racial identity, without due process or appeal. They were confined without regard to whether they had fought against the government. The vast majority, reckoned as "civilians," were required to obtain an official pass to leave the reservation—going AWOL could land a body in jail for up to nine months. Though not prisoners in a strict sense, they were mired in a legal limbo in which adult males could vote, but only in rigged referendums and with no understanding of when, or even whether, their detention would come to an end. The brutality of the modern concentration camp was still to come in the next century, but the Lakotas, and tribes like them, had a taste of its underlying principles while the Gilded Age was still aglow. The reservations were intended to confront an immediate and temporary "problem"—convincing tribes to disown their former ways and assimilate the habits of their white brethren—that proved, with time, to have no visible end in sight.[4]

Whatever the terms of their confinement, the Oglalas held fast to the land. Pine Ridge was a homeland well within the borders laid out in the 1868 treaty, a wedge of the territory promised Lakotas that later generations regard as one of the last assets—or blessings—left to the tribe. Pine Ridge wasn't the sacred Black Hills, and it wasn't the heartland of the area Oglalas roamed for decades along the Platte River in Wyoming and Nebraska. But it was better than the alternatives; the government had offered, for example, to move the tribe to Indian Territory after the dustup at Little Bighorn. Once the buffalo were gone and military resistance was suppressed, the reservation was their last best hope.[5]

Pine Ridge was an institution of sorts. Like Carlisle, it had its rules and boundaries, laws and punishments, the bulk of them designed and imposed by outsiders more than a thousand miles away. But there was nothing institutional about its appearance, sprawling as it did over some four thousand square miles, composed of streams and badlands, cottonwood-filled river bottoms and bluestem prairie grass that stretched as far as the eye could see. And yet for all the expanse of Pine Ridge, the comings and goings of daily life were closely monitored. The government tracked its denizens through an annual census. Names and numbers were carefully tabbed. Transactions were scrutinized by federal accountants. While the people weren't surrounded by brick walls or concertina wire, within a few decades the reservation would be fenced to keep livestock in and trespassers out and to maintain a visible border with the world beyond. The Oglalas were interned in a giant camp under the watchful eye of the Great Father.

In the days before they came to Pine Ridge, the Oglalas had lived and traveled in groups of a dozen or so extended families, each band consisting of a few hundred people in total. These *tiyospaye*, as Lakotas call them, came together in summer to celebrate the Sun Dance and visit and trade with friends and kin. But on Pine Ridge the traditional bonds of family and community were soon to be frayed. "These villages are made up of the refuse of the entire reservation," complained the agent in 1886. For him, the villages allowed leaders like Red Cloud to maintain a collective base of power in defiance of government rule. So the agent's first order of business was to disperse people far and wide across the reservation and break down the communities where they talked and gossiped and grumbled about the laws that now confined them. The strategy was ironic in that the people called themselves, in Lakota, *Oglala*, meaning "to scatter one's own."[6]

They were strewn to the four directions, cast out on the land where they settled along the creeks and streams that ran across Pine Ridge to feed the White and Cheyenne rivers. It was otherwise a dry land. Settling by the creeks meant they wouldn't have to drill wells, but irrigation was for naught because the creeks were too small and often too distant from the fields they would eventually plant. "The white man has taken from the Sioux pretty much all the land that can be considered arable," admitted one agent, a confession that one after another of his successors would affirm. If seven thousand white people, instead of Indians, tried to live there with seed and implements, he speculated, "they would die of starvation."[7]

They had lived in tipis of animal skin, cozy in winter with a smoke hole for fires, cool in summer with liftable flaps. But tipis were portable, and people who could easily pick up and move were hard to control. Only fixed abodes would keep Oglalas bound to the land. And so many of them, encouraged by reservation agents, went to work raising log houses with dirt roofs and floors by the time Clarence returned from Carlisle. The houses were small—a family of ten might live in a space ten by sixteen feet, a density that didn't change for decades. The people built the house frames; then the agency provided doors, windows, and nails to hurry them on their way to "civilization." After that the day schools spread across the reservation, just as the people did, a way to keep Oglalas confined to small groups not inclined to large assemblies except when food was distributed. And the food delivery was fragmented into substations for dispensing biweekly rations and herding the people into areas that ignored traditional ties of kinship and *tiyospaye*. As if that weren't enough, annuities like clothing were distributed to numerous band leaders rather than to a single chief, a way to further devolve power to an extreme. As Agent McGillycuddy noted, "It is to be hoped that the time is not far distant when there will be as many bands as there are families"; "in other words, every head of a family his own chief." The more isolated and fragmented Lakotas became, the easier they were to control.[8]

Just as it did at Red Cloud when Clarence was young, the government was itching to know how many people were in its custody. Census numbers determined appropriations, which in turn decided whether anyone would go hungry or lack proper clothing. The census also required proper Christian names and surnames so that everyone could be identified for heirship purposes. So the government did a tribal head count every year. Oglalas, hungry and confined, did what they could to protect themselves. When they saw the counters coming, they might pull children out of school to have them counted twice, or draw rations "for all their ghosts," as the government claimed. In 1886, while Clarence was working at the boarding school, police, employees, and interpreters marched out to the various districts sporting grim faces and toting official roll sheets. They counted up families, person by person, then turned the totals over to the police, who held the people under armed guard so they couldn't double back and be counted again. "There was no possibility of doubling or swapping babies as had been their custom heretofore," one official boasted. (The agent estimated the census would save Washington $50,000 on the next year's beef ration.) Like everyone else, Clarence's life was clotted with numbers. He was #1735 in the census that year. He was student #1876 at Carlisle—a number that recalled the year his people routed Custer. He would become allottee #2058. He would be a teacher at Day Schools No. 2, 3, 14, 19, 20, and 27. Enumeration was yet another way of tightening the government's grip.[9]

So huge was the fiefdom of Pine Ridge, stretching some ninety miles from east to west and fifty miles north to south, that bureaucrats struggled to manage its enormous girth. Officials carved the reservation into districts, nine of them eventually, based on watersheds like White Clay, Wounded Knee, Porcupine, and Medicine Root. Each was assigned a boss farmer responsible for monitoring school runaways, doling out money from individual accounts, and instructing whoever would listen on how to plant a field of corn or brand a calf. Government men drew lines on the map, ones that people couldn't see among the buffalo grass and bluestem, lines that would become more important than even the ridges and gullies that deeply scored the land. A portion of the land remained in tribal control, unallotted. But the rest of it was the business of the allotting crews, teams of men with compass and chain, with flagmen and interpreters and people to cook their food, men possessed of the secret of triangulation who would draw the plats that broke the earth into contiguous parcels of soil. They followed in the path of Washington and Jefferson and Lincoln, president-surveyors all, examiners often of Indian land because what could be marked off and measured could eventually be taken by science and law. Parceling out the land confirmed the scattering of the Oglalas, many of whom had planted themselves along streams and rivers in the early years, only to be allotted most of their land on the wide prairie. Owning the land would mold them into farmers and ranchers, then good community members, and ultimately American citizens once they had worked the land long enough to imbibe the vital virtues of patience, piety, and back-breaking toil.[10]

There was just one problem: the people didn't want the land in lots. In 1894, 90 percent of Oglalas, including Three Stars, opposed allotment. They petitioned, in vain, to have the reservation given to the entire tribe in fee simple, and the agent agreed with them: "The allotments of their lands in severalty will result in the degradation of this people and their speedy extinction." Nine years later, with allotment imminent, 90 percent still resisted the policy, while others, mostly "mixed-bloods" and white men married to Indian women, settled on the best pieces of land they could find in anticipation of the reckoning to come. It would take twenty years to fully allot the reservation, a span in which most of the Oglala estate was either leased, patented, sold, mortgaged, or when the banks had anything to say about it, foreclosed on and sold at public auction.[11]

The land allotted was less for ploughing and planting than for running herds of heifers and steers. "Agriculture is rather a precarious occupation in this climate," admitted one official. And tillable land, by the government's own reckoning, amounted to about one-fifth of Pine Ridge, much of it on its eastern flank. The problem of farming was often one of scale—early allottees had neither the machinery nor the know-how to farm sufficient acreage and harvest a sellable surplus. Ranching had similar drawbacks. Many Oglalas were "land poor," in effect, forced to lease their considerable acreage rather than ranch it themselves since they lacked the means to buy enough cattle to graze the land and fatten them for a profit at market.[12]

Every season was a mix of hope and hazard. The weather could be sunny and pleasant in the morning, raw and blustery by afternoon, and bring a raging storm by evening that could leave a freshet of rain or fifteen inches of snow. Temperatures ranged from 107 degrees above zero to 44 below. A host of challenges scared away many a white neighbor, but the Oglalas, rooted to the land by treaty, had little choice but to stand their ground. Every decade bore the scars of disaster. A drought in 1893 caused four-fifths of the reservation to be "burned over" by fires, and the hay crop fell short of filling barns for winter feed. Ice formed early in the winter of 1899 and stayed through the season, starving cattle who couldn't get to grass. The first good year for rain in half a decade came in 1901, but a severe snowstorm in April devastated many herds. Two years later, two thousand head of cattle were lost in bitter winter storms, while in 1906 a lightning strike in June destroyed the agency barn and with it 150,000 pounds of oats and hay. It could snow as much as fifty inches in a week—or the land could go weeks without moisture. "Sufficient rainfall was to be expected no more than one year in three," noted a visitor who marveled at the extremes of weather. They were dogged by intense heat, hailstorms (being in the "hail belt" meant insurers wouldn't underwrite them), drenching rain, flooding, grasshoppers, drought, and early frost.

"It is unfortunate that these Indians, once the owners of the fertile valley of the Platte and much other farming land, should have been relegated to a country like this," mused agent W. H. Clapp at the turn of the century, "where farming is impossible even for white men."[13]

When the land was dry, the threat of fire was never far. A flame whipped up by the wind could run faster than a horse and jump a road if it got out of hand. When smoke was sighted, men and women would pile into a wagon and head for the billowing cloud to help tame it. Fanned by the wind, a bad fire could burn for a week. Ranchers might kill a colt and cut the hide so it dangled in strips, then rope it on head and hind feet and drag it along to snuff out the edge of a blaze. In good times they would have cattle graze down a catch pasture in front of their buildings to keep the flames at bay, or they would plow a firebreak around a barn and haystacks and just hope for the best. The damage in dead cattle and horses could stagger a ranch; even harder to stomach were the animals maimed and burned beyond help. But it was no different than the big city; Clarence had seen in Philadelphia how a blaze could bring down a building or reduce a city block to a layer of rubble and ash in a matter of minutes.[14]

The Oglalas tilled where they could on turf they were assigned using the tools they were bestowed. The first allottees were granted two mares and a pair of cows with a wagon, plough, harrow, harness, and axe. Later they were given twenty heifers in lieu of tools, and by the 1920s, when the agency grew tired of dealing in dry goods and livestock, the offer was just a handful of cash. They fenced off vegetable gardens and dug root cellars. They built barns and herded cattle. Those who had farmable land and sufficient tools grew oats, corn, potatoes, and wheat; those who didn't raised herds they bought and sold on and off the reservation, though the nearest rail head was dozens of miles distant. By the time William McKinley became president, Three Stars had dozens of cattle and his own brand, making a good living in the days when Pine Ridge still offered small ranchers a modicum of hope.[15]

But prohibitions were everywhere. No one could sell stock without the district farmer's permission. No one could sell Pine Ridge timber off-reservation. No one could dispose of an animal without the agent's consent in writing—those who killed breeding stock in winter, when the beef ration fell short, were punished. One needed permission to kill cattle even for a celebration or feast, and no cows could be felled unless barren, no steers younger than three years old. There was a lack of credit, a lack of seeds, a lack of fencing and tools. The people were issued stirring plows that couldn't break the earth. Then breaking plows came, and mowing machines were loaned out because hardly anyone could buy them outright. Equipment loans came due within five years, but most families couldn't put food on the table, make improvements on the land, and save enough to settle a debt all at once. For many, the land became a burden rather than a blessing.[16]

Despite it all, descendants of Lakota hunters turned to herding with a passion. By 1895 Oglala ranchers were raising two million pounds of beef per year, proof of what they could muster in spite of abundant obstacles. Medicine man Frank Fools Crow remembered the period from the turn of the century until the First World War as one in which his people "learned what unity was; what it was like for a family to work together, and what it was like to co-operate with relatives and neighbors." After the difficult period of Wounded Knee and its aftermath, many Oglalas warmed to the task of remaking their lives—that is, until the Great War brought loss of livestock, wide-scale leasing, and returning Lakota doughboys who had seen another world and were no longer satisfied with the old ways.[17]

Life got leaner and harder. Assets leaked out of Oglala hands like water from a broken hydrant. The Homestead Act was amended to increase land grants from 320 to 640 acres, leading big cattlemen to look for undeveloped land, usually on reservations, where they could run their herds. Leasing was the main culprit. Nonpayment of leases was widespread, but the Indian Office claimed it didn't have the personnel to process complaints. Leased and trespassing cattle headed for the creeks, fouling water used by "full-blood" families and leading to bouts of trachoma and other illnesses. Though it provided a steady income, leasing removed land stewardship from Oglala oversight. It was as if the Indian Office had thrown a rope to rescue Lakotas—then tied them in knots once they managed to gain a grip on it. And the coming of the Great War would only intensify the problem.[18]

For the average Lakota, owning land wasn't the same as keeping it. Washington created competency commissions to determine which Indian lands could be taken out of trust by decree and then fee patented. For years the superintendent had the unilateral right to grant such certificates of competence. Many were those Oglala declared "competent" to patent their allotment—and thus pay taxes and become American citizens—even if they were illiterate and unable to speak English. They were citizens by decree, not by choice. On Pine Ridge, Three Stars became president of the Indian Protective Association, a group of activists who complained to the commissioner if lands had been patented, and thus subject to taxation and foreclosure, without approval by the allottees. Families who had been kept in wardship status for years were suddenly exposed to tax bills they couldn't pay, in which case the land would be mortgaged and removed from Indian hands.[19]

To buy a roll of fence or a new plow or even a fancy Stetson from Dawson's dry goods, allottees had to be resourceful. Money from land sales, leases, and allotment benefits were put in Individual Indian Money (IIM) accounts, closely monitored by the government. Small amounts were given to account holders on request, but usually in draft order scrip redeemable only with local traders. Frustrated by tight purse strings, Oglalas spent a lot of effort trying to get IIM money at any cost, to the point where some would buy useless or questionable machinery just to see their assets put to use: "Every scheme imaginable is invented for an excuse to get his funds," complained one official, "and he will never rest until the last dollar is withdrawn." Sometimes the purpose of buying "useless" machinery was nothing more than to sell it to a white man for cash. Just as Pratt designed a system where students could only draw their earnings with the Captain's permission, so did the IIM balance sheet, administered by a trustee, resemble a cross between a community savings bank and the tight-fisted credit ledger of a company store.[20]

Cash was hard to come by; families scrambled for work—not always of the paying kind. For years every able-bodied Indian male aged twenty-one to forty-five (teachers and missionaries excluded) was required to do two to five days of unpaid road work annually, and more in case of emergency—what was called a *corvée* during the Middle Ages. Occupants of Pine Ridge jail were drafted for roadwork, and Indian convicts, most doing time for trivial offenses, put up fifty-five miles of telephone line connecting all subagencies with Pine Ridge village. Those not incarcerated were introduced to the wage economy: felling trees and hauling them to the agency sawmill and then driving the piles for foundations of bridges and dams. In summer thousands were removed from ration rolls to do repair work or haul freight for modest pay, while others toiled for railroads as coal tenders and section hands. By the 1920s, 40 percent of Oglalas earned a living by working in towns or doing stoop labor in Nebraska potato fields, abandoning their own land and holding their children out of school so the family could earn enough cash to get through the winter if rations ran short. They worked when there was work to be had, they consumed their rations when times were hard, and—in the absence of tillable fields—sat around "waiting for [their] cattle to grow," as one official put it. If the men didn't have their hair cut short, they weren't given any work at all.[21]

Oglalas figured the Great Father owed them every single gunnysack full of sugar and flour the drovers could haul up from the Nebraska rail line. The Black Hills agreement of 1877 said, "[Rations] shall be continued until the Indians are able to support themselves." By the time Clarence was a veteran teacher, every head of family counted in the census received a monthly ration of forty pounds of beef, gross; two ounces baking powder; one pound beans; one-half pound coffee; three pounds corn; twelve pounds flour; two ounces salt; one ounce soap; ten ounces sugar; and two pounds bacon. Old and sick people were given extra shares. But ration weights could lie as much as census numbers—what was forty pounds of beef, exactly? The meat wasn't always edible; beef on the hoof could shed 50 percent of mass during a long Dakota winter before butchering; and from time to time the government was known to lay a heavy thumb on the scales when no one was looking. Washington intended that the Oglalas should work at becoming self-sufficient. But in Lakota eyes the rations and annuities amounted to tribute the government paid for annexing the Hills in the first place. In 1901 Superintendent Brennan ordered 857 able-bodied men to be cut from the ration rolls, among them Three Stars, who admitted he was self-supporting. From that point on, the family raised and traded for its own fare from the Three Stars ranch and the little red schoolhouses they managed, with gardens and fields at their bidding.[22]

As expert hunters, Lakotas had learned for generations to feast when they had the chance—the next good meal might be days away—a habit that continued on the reservation. Sharing with anyone in need was, and is, a stock Lakota virtue. Giveaways were standard for every major life event, and public gatherings provided a meal for everyone and leftovers to anyone who came with a vessel to carry part of the feast away. Being stingy was a sign of meanness, even indecency. And yet the government frowned on sharing. Once a family received its biweekly rations, their food might be gone in a day or two, so willing were Lakotas to share with extended family. Officials fretted that anyone with a steady job would be beset by relatives for food and raiment—which no one could refuse and which might discourage any inclination to work at all. The ethos of community clashed with the credo of the individual, a gulf that made the prospect of assimilation difficult for many Oglalas.[23]

Considering the frequent shortages, the difficult odds, and the byzantine legal restraints, one would think that reservation crime was commonplace. But most infractions were sparse, if they could even be called criminal in the first place. Loafing, or vagrancy, drew a five-dollar fine or ten days in the poky, ten dollars or thirty days on the second offense. (Given the later popularity of leasing land, almost anyone could have been hauled in on that charge.) During fiscal year 1904, for example, there were ten cases of drunkenness, thirteen of fornication (unmarried intercourse), eighteen of adultery, eight of spousal assault, five of common assault, nine of horse stealing, four of changing brands of stock, and random others. Such numbers seem remarkably small for a reservation of 6,700 people. Though agents might have been tempted to underreport antisocial behavior to burnish their reputations, the fact that serious crimes were investigated by federal authorities would have limited chances to fudge the numbers. Penalties for violations could be harsh, however. The sentence for being drunk, said Fools Crow, was a year and a day in the village jail. Charlie Black Horse Jr., issued two horses for allotment benefits, sold them to a white man without permission of the superintendent and got ninety days in the slammer for his trouble.[24]

Given the low rates of violence, Indian police turned instead to tracking misdeeds of moral trespass, especially those that figured in heirship claims. Such was the need for documenting legal possession of land that anyone married by custom ("Indian marriage"), as opposed to formal ceremony, spent time in the guard house, not the least popular place on Pine Ridge. Many Oglalas were so destitute they hardly considered a week in lockup an inconvenience. By 1910 marriage licenses were required by the agent, a pricey ask for people perennially strapped for cash. A decade later the licenses were being issued free to noncitizen Indians, but many lived so far from the issuing place they simply didn't bother. Since divorces also cost money in the state courts, many Oglalas resorted to a simple form of separation or another custom marriage to annul a previous union. Clarence and Jennie chose a church ceremony in 1892, a sign that they were amenable to strictures of both law and church.[25]

It's not that violence didn't happen. Three of the day schools were torched during the Wounded Knee campaign. The No. 2 day school teacher, Frank Lewis, was murdered in 1890, shot by a man named Eagle Horse, who suffered from tuberculosis. Eagle Horse was said to have murdered Lewis so that a white man would accompany him to the spirit world—after which he went up on a hill and shot himself. In 1899 locals burned down a slaughterhouse in the White Clay district to protest the issuance of block meat rather than beef on the hoof. Horse thieves were considered worst of all, and if cornered, were likely to kill themselves rather than go to trial. When a major crime was committed, one agent noted, Indians dread "going over the road to Deadwood" to be tried, but such occasions were exceptional, especially for a people living under pressures that white American communities could hardly have imagined.[26]

Amid relative peace and calm, despite plague and epidemic and harsh weather, the population of Pine Ridge quietly grew. With their seven children, Jennie and Clarence were hardly unusual for the time. One physician wrote of the Oglalas, "They would multiply and overrun the country"—if not for tuberculosis. And though challenged with the pressure of assimilation, many of the old ways continued. Births were handled in the family. Indian women in the early years didn't ask for doctors and, surmised one official, were in better shape than white women because they worked harder and didn't wear corsets. They could bear up under more pain than white women, he added, and some would rather die than be aided by a man. Abortions occasionally happened and were sometimes fatal, but whatever the procedure, many families only called a doctor when death was near. Still, over the course of half a century, the tribal population increased from 7,200 in 1880 to 8,000 in 1928, notwithstanding tuberculosis, Spanish flu, high infant mortality, and attendant deaths such as exposure and starvation in the rugged badlands and enormous prairie expanses of Dakota.[27]

Through it all, Lakota culture adapted and endured. Oglalas found ways to challenge their reduced circumstances, profit from them, learn from them, coexist with principles that might have merged with their own. Ceremonies like the Sun Dance and *yuwipi* (a healing rite) were prohibited by priest and agent but survived by going underground far from the prying eye of authorities. "Full-blood" men like George Sword filled enforcement jobs as policemen, a position that rewarded the warrior ethic so prominent in Lakota life. Judges on the local Court of Offenses, a panel that long suffered for want of funding, eventually practiced as justices of the peace, a role that remembered the authority of elders in prereservation days. The *tiyospaye* transformed from a group of nomadic extended families to a church-based and school-based community that still relied on the traditional virtues of generosity and cooperation. On issue day the people played their games of shinny, as they long had, a rough and tumble game of field hockey with hand-carved sticks and balls made of rags, running the length of fields and pastures for hours on end in contests that might cover half a mile and more. Oglalas were creative when life was hard. The telegraph line to Chadron was plagued by mysterious prairie fires that burned down the poles, the unfortunate result, officials suspected, of people commandeering posts for firewood to cook their rations—until a new line was built with two-inch metal piping to protect it from mischief. Just as Carlisle had its runaways, Pine Ridge had dissenters who wouldn't yield easily to the new ways of the *wasicu*.[28]

Back and forth the people went. Progress brought them log houses, warm and dry if chinked and shingled, but houses couldn't be moved like a tipi. Progress brought them doctors with black bags and elixirs, but they knew nothing about plants and herbs. Progress brought them sacks of sugar and flour, but the mush they ate made their teeth go bad. It was progress that brought them judges and teachers and agents, but why did none of them speak Lakota? Progress, too, brought them children who could read words from a book but not the trail of scat left by a herd of deer in broad daylight. Progress brought them gingham dresses and hand-tooled cowboy boots but also the sting of whiskey and the night of incoherence and numbness that followed. Progress brought them the piece of land where they settled, but it also brought them the fence line that reminded them their days of roaming were over.

The old ways were changing, and no one could stand in the way. Young and old, Clarence among them, took up smoking cigarettes, aggravating lungs already scarred from TB. The use of intoxicants was spreading. Liquor was prohibited, distilled patent medicines too, but some "full-bloods" were using canned heat to get high before long. Even childish amusements like chewing gum became trendy: "The inordinate use of the muscles of mastication is conducive to nervousness; the continuous stimulation of the salivary glands produces glandular irritation and perversion of the normal secretion," lectured one agent, rather pretentiously, who warned that gum should be prohibited in the schools.[29]

The hunt became a shadow of itself and then just a memory. On the early reservation, people gathered at the corrals, and a crier called out the name of each family in turn. As each group of cattle was released, several Oglalas on horseback rode them down and shot them with repeating rifles, as on a buffalo hunt. They felled, butchered, cooked, and ate some of the kill on the spot, drying the rest for later. Then, in the 1890s, it was determined that beef would only come butchered on the block in future. The beef sinew was still good for stringing a bow, and the buffalo liver was a delicacy when roasted, but the days of the hunt, when the whole animal was prized, were gone.[30]

Everywhere, old and new consorted. The first annual Pine Ridge fair was held in 1915, with juried prizes for contestants: best beaded saddle blanket, best onions, best draft gelding, and best "full-blood" Indian baby (four dollars awarded the family of David Red Star). And just before July

4, Oglalas would gather near Allen for several days to prepare a reenactment of the Custer battle. White people would gather from far and wide and camp in a big tent on top of a hill, the target of the "attack." Early on the morning of the fourth, a large band of Lakotas in their buckskin and beaded finery would ride their best horses and charge up the hill, shooting blunted arrows and yelling war cries to electrify an audience that had gathered to feel the shiver of combat. Eventually people tired of the Sunrise Battle, though. Later on, thousands would still gather to watch as hundreds of Oglalas paraded in the wee hours of Independence Day morning. Their headdresses reaching as far as the ground, the bells tied to their horses' bridles jangling, they rode on their best mounts with beaded saddles and colorful blankets before the signal came—at which point they would charge to the top of the hill to ward away the darkness and greet the morning star at daybreak. The old fight may have been gone, but the dignity and honor were still intact.[31]

The Indian agents of the Great Father, venerable headmasters of the reservation, were rarely great. The Indian Service routinely moved agents (later called superintendents) every few years, whether to sidestep personality conflicts, dodge the trap of drudge and boredom, or promote the best of candidates and punish the worst. The policy meant that reservations like Pine Ridge had to frequently adapt to a new agent who brought with him a unique temperament and vastly different life experiences than his predecessor. Some were military, others not. Some were businessmen, others bureaucrats. Like a nobleman on a remote feudal manor, the agent possessed grand powers over the daily lives of his charges, scattered across a large federal estate, his primary mission to follow the letter, and then some, of Indian Office law.[32]

John Brennan was Pine Ridge superintendent from 1900 until World War I, a large and productive slice of Clarence's life. Brennan liked Three Stars, which set him apart from many of those who filled the post before and after him. He supported Clarence's application for a land patent, arguing that a decade of teaching in the day schools made him "qualified in every way to manage and handle his own business affairs." His yearly evaluations were respectful, if sometimes moderate: "Couldn't pass a civil service examination to save his neck," Brennan wrote, "unless it would be on native ability and acquired ability." He knew that Clarence had little more than a grade school education after his years at Carlisle and the Lincoln Institute: "While it might be hoped that his scholarship was better, yet, taking it all in all, his results may be as good as a white man whose education is better. . . . No one plans his schoolroom work any more carefully." Clarence had to be more adept than his white colleagues to prove his mettle.[33]

Surely no agent filled the office of reservation bigwig better than Valentine T. McGillycuddy, who arrived at Pine Ridge the year Clarence set off for Carlisle and stayed as agent for seven years. McGillycuddy knew something about the Oglalas, having been post surgeon at Fort Robinson when Crazy Horse was killed there in 1877. A martinet by inclination, he ruled the agency with tightfisted assurance, an unrepentant foe of Red Cloud to the bitter end. "An Indian can no more serve two masters than a white man," he wrote of the warrior, his rival in a personal competition that the good doctor eventually lost. Like many agents, he kept a hobby horse or two in his personal corral and was especially effusive on the subject of Indians and food. He called Indian treaties "nonsensical" because they provided beef for people who then didn't have to work for a living. He approved of punishing indiscretions by withholding rations: "Poor Lo, not unlike his white brother, is peculiarly sensitive in the gastric region." He opined, "[The Indian] has not much use for grain unless he can have it served up in the shape of hot rolls and buckwheat cakes in a Washington hotel." McGillycuddy, though divisive, ran Pine Ridge with considerable efficiency. He admitted that arable land was hard to find; he noted with satisfaction that crime was rare. But the great Red Cloud was his obsession, a nemesis he accused of imbibing alcohol, killing cows for feasts rather than raising them for stock, and maintaining "his ridiculous assumption of authority," a general subject that McGillycuddy was rather well versed in from personal experience.[34]

Then there was agent H. D. Gallagher, a man who stayed for a few seasons but couldn't for the life of him appreciate Oglala funeral rituals. Given that Lakotas destroyed or gave away property after a loved one died, a practice Gallagher abhorred as pagan, he determined to forbid it entirely on the reservation. Oglalas discovered a workaround, as they so often did: many families would start with the giveaway, cut themselves as custom required, and perform other rites before the death even happened, avoiding any punishment for breaking the ban. The giveaway wasn't a difficult concept to understand. "We don't believe in a family getting wealthy through inheritance," explained Lakota medicine man John (Fire) Lame Deer. "Better give away a dead person's belongings. That way he, or she, will be remembered." Gallagher, opposed to many local undertakings, vilified those like Luther Standing Bear, Clarence's old schoolmate at Carlisle, who rode with the Wild West shows and returned home "perfect wrecks, physically, morally, and financially."[35]

A successor to Gallagher was Captain W. H. Clapp, the military man who could barely hide his disdain for Clarence. "He is well educated for an Indian, having been for several years at Carlisle, Pa." he informed the Indian commissioner. But he could be a troublemaker just like his father, the captain noted, irritated with Clarence's refusal to be transferred off-reservation. Clapp was prescient about Clarence's sway in the community, if disparaging about its effect, writing, "His influence among the people is bad and is expected to so continue. He is essentially a man with a grievance, and what he says should be taken cum grano salis." Clarence indeed was aggrieved, and his resentment would fester by dint of diminished treaty provisions, the disintegrating influence of allotment, and the narrowing range of choices Lakotas faced as the years went on.[36]

Brennan, who took over from Clapp after a brief interim, brought some continuity to the job. An accomplished community booster, he was a founding father of Rapid City, the first municipal fire chief and first county school superintendent. Oglala elder Frank Fools Crow praised him for his willingness to learn Lakota and maintain an active presence in the communities. He was also a successful rancher and member of the Western South Dakota Stock Growers Association executive committee. In fact, Brennan embodied big cattle interests in the state and worked hard to open Pine Ridge for leasing to white ranchers. He argued for the sale of Indian land to whites so as to bring "civilized community" onto Pine Ridge and increase land values. Brennan oversaw many "improvements" during his tenure: eight thousand allotments compared to none before;

Oglalas scattered far and wide instead of clustered in villages; only one-third of them on the ration rolls; and the reservation strung from end to end with three-wire fence.[37]

Pine Ridge, then, was a very big house, even for the people of Crazy Horse and Red Cloud. But was it big enough? No matter how many times he had been schooled and unschooled and reschooled, Clarence's world was confining still. Pine Ridge wasn't a total institution like Carlisle, but its demands were great. Its mission was to make converts of the Oglalas—good wage earners, pious worshippers, loyal patriots. Men were to wear their hair short and don Western garb. Women were to learn the higher reaches of the domestic arts. Money was to be dispensed prudently because, after all, a fistful of cash could be the low road to ruin. Young people were required to read and recite in a house of education, their parents to pray and recite in a house of God. And the partition of the land was how they would finally be pinioned to the earth, at least those who could hold on to what they had been handed of it in the first place.

Through the eyes of the agent, the Father was everywhere or could see everywhere, his field of vision spreading out like a February quilt of snow from Allen to Wounded Knee and all the way up White Clay Creek to Oglala, covering everything as it fell, leaving no man, woman, or beast untouched. The Great Father was more than just one man, more than the great obelisk to Washington raised in the city named in his honor. His picture looked back at them from the paper money. It was there in the portraits that had hung for years, with malice toward none, in Clarence's classroom. And the Father was Captain Pratt and Mr. Wanamaker, too, giving instruction in the lessons of a world that never stopped pulling at him, insisting he do the bidding of formidable, but now absent, men, the teachers he had left back east who spoke to him now across hundreds of miles, not to mention two decades and more of searching.

10

Lightning Creek

Years of missionizing and day-school teaching on Pine Ridge may have convinced most people that the violent struggle between *wasicu* and Lakota was over. But one incident early in Clarence's years as an educator reminded people that violent racial animosity, far from being a relic of the old days, was still a simmering and dangerous fact of life. The root of the problem lay in how local officials administered treaties with Plains tribes. As Three Stars and his colleagues had argued in Washington a few years earlier, the beef ration was measly, mismeasured, and often inedible; Indian ranchers were cheated out of earning market price for their cattle; and the issue stations had stopped allowing Lakotas to kill their cattle on the hoof, instead issuing cuts of beef that denied them internal organs and hides. Many Lakotas were restless and hungry as a result. Though treaties had given them wide swaths of unceded land in Nebraska and Wyoming, where they were allowed to hunt, that privilege eroded as the borders of Pine Ridge came to be enforced as though they were walls. Surviving meant standing in line at the issue station for government commodities rather than hunting game in the grasslands and hills beyond their allotted homeland.

In late September 1903 Clarence's sister-in-law Lizzie Dubray and her husband, William Brown, obtained from Pine Ridge agent John Brennan a sixty-day pass to leave the reservation. Unallotted Lakotas weren't allowed to venture off the reservation without permission of the agent, a long-standing policy that endured into the twentieth century. The Browns and their party were given a permit to gather berries, roots, and herbs for medicinal purposes—but not to hunt game, a restriction that would have puzzled, if not dumbfounded, their ancestors. Charles "Charlie" Red Hawk Smith led a second party also headed west toward the Black Hills. Lizzie, William, and Charlie were all returned Carlisle students.[1]

That October, both groups, numbering about thirty Lakotas in all, rode westward. Their intentions were peaceful. Not only did the two bands include women and children, but few of the men were of fighting age. Riding through the Black Hills separately for several days, the two parties inadvertently drifted over the Wyoming border, at which point they rejoined and camped together to plan their eventual return to Pine Ridge.

On the afternoon of October 30, a posse under Sheriff William Miller entered their camp to inform them they had violated the game laws of Wyoming. According to one report, Miller assumed they were hunting because he saw an antelope hide draped over a horse. The Lakotas said they had bought the hide, not hunted it, along with others in their possession. Not to be deterred, Miller said he planned to take them all to jail in nearby Newcastle, willing or not. Group leader Smith refused the invitation, pointing out that he was a resident of Pine Ridge and subject only to its jurisdiction. As evening fell the posse didn't budge, and Lizzie Brown, dusting off her best manners, went to the trouble of cooking them all a meal. Before the posse left, Miller walked up to her husband and warned him, "I am after you." Brown replied, a little mysteriously, in his accented school English, "All right." "That's good," the sheriff said. "I'll be back in the morning."[2]

The Oglalas didn't wait until morning. They broke camp that night and headed for Pine Ridge, refusing Miller's invitation to host them in the Newcastle jail. By the afternoon of October 31 the ragged fleet of some fifteen wagons and a small herd of ponies had made seventy miles to the east and was following a road along Lightning Creek with the sun at their backs and autumn shadows before them. The wretched story of what happened next had more than one version.

About four o'clock, the Lakotas said, they came across a wire fence on the road. A young girl jumped down from her wagon and opened the gate so a boy leading the herd of ponies could pass through. A couple wagons had already followed him past the gate when he came riding back, yelling, "Look out! White men with guns!" The boy and his mount were killed instantly by a volley from Sheriff Miller and a posse of thirteen men. The shots poured forth, and Indians in the front wagons returned fire. The shooting caused the horses to stampede, and William Brown grabbed his wife, Lizzie, and children and fled the scene in a smaller wagon. The family drove hell-bent for Pine Ridge, fired on by strangers along the way, before they made it safely to the agency. It was a far better fate than what awaited several of their companions.[3]

Miller's men told a different tale. The Indians dismounted from their wagons and retrieved their weapons as soon as they saw the posse. When the sheriff approached and told them to surrender, the Lakotas fired shots from the rear of the wagon train. Three or four minutes of gunfire ensued as the posse sought to fulfill its assigned duty. The Indians fired first, they insisted, resisting lawful arrest.[4]

About the only thing the two sides agreed on was that the skirmish took all of five minutes. Sheriff Miller died after bleeding out from a gunshot wound in his thigh; one of his deputies, Falkenburg, was killed by a crack shot. The posse did even more damage. They killed Black Kettle, who was fifty-eight years old and a former policeman. Philip White Elk, the boy at the gate, was eleven; the top of his head was shot off by a bullet fired at close range. Gray Bear, whose wife and daughter accompanied him, also died, aged forty-eight. And Charlie Red Hawk Smith, late of Carlisle Indian Industrial School, aged thirty-seven, was felled by a bullet that broke bones in both his legs and rendered him helpless. He crawled under a wagon, having survived the immediate scuffle, and as a member of the Kitfox (Tokala) warrior society, he sang his death song while still gasping:

> Lo, the Fox, the Fox am I!
> Still the Fox a moment yet,
> Then the Fox shall be no more.

He barely survived into the next day, his body rimmed with frost, and died the night of November 1. His wife was wounded in the shoulder. Last Bear, aged seventy, was shot in the back, the bullet exiting out the other side and thus saving his life. A hunting infraction, if infraction it even was, had turned into a mess of dead and maimed.[5]

Nine of the Indians were arrested and charged with murder. All were acquitted in Wyoming for lack of evidence. The Lakotas swore that the posse had fired first. Because the white men didn't identify themselves, said the Oglalas, no one knew they were the same men who visited them the previous night. The posse's story was suspect: if the Indians had prepared an ambush, as some of the white men alleged, having their wagons strung out along the Lightning Creek road was a bad way to do it. Neutral parties like Pine Ridge agent Brennan sided with the Lakotas, even if the confusion over the incident troubled him. He conceded that to refuse the posse, as Smith did, was a rash act. But the aggressive tactics of Miller's men and their failure to identify themselves left him deeply suspicious of their version. As George Sword later reported on behalf of the tribal council, the 1868 treaty gave Lakotas the right to hunt in unceded territory. The ambush, they reasoned, not to mention the Wyoming proscription against hunting, was a treaty violation.[6]

Local newspapers protested that the posse had been surrounded by Indians and fought to avoid a Custer-like debacle. Others conjectured that the fuss created in the Wyoming press had an ulterior motive. After all, Indians were good for local business. These observers argued that western communities griped about Indian incursions of any sort, hoping the government might just dispatch soldiers and build a fort that would have to be provisioned by local ranchers and merchants. It was the same motive that led many off-reservation communities to support the building and maintenance of nearby Indian boarding schools.[7]

When he heard about Lightning Creek, Three Stars was livid. In a densely written, seven-page letter to a Carlisle official, he complained that Smith and Brown were merely out on a hunting trip, a pastime even President Roosevelt enjoyed. His letter was spurred by a personal visit from Brown, his wife's brother-in-law, who told Clarence more than he had revealed in his testimony to the U.S. attorney. "He did not tell all that he knew because he was scare, at the time," Three Stars explained, "but now he tells all of it." The excursion leaders had hardly been Pine Ridge ne'er-do-wells, Clarence explained: Brown was a respected rancher, and Smith was on the Pine Ridge payroll as an assistant farmer. They both knew Wyoming, and they knew their rights.[8]

In December the Carlisle paper *Red Man and Helper* published a lightly edited version of Clarence's letter. The ex-Carlisle boy could see the irony of several of Pratt's former students being ambushed by a sheriff on the trumped-up charge of killing game, an accusation that didn't merit bloodshed in the first place. The roles in the proverbial Indian massacre were reversed. The Lakotas clambered along in wagons with their families, while the posse hid in the trees waiting to bushwack them. Like Wounded Knee and the Grattan battle and others too numerous to mention, white people alleged that the Indians fired first. But the evidence didn't support it. Three Stars called the whole fracas a "paleface uprising of Wyoming."[9]

His anger was edgy: "The whites never warned the Indians as they should do, but lay in a hole, like a snake, although snakes warn people, but these snakes would not." The posse fired first, he wrote, and the Indians responded in self-defense, a verdict almost everyone apart from the posse and a few newspapers agreed on. The two white casualties were shot down "in a twinkling of an eye," Clarence wrote, a phrase that suggests he wasn't all that disappointed by the result. He surmised that the attack was an attempted robbery and that "the whites were under the influence of mysterious water," a detail that Brown may have given him when they met.[10]

The morning after the "battle," as the press called it, several Lakota women returned to the wagons. There they found the posse, guns in hand. The daughter of the deceased Gray Bear stepped forward and accosted them as cowards, even daring the posse to shoot them down. At that point, after everything that had transpired, an emotional tipping point occurred. The diatribe by an unarmed woman seemed to disarm the posse. As Clarence had it, the "men put down their guns and cried like babies." And it didn't end there. Three Stars added "the girl went around and shook hands with the men," whether in an act of conciliation or emotional triumph is unclear. It was a bizarre end to the Lightning Creek incident, as the skirmish came to be known. Three Stars concluded, "[The girl] can and will tell this story often in camp among her friends." It was a brave deed for an unarmed witness and a reflection, if an extraordinary one, of how Lakota warriors recounted to tribal audiences their own exploits in battle. The girl was named Hope Clear. In the face of guns pointed at her party, Hope challenged the men, insulted them, and then touched them with her hand—and lived to tell about it. She had, in the traditional way, counted coup on the enemy.[11]

The ambush was an assault on Carlisle and all its tribe, and Clarence felt it deeply. Only four years earlier, in 1899, he had returned to Carlisle at Pratt's invitation to speak at the school's graduation ceremony. Pratt had introduced him to the crowd of seven hundred gathered in the gymnasium as a member of that first arriving class, from twenty years before, a sterling example of the men that Carlisle made. And Clarence repaid him the compliment: "I try to improve myself and use my education in such a way as will be a good example to my people," he began. His own plan for self-improvement had led him to books, "nothing but good books," which brought another healthy round of applause. "I feel as I stand before you," he confided, looking out over the large assembly, "that this is the real home of mine. . . . The reservation is only a temporary home." It was temporary, perhaps. His speech was an outpouring of nostalgia for a place he felt ambivalent about, probably more sentimental than accurate. After much applause, he shared the platform with Charles Eastman and Carlos Montezuma, both renowned Indian physicians who had worked at Carlisle and made national reputations in their own right. By that point in his midthirties, Clarence was still, at least on the speaker's dais, a Carlisle boy. And the attack on Charlie Red Hawk had been an attack on all of them.[12]

The fracas touched the Three Stars family in a personal way. Jennie's elder sister had come within a few feet of being shot by a group of vigilantes, and for nothing more than gathering plants and buying hides on land where such was their right by treaty. Lizzie had even prepared dinner for the posse on the night before the assault, a gesture of good faith probably interpreted by Miller and his men as a sign of weakness.

The Lightning Creek attack had an odd parallel in Three Stars family lore. Fifty years before, Clarence's grandfather High Forehead had shot a cow, and now Charlie Smith, a family acquaintance, was accused of killing antelope. In each case the trespass was small, but both men were hunted down for their indiscretions. Neither fired until fired on. The ultimate response was a hail of bullets and bloodshed. The two incidents bookended the Lakota war with whites, spanning half a century, like a pair of grim watchmen. To a Lakota like Clarence, who contemplated the scales of American justice from his modest position as a government ward, the law must have seemed a fickle and perilous thing.

11

A Taste of the Law

It was about the time Louisa died, during his teaching years, that Clarence began laying the foundation for a second career: the study of law. Indian tribes had not done well by the highest court in the land during his adult years. *Ex-parte Crow Dog* (1883) led to the Major Crimes Act of 1885, which transferred prosecution for major crimes from tribal to federal control. In *Elk v. Wilkins* (1884) the Supreme Court ruled that an Indian who maintained tribal allegiance didn't qualify as a U.S. citizen. In *Lone Wolf v. Hitchcock* (1903), the court took its biggest step, ruling that Congress had the right to unilaterally revoke treaty provisions if it determined Indian people would benefit. For decades the court had been withdrawing basic rights from Indian country and delegating them to Congress under the theory that Indians were second-class citizens and not even really citizens at all.

The heart and soul of the law long intrigued Clarence. His 1891 junket to Washington had endeared him to the city where politics was king and where the din of disparate voices was transmuted into the rule of law—whether by hook or by crook or by just the downright venal and crooked. The visit must have inspired him, because two years later, newly married and assigned his own schoolhouse, Clarence applied for a job in Indian Office headquarters with an eye to attending law school in the city. Fluent in Lakota and English—and literate in both—his value to the Interior Department would have been considerable. But the request went nowhere. The new husband of Jennie, father of Sophia, and master of Day School No. 19 had to bide his time before the mysteries of tort law and criminal jurisdiction would be revealed in all their glory.[1]

He never quite let go of that dream. At some point Three Stars enrolled in what turned out to be an early twentieth-century version of the internet—a correspondence school. The one he chose, the Columbian Correspondence College (CCC), was housed just across the street from the new Beaux-Arts Library of Congress building on Capitol Hill. "A greater number and variety of subjects are taught by this College through its original correspondence methods," the school ads boasted, "than are included in the curriculum of many resident universities favored by prodigal endowments and the prestige of long careers." The school offered an education to the "ambitious poor," of which Three Stars was arguably a member, as well as the middle class. Its promise of self-paced knowledge was just as entrancing for a young teacher from the Dakotas as it would be a century later for lifelong learners of the information age.[2]

The typical correspondence school wasn't just a fly-by-night operation touted in a newspaper classified. It was a burgeoning industry that offered a viable alternative to public schools, on the one hand, and the industrial education championed at places like Carlisle on the other. By 1910, about the time Three Stars was likely enrolled at CCC, there were over two hundred proprietary correspondence schools across the country, and their popularity was spreading. The International Correspondence School (ICS) of Scranton, Pennsylvania, boasted one hundred thousand new students *every year* in the early part of the century. The schools spoke to—and played on—the fond American myth of home education embodied by Ben Franklin and Abe Lincoln, not to mention the contemporary bootstrap success stories of Horatio Alger Jr.[3]

Though the schools offered formal degrees, most students enrolled for pragmatic reasons. Enrollees could choose from extensive offerings in modern occupations like plumbing, bookkeeping, advertising, car mechanics, and the law. It was one thing to be a blacksmith, like Edgar Fire Thunder, hammering out a hot poker in a Carlisle workshop; it was quite another to be a man garbed in hat and suit who had dabbled in *Blackstone's Commentaries* and knew a thing or two about *Lone Wolf v. Hitchcock*. The ICS offered five hundred different subjects in its curriculum by 1906, a variety difficult to find at the land-grant colleges, much less the Ivy League. Although the Columbian school was small by comparison with some rivals, it maintained a presence in the capital for nearly half a century.[4]

The schools thrived because they were selling special skills, not broad curricula, and didn't need to defend the usefulness of a liberal arts education. Their purpose was to make money in selling marketable skills, and make money they did. The Columbian Correspondence School, incorporated in West Virginia, bragged, "Correspondence instruction has advanced to a degree of perfection which seriously menaces the supremacy of resident universities." Schools like the CCC were a major force in American education up to the time of the Great Depression.[5]

Like many online learners today, correspondence students were invisible. Through the medium of the U.S mail system, no one could be distinguished by skin color, accent, or general appearance, a distinct advantage for the underprivileged. Clarence, whose English was strongly accented, knew only too well the gulf between the rural isolation of Pine Ridge and the bustling urban centers of the East. He also knew the humiliation that could befall one in a classroom, as had once happened to him at Carlisle. Reading the law by night, after delving into the mysteries of the *Third Reader* in daylight hours, was an enticing prospect for a man who had, to that point, received little in the way of vocational education beyond the finer points of handling a tailor's scissors and tape. He had worked in a manual trade that was, in the eyes of most educators of his time, more befitting an Indian than the law would have been.

The Columbian College, an elaborate brick facade near the Capitol, had been well known since its founding in 1897. By the time Clarence enrolled, he knew the city firsthand from his delegation visits in the 1890s. He had seen the streetlights, the extending radial avenues, the Smithsonian castle, and the skyline dominated by the obelisk dedicated to Washington. By 1910 the city had more than three hundred thousand inhabitants (small compared to Philadelphia), with three hundred miles of paved streets, a bustling streetcar system, thirty-two fire stations, and a police force that numbered over seven hundred. What's more, there was a public library system with over one hundred thousand volumes; a network of forty thousand telephones; and the beautiful, vaulted Union Station, triumphal arches, statues, and all, a colossal edifice that would have enthralled boorish yokel and trendy flaneur alike. The CCC was only one among a hundred "miscellaneous" schools that populated the city, in addition to three universities and a passel of public and parochial institutions. Since Clarence couldn't see much of this from faraway Pine Ridge, except the school advertising circulars, the experience was rather like a pale taste of Philadelphia, only nearer the beating heart of power.[6]

The offerings at CCC ranged from stenography and bookkeeping to literature and journalism to civil service and the law. The law program Clarence chose was headed by Charles Andrew Ray, former chief justice of the Indiana Supreme Court. It was a three-year program that students took at their own pace. At year's end the school examined each student near their home locale, preferably proctored by an attorney, and awarded certificates to those who passed. Candidates who successfully completed the final year earned the degree of LL.B. Annual tuition was twenty-five dollars (cash)—about two weeks wages for Clarence; books were free the first year and then rented for five dollars the next. It was a poor man's credential, to be sure, but more formal training than Abe Lincoln would have had seventy years earlier when he was licensed to practice law in the 1830s.[7]

Judge Ray was an accomplished professional in his own right. Born in Indianapolis in 1829, the son of a prominent civic leader and educator, he went to grammar school with Lew Wallace—future territorial governor of New Mexico and author of *Ben Hur*—and later did limited stints at Brown University and Harvard, where he studied law. In 1861 he was appointed to the bench and three years later, elected to the state supreme court of Indiana where he served as chief justice in rotation. A decade after leaving the court, Ray was appointed law clerk for the postmaster general in Washington and was instrumental in allowing Walt Whitman's *Leaves of Grass*, a controversial and much censored volume, to be moved through the mails without fear of suppression. Ray may have been sympathetic to Whitman's barbaric yawp, thinking it should be allowed to echo over the roofs of the world, but it wasn't long before the judge himself would be the attorney of record representing a suit against the postmaster general himself.[8]

The Indiana justice may have been the most important teacher Three Stars ever had, though the two probably never met. Although Clarence noted in a job application that he studied with the judge, it doesn't mean they ever talked over the same table, not at a school that declared, "All work is by mail." Unlike Clarence's instructors at Carlisle and the Lincoln Institute, Ray was a man of standing in his profession. The judge authored legal tomes with lumbering titles like *Negligence of Imposed Duties and Contractual Limitations, Including Trade Strikes and Conspiracies, Corporate Trusts and Combinations*, the former receiving high praise in the *Harvard Law Review* even if the critic did note a penchant for repetition.[9]

Clarence was likely more familiar with Ray's *Quiz Book*, a review of criminal procedure the college published in 1900. The *Quiz Book* was a rote slate of pedagogical call and response, a method Clarence's rigid training had prepared him for:

> Q: "What can you say of the hue and the cry?" A: "Hue and cry was a common law method of chasing the felon with horns and voice."
> Q: "Could an atheist testify in court?" A: "An atheist can not testify . . . [however] . . . This rule is now changed."
> Q: "Who is eligible to serve on juries?" A: "In one or two States females are competent jurors."[10]

The book was chock full of nagging questions—and unequivocal answers—big and small. What can you say of the right to a trial by jury? When may a verdict be delivered into court? Must the court accept the verdict? May a juror by his affidavit impeach the verdict of the jury? And so Dr. Ray's guidebook, almost one hundred pages deep, worked its way through a maze of criminal procedure for aspiring legal candidates who were never destined to meet him in the flesh.

Ray was a noted author, magistrate, and when he accepted the position of dean in the school law department, an editor for the Washington Law Book Company. His boss at the school was Daniel A. Edwards, who had graduated from the University of Michigan with a master's of law degree in 1896 and founded the CCC the next year with his brother James. Daniel was a leading civic figure of the district, serving as president of the Washington school board and a trustee of the Washington Carnegie Library, as well as president of the Lincoln Park Citizens Association, all while being a fourth-degree member of the Knights of Columbus. He also had a proclivity for financial doings, serving as auditor of the Congress Hall Hotel and director of the Savings Security and Commercial Bank during more than forty years in the capital. The school looked mighty professional from its directory.[11]

But something shady was going on at 223 Pennsylvania Avenue SE. In 1915, not long after Clarence had done his coursework and was settling into his own legal career, CCC opened the Columbian Information Bureau and began hiring college graduates "who commenced writing addresses for all classes of people as they were ordered." The bureau contracted to write essays for hire—speeches, debates, even valedictory addresses. Pupils in the eighth grade and other customers paid four dollars for an original composition and fifty cents for anything in the school archive, which was marketed through thirty-two-page advertising circulars that noted Edwards's membership on the board of education. There were addresses for presenting diplomas, discourses for requesting funds, even full-blown speeches for congressmen as the school moved its business into the nooks and crannies of official Washington. By 1922 they had almost 1,300 papers in the bureau archive.[12]

To upstanding outsiders, it smelled a lot like a paper mill. After all, there had been questionable doings at the college before. The CCC had been sued for $5,000 in 1900 by a man who alleged the college was selling his work under a variety of false names. School superintendent Frank Ballou savaged Edwards before the district Subcommittee for House Appropriations on the issue of selling made-to-order essays: "I would like to say that I have no sympathy whatever with this enterprise," Ballou testified, "and I certainly condemn it very vigorously from the standpoint of education." But Edwards was obdurate: "We do not know what use is to be made of these addresses nor do we inquire. We are simply authors and publishers. No one would question our right to publish these addresses in book form and sell them to all who wanted to buy them or hold us responsible for the use the purchasers made of them. . . . If it is wrong for young people to have help along these lines, then it is wrong to have in the library books containing orations and essays." When asked what he would do if he learned that students had submitted one of his publications for classroom credit, Edwards responded, "I would simply say that I had nothing to do with the case at all."[13]

Would Clarence have even been scandalized by the controversy? In one sense, the school archive was a written counterpart of a collective "tribal" memory. Statute law had precedents and conventions, just as Lakota tradition did, and access to them was important. For that matter, the rote copying and memorization of his own schooling, from Carlisle through Columbia, spoke to the importance of pooling knowledge for the benefit of community, particularly for oral use. There must have been times when the concept of ownership in the white man's world, particularly of the written word, mystified the son of Yellow Knife. The needle wobbled back and forth between individual and tribe in the spiritual compass of a man who was trying to live, unfettered, within arms' length of both.

If the vision of a populist, professional school serving the ambitious poor proved to have a seamier side, it couldn't have surprised Three Stars. His alma mater, the Lincoln Institute, was denied federal funding because of harrowing reports of mistreatment. The land commissions that set up shop on Pine Ridge were little more than coercive taskforces dressed in the sheep's clothing of government largesse and roundly criticized as such. His home agency was run on business principles that would have made Tammany Hall blush. And perhaps the Columbian school was of the same cloth. If Clarence's goal was to become an edgy advocate for reform, the inspiration for change was all around him. It was no wonder he wanted to learn the law.

He had come a long way from his first days at Carlisle. There had been pitfalls on the path that no book could have portended. What if Clarence, the successful schoolteacher, was really the one being instructed, the one being trained by habits unaware? What if the notions of the Indian Office would leach into his blood? Maybe he would become an agent of the system he wrestled with, and maybe the government would take his passion for teaching and twist it into a game of making the untutored march in place from dawn to dusk. And so what if he did? Wouldn't that, after all, make the young ones better behaved when they lined up for commodities? Wouldn't that make them less likely to speak out and endanger their families? Didn't Agent Brennan and the Great Father claim that all Indians really needed in life was instruction, with a healthy dollop of discipline on the side? The answer was never simple. Teaching could take the form of refusal and negation, too; it could be recitation of dry rot or offering the wrong things to remember and the wrong people to please.

There he was, a model of the white man's school system, on the verge of becoming an arbiter of law, a man educated beyond the limits of what an Indian was "supposed" to learn. Laws were meant to keep Indians in line, not to be studied and parsed and debated by them. Boarding schools provided cheap institutional labor and educated students for a lifetime of drudgery. But becoming a lawyer defied all this at a time when most Indian boys were being tutored in how to shoe a horse or plant potatoes or pound a rod of red-hot iron. The assimilation many advocated only brought students into the lower orders of the social ladder. Clarence would soon decide not to earn his living—that is, teaching—by using his hands, nor to reside any longer in the confines of a little red schoolhouse and its garden.[14]

By his own account he graduated from CCC, though the practical value of his coursework may have been worth more than a framed diploma in the world beyond Day School No. 27. Three Stars had indeed become what Governor Warner called a "professional Indian." He wrote angry letters, visited Washington, translated gripes, and signed petitions. Isn't that what Captain Pratt had said he should do all along?

His study of the law would teach Clarence the truth of what his grandfather had learned the hard way—that Indian rights were written on a flimsy scrap of paper in the white man's book of the world.

And there was a price to pay for everything in that world, even for a lame cow.

12

The Pipe, the Cross, and the Eagle

The day he was baptized into the Episcopalian faith in 1880, Clarence Three Stars was neither infant nor adult. It seems only fitting of his journey between the Lakota and *wasicu* worlds that he was also in transit between the stages of life when the priest touched his head with holy water. He was an adolescent at the time, barely sixteen, neither totally innocent of the consequences of such an act nor fully cognizant of what it portended. He became an Episcopalian, just as he had become a Carlisle student, more by fiat than personal choice. On his return from Pennsylvania he found that a proper church of his denomination had been erected in Pine Ridge village, a place of worship just as much for those recruited and converted with a heavy hand as it was for families who had practiced the faith for generations.

Episcopalian missionaries began working the Dakota Territory in the 1860s. Key to their efforts was Samuel Hinman, who missionized among the Santees, an eastern branch of the Sioux, and translated a good part of the *Book of Common Prayer* into Dakota, a sister language of Lakota, by the time Clarence was born in 1864. Hinman had stood steadfast with the Santees even when he was beaten unconscious by angry settlers after the Dakota War of 1862. He is remembered by the Lakotas, farther to the west, in a darker light, however. Not only was he a member of the 1876 commission that seized the Black Hills, but he outraged many Lakotas in 1882 with his work as interpreter for the government commission that first tried to grab nine million acres from the heart of the Great Sioux Reservation.[1]

The first Episcopalian confirmation on Pine Ridge happened in 1880, and among the new converts was Lakota chief of police George Sword.

The next year the village church was finished, the same place where the Wounded Knee survivors would be doctored a decade later. As early as 1886 Clarence, who had recently returned from Carlisle, was calling roll for Sunday school at the new church, passing out hymn books and catechizing children in English and Lakota, foreshadowing his long bilingual teaching career. As the collection plate was being taken forward to the chancel, the children stood up to sing "Praise God from Whom All Blessings Flow," both in the tongue of their parents and that of the presiding priests.[2]

Religion was nothing new to Clarence. His people had prayed with the pipe for centuries. Lakotas told how Wakan Tanka, the Great Holy, had first breathed life into the world; how the people emerged from underground, lured by the trickster Iktomi; how the sun and moon and stars came into being; how lightning creased the sky and the seasons were created. The pipe had been brought to them generations before by the White Buffalo Calf Woman, and it was the pipe that became the instrument by which Lakotas spoke with Wakan Tanka. They built altars and smoked the bark of red willow trees and prayed for good health, for brotherhood, for wisdom, for peace. They had medicine men and women who doctored and healed. Packs the Dog was raised in this world until his teenage years and would have seen full evidence of Lakota harmony (*wolakota*) everywhere—heard the prayers and sung the songs and learned the faith of his ancestors—until, that is, the day he was taken to Carlisle and the pipe, replaced by a cross endowed with a different kind of *sicun* (power), was no more with him.[3]

The church accommodated many Lakota beliefs and customs. Mourners were allowed to place food on the graves of the dead, and giveaways after a funeral were permitted on church premises, both echoes of the past. Even the traditional Sun Dance, a summer ritual where large numbers of Lakota bands gathered, bore more than a passing resemblance to the Niobrara Convocation, a midyear ceremonial where as many as ten thousand Episcopalian Sioux camped out to celebrate social and religious ties, an assembly that continues to this day. In 1927 President Calvin Coolidge visited the jamboree held that year on Pine Ridge, where Three Stars was a special committeeman. But the convocation accepted as gospel many tenets of American society that ran contrary to Lakota beliefs: the husband was the unquestioned head of family and owner of family wealth; arranged marriages and polygamy were prohibited; and land was to be owned individually, not shared in common. At times, the congruence of sacred and secular couldn't even be counted on in the white world. Rev. William Hobart Hare, long-standing Dakota bishop with whom Hinman had once feuded, opposed an 1890 prohibition bill that would have outlawed the use of fermented beverages in the taking of communion.[4]

Episcopalians, like other denominations, worked to outlaw many popular practices. Clarence was part of a church committee that condemned Native Indian dancing as "disgraceful" and "harmful." Though the Sun Dance had already been prohibited, Omaha and other dances were still popular with Oglalas, if openly discouraged by the agent. The committee offered, "[We] see hopeful signs of the dying out of the vicious features of the dances. . . . We hope to see all encouragements of the Government officials withdrawn and our own Christian people learning to stay entirely away from such affairs." The year Clarence returned to Pine Ridge, 1884, the Sun Dance was publicly banned on the reservation, a policy that continued well into the twentieth century. By 1916 Indian dances of any kind were permitted only two nights a month and on the Fourth of July.[5]

Clarence's church disparaged another practice considered even more insidious: "With regard to the Mescal bean cult we hear with great satisfaction that Commissioner Sells and other good friends will entirely oppose the evil custom which is rightly counted with whiskey and opium, and is a most harmful indulgence." Indeed, Clarence had applied, without success, to be the special officer in charge of suppressing liquor traffic in 1914, an illicit trade the church believed was related to "the bean cult." Three Stars had been thoroughly assimilated in matters of the spirit, expressing his disavowal or denial of hazardous "intoxicants," whether they took the form of dancing to the beat of a communal drum or being literally ingested by mouth.[6]

The committee, it turns out, had confused the "mescal bean" with peyote, a common mistake of the time. The mescal bean grows in northern Mexico and the Texas borderlands, derives from an evergreen bush, and is an extremely powerful intoxicant. The peyote cactus, which grows in roughly the same area, yields buttons that, when dried and eaten, offer hallucinogenic visions; spiritual seekers found such visions could be a vital part of religious meditation. It was peyote that spread northward from Mexico across Indian Territory and the southern plains and reached the rambling prairie of Pine Ridge by the early twentieth century. Although not an addictive substance, peyote was arguably, though not specifically, included in the generic federal prohibition of 1897 against "intoxicants," and the campaign against it was closely related to the suppression of alcohol. Though proscribed by some state laws, peyote wasn't singled out as a dangerous drug by the federal government until 1965.[7]

Peyote had been used for centuries as a medicine, a stimulant, a way to foretell the future, and a road to religious enlightenment. The sacrament, developed in the American west in resistance to church missionizing, consisted of eating the bitter peyote button and communicating with the Great Spirit through song, prayer, and introspection. The religion that was founded to protect the sacrament from attempts to ban it—the Native American Church (NAC)—was incorporated in Oklahoma in 1918, a fusion of indigenous and Christian rites that subscribed to a belief in a supreme being. Three Stars would have been shocked to learn that, a century later, some three hundred thousand adherents of this pan-Indian movement would be *protected* by federal law in practicing their peyote rites, provided they were card-carrying members of the NAC.[8]

Peyote ceremonies mushroomed in the early twentieth century. By 1919 some 5 percent of reservation Oglalas were said to be participants. Although peyote usage was not an epidemic, it was enough to frighten authorities, not least of whom was Superintendent Brennan: "If the peyote habit gets a firm hold on the Sioux Indians it will work to their everlasting harm and make them unfit for industrial and helpful occupations." The next agent described it as a "poison," and by 1923 most peyote "addicts" on the reservation were based in Bennett County, where Three Stars lived. Since mostly trust-status Indians, whose rights were regulated by federal jurisdiction, were involved, they were immune to a South Dakota law that forbade use of peyote. The headquarters of the Native American Church on Pine Ridge was in Allen, near the place where Three Stars once tended store and not many miles from the land his family was allotted.[9]

Plenty of white and Indian Brahmins lined up to deplore the humble cactus. Charles Eastman told a congressional hearing in 1918, "Some of the brightest boys that were ever educated at the Indian schools have become peyote eaters, and those men have been ruined in their character." Gertrude Bonnin, secretary of the Society of American Indians, warned that among the Utes "an unscrupulous organization, through its agents, [was] promoting the peyote cult, under a religious guise, solely for the easy money gotten from their superstitious victims." But the courts didn't concur. A 1916 case against Pine Ridge peyotist Harry Black Bear was dismissed by a judge who didn't accept that the prohibition against alcoholic intoxicants included peyote. Two years later a federal law that would have outlawed peyote died in the Senate; even Congress couldn't agree that the need to ban the cactus was pressing. But the enemy was closer to home than one imagined. None less than Richard Henry Pratt testified during the hearings, "Peyote has had a very demoralizing effect on some very excellent products of the Carlisle School." Clarence's own cousin, Paul Black Bear, ever the practical joker, informed school authorities in 1910 that he was a laborer with an interest in "mescal."[10]

Carlisle, it turns out, was a breeding ground for peyote enthusiasts, no surprise given the diversity of tribal cultures that mingled at the school. Over one hundred Carlisle students were estimated to have been peyote adepts at one time or another, the most notorious, by some accounts, being Sam Lone Bear of Lone Bear Creek, South Dakota. Sam, whose father was a tribal policeman, enrolled for five years at the school and left in 1897 in his later teens. After his Carlisle stint, some have alleged, he enlisted in Buffalo Bill Cody's Wild West show and became one of the most popular riders during the European tours of the early 1900s. The saga of Samuel Lone Bear then grows murky. Some have claimed that he went on to live and die in relative obscurity, while another man of the same name took up the peyote sacrament. Others maintain that it was the same Lone Bear who, after his return to South Dakota from Europe, adopted the clandestine rite and toured the intermontane West for nearly three decades, preaching peyotism to anyone who would listen. Nebraska, Utah, Oklahoma, Colorado, Wyoming—Lone Bear barnstormed across the West as a peyote missionary with all the wanderlust of Colonel Cody's show. But the lust was more than metaphorical. Sam, who traveled under pseudonyms like Cactus Pete, Roan Bear, Sam Loganberry, and Leo Old Coyote, was renowned for his dalliances with teenage girls and eventually accused of kidnapping, theft, and rape, among other indiscretions. Though never punished by any state laws that sanctioned peyote, he was convicted under the Mann Act for transporting a woman across state lines for immoral activities and served more than a year in federal prison in Washington State. Sam Lone Bear wasn't the kind of returned student—if it was the same Sam Lone Bear—that Captain Pratt liked to talk about.[11]

While Lone Bear brought peyote practitioners a bad name, another adept, James Blue Bird, took the high road. Blue Bird entered Carlisle in 1910, a strapping twenty-one-year-old enrolled in the fourth grade. He was a peyote user before he even got off the train, beginning with the Oklahoma ceremony he attended at age fourteen with the famed Comanche chief Quanah Parker. Blue Bird was discharged from Carlisle after less than a year, branded in his file as a "deserter." But he seemed grateful for the experience anyway: "I am thankful for what I've learned at Carlisle," he wrote in 1913. "Altho I am sorry to say that I didn't stay as long as I ought to." He did an outing during his short tenure at the school but still hadn't received his back pay some seven years later, by which time he registered a formal complaint that probably never yielded a penny. Blue Bird went on to ride with the Miller 101 Wild West Show, a familiar trade for Oglala males of the time, before he settled down and became a peyote spiritualist and roadman (ceremonial conductor) on Pine Ridge. In years to come, whether working the harvest or driving a truck for the South Dakota Highway Department, Blue Bird went far and wide in service of peyote, just as Lone Bear had, but he inspired trust and respect rather than conflict and controversy along the way. When Lone Bear fell ill during the dog days of the Depression, dirt poor and living in an abandoned shack on Pine Ridge, Blue Bird brought him food and conducted a peyote service at Sam's own request before the man known as Cactus Pete passed away in 1937.[12]

Blue Bird, son of an Episcopalian minister, regarded the peyote rite as a unique Native blending of biblical scripture and Indian belief. But Clarence Three Stars saw the sacrament for something different, a threat to everything he had learned back east: a form of intoxication imbibed during secret sessions, a ritual that ran counter to the trappings of discipline and self-denial so integral to church and school. Peyote presented yet another legacy of returning students who fanned out across the country carrying with them a mixed message; they were educated disciples, but they were also "under the influence." Some found genuine spiritual guidance in the button's sacrament, while a few, like Lone Bear, discovered in its power an excuse for deception, fraud, and rank abuse.

A yeoman of God and church was Clarence Three Stars, a figurative plowman in the fields of the Lord. He was a church helper at Trinity Station and Advent Station and then a catechist at the Good Shepherd Station of Corn Creek District. He served as a committeeman at the Niobrara Convocation. He was a leader in raising money for missionary work overseas. He did what a devout man could. But if he harbored any dreams of one day leading his own congregation, the path for a "full-blood" Lakota in the ministry was a difficult one.[13]

Perhaps more important, the church allowed Clarence to sing. He had taught his students the wonders of anthems and carols, accompanying them on what was (probably) a portable harmonium. They would sing "Our Native Land," memorize short songs, and chant when they tired of dry book learning. With children there seemed to be a song for everything, and so it was with worship. There were hymns for circumcision and the Epiphany, for the Ascension and Advent, hymns for catechism and burial, for offertory and matrimony, for Thanksgiving day and the virtues of temperance; there was "My Country Tis of Thee" and "The Battle Hymn of the Republic" and "We Three Kings" and "The First Noel." There were hymns for those who had died and those who were remembered, mournful in the undertow but always with a triumphant, if grave, sense of renewal. They had songs for the classroom, too:

> We build our school on thee, O Lord
> To thee we bring our common need
> The loving heart, the helpful word
> The tender thought, the kindly deed.

And so Clarence raised his voice to God in a congregation of neighbors, family, and friends in the small frame churches that dotted the Dakota prairie. It was almost like the camp life of his childhood, but with a frame roof and a promise of heaven over their heads.[14]

His devotion to liturgy didn't serve him well with everyone. A case in point was Dr. James Walker, who enlisted Clarence for one of the most extraordinary research projects ever undertaken on Pine Ridge. Walker was the doctor who had done valiant battle with tuberculosis on the reservation. He was that most talented of types in the American West—a proven professional who performed fundamental research in a field that took him far beyond his training, often as a passionate hobbyist in his spare time—one thinks of George Bird Grinnell or John Wesley Powell as kindred spirits. For all he would accomplish in his adult life, however, Walker's origins were hardly promising. A farmer's son, he was born in a log cabin in 1849. He ran away from home at age fourteen, pretending to be older than he was, and enlisted in the Thirteenth Regiment of Illinois Cavalry Volunteers to serve in the Civil War. He soon contracted dysentery and was discharged from service in 1865 after serving in the U.S. Sanitary Commission, a government-chartered agency that tended to sick and wounded soldiers during the war. He would battle the illness for his entire life.[15]

Perhaps spurred by his chronic condition, Walker took a degree as doctor of medicine at Northwestern University in 1873. For much of the next two decades he served as Indian physician and overseer at Leech Lake Chippewa (Ojibway) Reservation in northern Minnesota. Among the Ojibways he successfully combatted and contained a virulent smallpox epidemic through the use of quarantine and vaccination, his efforts later honored by President Theodore Roosevelt. Walker was also responsible for keeping the Ojibway reservations clean of vices like drinking, gambling, and dancing, an assignment that would have earned the respect of a pious Episcopalian like Three Stars. In 1893 Walker accidentally shot a Native man at Leech Lake while trying to enforce a whiskey ban and was threatened with his life by an angry mob. The victim suffered only minor wounds, but the doctor was summarily transferred to Colville Agency for what the Ojibway agent termed his unnecessary "rashness" in almost starting a riot.[16]

Following a brief stay at Carlisle Indian School, Walker was assigned as physician to Pine Ridge Agency in 1896, where for the next eighteen years he undertook a long and productive residency among the Oglalas. Early in his stay he brought the tuberculosis epidemic under control and lobbied to build a sanitary camp for tubercular patients, a project that was never funded. Such was Walker's reputation on Pine Ridge that at one point he was recommended for the job of superintendent at the notorious Canton Indian Asylum, another notion that never came to pass, perhaps regrettably. Had Walker been appointed, it likely would have had a salutary effect on the asylum's patients, one of whom would turn out to be the eldest child of Clarence and Jennie Three Stars.[17]

Walker wasn't just a capable doctor. He made it part of his regimen, and his professional practice, to learn the ways of Oglala medicine men. During his two decades on Pine Ridge he became a "secret sharer" with these healers, teaching them aspects of Western medicine while he interviewed them as cultural informants and participated in their healing ceremonies. Forging an alliance with anthropologist Clark Wissler of the American Museum of Natural History, Walker wrote articles about Lakota lifeways, compiled demographic data, recorded music on wax cylinders, and undertook a staggering project to salvage what he could of "primitive" Lakota rituals and beliefs that he was certain were bound for extinction. He came to be regarded among traditional Oglalas as a *wicasa wakan* ("holy man"), a singular honor for a white man on Pine Ridge, both in his time and ever after.[18]

No one was more important to Walker's research than George Sword, a man well known to Three Stars as Oglala police chief, Washington lobbyist, and shrewd tribal spokesman. Born in 1847, Sword—a nephew of Red Cloud—was almost a generation older than Clarence, old enough to have fought in the Fetterman battle (1866), where he was wounded, and the Wagon Box Fight (1867), both with distinction. He was that rare man who thrived in both the Lakota life of the high nineteenth century and the coming white world of the twentieth. He danced his first Sun Dance at sixteen, counted coup on Crow warriors and white soldiers, received training as a shaman to practice the holy art of bear medicine, and once wrote that he killed an eagle with his bare hands whenever he slew an enemy; he also became an Episcopalian deacon, a judge, and a chief of police—the first chief of police on Red Cloud Agency, and later Pine Ridge. Known as Growling Bear and Takes Revenge on Them in his youth, Sword took his later English name from an older brother, honoring the weapon worn by white officers in the field. His new name was a pointed way of crafting a fresh identity in the hazardous, and often contentious, world of Pine Ridge.[19]

It's hard to imagine a man more alive to the incongruity of two colliding cultures than Sword. He not only knew the contradictions of those cultures but embodied them. The scars on his body bore testament to participation in fierce battles as well as sacred ceremonies. He had led war parties in his youth but was a member of the parley that convinced Crazy Horse to surrender in 1877. Though related to Red Cloud, he was forced to side against him repeatedly during an 1880s feud with Agent McGillycuddy. He was a shirt wearer, chosen by band leaders to mediate disputes and serve as peacemaker, while at the same time he worked with the government to stem the Messiah Craze at the time of Wounded Knee. And while Sword claimed late in life that he couldn't speak English (though he did understand it), he was fully literate in Lakota and devoted much of his life to writing down traditional lifeways in a native tongue that reservation authorities were determined to erase. If one could have taken the two cultures and violently shaken them together to see what kind of strange hybrid would result, a figure like George Sword would have emerged, a man of peace and war, of killing and healing, of brutality and grace, and beyond such contradictions, a keeper of cultural wisdom carefully salvaged by long hours, even years of devotion. Since he believed that after death his spirit would go to the land of the Lakotas, his ultimate loyalty was with the people of Red Cloud.[20]

Sword would become a key informant for Walker's project to record Lakota myths and legends. Since most of his Lakota informants had only a sketchy grasp of English, the doctor needed translators who were fully bilingual. So it was he turned to Clarence Three Stars. Clarence was a logical choice: a prominent returned student, a popular teacher, a fellow traveler with Sword in the vice-fighting Christian world, and reputedly well versed in Lakota ways. In 1909 Walker assigned him the project of translating some of Sword's Lakota manuscripts into English. It should have been an ideal project for a boy from the Kiyuksa band who had been reborn in an English-only boarding school before turning to the task of balancing both languages in the local day schools. He had done duty as an interpreter and came from a respected family. He knew Sword personally, having travelled with him to Washington in 1891, and had no doubt dealt with him over truancy enforcement in the schools. The prospect of the two men transforming Lakota traditions into Clarence's adopted tongue was promising. But it wasn't long before Walker would come to see that his translator's awkward path to assimilation had taken him half a world away from the stories that Sword was so diligently transcribing. It was a problem he would have for many years and with many informants.[21]

As Walker tested him with assignments, Clarence struggled. He brought a considerable burden to the task: not only the weight of his Carlisle education but the immature baggage of his traditional learning, prematurely cut short by Pratt. The instructor from Day School No. 27 was taking stories and myths from Sword and converting them into the English of a man cultivated on school primers and the *Book of Common Prayer*. His labors paid fifteen cents a page, and the Carlisle veteran took up his new job anxious to display his erudition. But he didn't just render the material; he shaped it. He translated *tipi* as *house*; a *disaster* became a *sin*. His tone recalled something out of a King James verse: "There is a house, high up in the Heavens, and in the house, there were Creatures, resembling the Bears, sitting up therein." It didn't help that Sword spoke and wrote an older, more formal version of Lakota that younger people didn't grasp. Impressed with Three Stars at the outset, Walker grew disillusioned. "His work is not at all satisfactory to me," he confessed to Wissler in 1910, "for he has given so liberal a translation that it has destroyed the ethnological value of the work." Not only were his English work-ups incompatible with the letter and spirit of the originals, Walker maintained, but Three Stars even added details that he thought Sword had left out. The stories were being transformed more than translated.[22]

Walker had his critics, as did Sword. Some have questioned the extent to which the doctor was truly initiated in shamanistic rites. His desire to synthesize different renderings of a story into a single composite version has been subject to some debate. As for the chief of police, doubts have been raised about whether Sword's role as informant to numerous white authorities undercut his loyalty to Lakota culture, even if one could argue that his ethnographic work was subversive of government control. Edgar Fire Thunder, for one, would complain much later that Walker, even with his informants, didn't understand the Lakota language well enough to accurately render its stories. As it turned out, it wasn't long before Walker cashiered Edgar's old friend Clarence. Three Stars had become more acculturated than the white doctor-cum-shaman could tolerate.[23]

The church meant community, and Clarence belonged to communities near and far. Not all of them were strictly religious, however. Three Stars was a charter member of the Society of American Indians (SAI), originally called the American Indian Association when it formed in 1911. While the Society may not have decisively influenced his life, it was composed of men and women who were, in fact, Clarence's cohort: educated professionals who were self-made men and women by act and notion and who possessed a public platform, be it local, regional, or national. SAI members read like a roster of distinguished Indian intellectuals of the era: Carlos Montezuma, Henry Roe Cloud, Arthur Parker, Charles Eastman, Henry Standing Bear, Angel De Cora Dietz, and Gertrude Bonnin. The organization was to be run by Indians, not by sympathetic whites who had advocated so many dubious reforms from land allotment to suppression of Indian cultures. Over time the society endorsed a number of different views, some of them contradictory, and schisms eventually divided its membership until it disbanded in 1923.[24]

The SAI was a middle-class reform organization born of the Progressive Era. Although it aimed to improve the quality of Native life, it struggled during its short life span with the question of how someone could be both Indian and American, a controversial topic for many at the time. The society chose the American eagle as its symbol, borrowing a beloved national icon as an affirmation of its patriotism; the eagle, it so happened, was also a potent figure among Lakotas, a winged messenger of great spiritual power. The blend of national and pan-Indian interests was complete when the organization selected Washington DC as its headquarters. The telling motto of its professional journal was "For the Honor of the Race and the Good of the Country." Though not a religious society, the SAI was the next most pious thing—a civic organization with a devoted following and a bucketful of lofty goals.[25]

The SAI was pan-Indian in scope, appealing, in principle, to any tribal member in the country. Active members were required to have at least "one-sixteenth" Indian blood, as measured by the race of their parents and grandparents, or be enrolled tribal members. People of other races could join as associate members with limited privileges, as did luminaries like W. E. B. Dubois and theologian Lyman Abbot. Whatever its pan-Indian ideals, the society wasn't representative in the broad sense. It appealed to an educated elite, of which Three Stars was a member, not the communities his students and their families came from. The society had a broad agenda: sponsoring annual conferences, often held at colleges or universities; lobbying for legislation; publishing a professional journal; providing legal assistance; and celebrating a special day when Indian achievements were recognized, anticipating the ethnic days and months that mark our calendars today. It successfully argued to establish a U.S. Court of Claims to adjudicate Indian cases rather than through special congressional acts, a decision that allowed the Lakota Black Hills claim to advance in future years. It also actively pursued citizenship for all Indians, a goal finally achieved at the federal level in 1924. Even so, the society was once described as "a reform organization which could not achieve reforms," owing to its modest budget and slender political influence in the capital.[26]

Beyond the aspirations that united the SAI were issues that bitterly divided it. One such dispute where the society and Three Stars were in broad accord was peyote. In the same spirit of temperance that would lead to Prohibition, the SAI condemned peyote and advocated for its criminalization in 1916, despite the fact that many peyotists were society members in the early years. The peyotists, however, were bitterly opposed to alcohol, creating an ironic undertow in the temperance movement against spirits. Three Stars would have almost surely agreed with legal Prohibition, given his earlier attempt to join the liquor-suppression brigade. But his condemnation of peyote, like that of many peers, was at least partly based on the confusion between mescal and peyote, between a distilled brandy used for intoxication and a hallucinogen that led to religious insight. The argument over peyote was acrimonious, and many non-Indian associate members supported its suppression, which only moved the society further from Plains Indian communities where the sacrament was increasingly popular. The controversy coincided with diminished membership and disagreements over whether the Indian Office should even continue to exist, and it wasn't long before the society closed its doors.[27]

Three Stars believed in his church, his community, his people. But his country, the nation of the eagle grasping arrows and olive branch, was something just out of reach. He had been a communicant and catechist since his youth. But a citizen? That was something he would have to prove, and the proving would be a struggle.

13

Citizen Three Stars

In the spring of 1909, two years before the Society of American Indians was founded, a distinguished-looking gentleman of some seventy years wearing a white handlebar mustache and dapper suit rode into Pine Ridge on a mission to discuss a nagging little real estate matter: the "opening" of Bennett County. Established that year by the South Dakota legislature, the county comprised the southeastern quarter of Pine Ridge Reservation; opening it to settlement meant that white farmers and ranchers would be able to buy surplus reservation land on the open market. Many "full-blood" Lakotas were dead set against the maneuver, seeing it as yet another land grab that would further erode what their parents had known as the Great Sioux Reservation and what their grandparents had seen as part of the vast Lakota realm that stretched across millions of acres of western prairie.

The visitor was James McLaughlin, hard-boiled government envoy and crack negotiator. Canadian by birth, McLaughlin had a long and checkered history in Indian country, having been the agent at Standing Rock Reservation who ordered the arrest of Sitting Bull; the U.S. Indian inspector since 1895; and a diplomatic arm-twister of significant renown whose soon-to-be-published autobiography was titled, if somewhat dubiously, *My Friend the Indian*. Pine Ridge had seen its share of Washington bigwigs over the years, from military brass like Crook and Pratt to civilian governors like Charles Foster and William Warner. But the difference between McLaughlin in 1909 and the Crook Commission of twenty years earlier was breathtaking. While both had come to obtain "surplus" land from the Lakotas, the inspector general, known by the honorific "Colonel

McLaughlin," arrived with little baggage in the way of legal humbug. Gone was the pomp and glamor of an official commission with days of feasting and impassioned speeches. Gone was the pretense of a formal vote and the accompanying incentives that would, through bribes and intimidation, gain the majority of three-fourths of adult males. Gone, too, was the idea that the Oglalas had some kind of decisive voice, individually or collectively, in deciding their future.

What had changed since the Crook commission was a Supreme Court decision that fundamentally altered the course of Indian law—and Indian life. The case stemmed from an 1892 commission that allegedly gathered sufficient signatures to allot the Kiowas and other tribes and sell their surplus lands. The tribes felt cheated even before the negotiation had ended, however, and so began a long court battle to overturn a pact apparently achieved through misrepresentation and fraud. After Congress passed a bill ratifying the agreement in 1900, the plaintiffs, led by a Kiowa man named Lone Wolf, pleaded with President McKinley and appealed all the way to the Supreme Court. The court finally ruled, in *Lone Wolf v. Hitchcock* (1903), that Congress had full power to ignore and annul any Indian treaty or agreement absent tribal consent, provided the legislature deemed it in a tribe's best interest. In a single swipe, *Lone Wolf* crumbled the foundation of American treaty making and, in the process, erased the principle of supermajority assent stipulated for the Lakotas in the Fort Laramie treaty.[1]

As he addressed two hundred Oglalas at Pine Ridge in early April, McLaughlin, who would make Washington's hard-sell pitch countless times in Indian country, alluded to *Lone Wolf*: "The fact, which I wish you to not overlook, is that Congress may enact legislation for the opening of Indian reservations without consulting the Indian occupants." The meeting was only a formality, then, though McLaughlin assured his listeners that Washington would prefer to have their approval. The audience, composed mostly of "full-bloods," listened mutely as the visiting emissary took a full hour to read, verbatim, the entire Senate bill to open the county. Many of them couldn't read English or even speak it, but the recitation satisfied the government condition that the delegates hear the words of the bill, first in English and then Lakota. Section after section of the densely worded text passed over the crowd like a threatening thundercloud, with nothing to protect them during the weeks and months to come from a thorough and memorable drenching.[2]

Several listeners rose to dispute the colonel. Charles Turning Hawk, president of the Oglala Council, rejected opening up Bennett County because selling land to white settlers shouldn't have precedence over the thousands of Oglalas (and their descendants) who hadn't been allotted yet. George Sword, warrior turned Episcopal deacon, lectured McLaughlin that twenty years before, the Oglalas resolved not to give up any more land, and they weren't about to change their minds now. Red Hawk said they would need the land for the increase of their children. Then Lawrence Industrious advised that Washington officials only seemed to come to Pine Ridge on the mission of getting *more* land. He said, "I would like to see a Government official come here, who would advise the Indians not to sell their land and to hold on to it to the very last and keep holding onto it for their children." And Joseph Eagle Hawk spoke, and so did Plenty Bear and Amos Lone Hill and Fast Horse and John Little Commander, and even Jack Red Cloud, descendant of the great leader who would die later that year. Clarence Three Stars, if he was present at all, spoke not a word for the record.[3]

McLaughlin wrapped up the three-hour council with a caution: "I do not wish to mislead you in any way by having you think that your refusal to this proposition ends it." In fact, he was back a few months later to coax and cajole some more. On September 1 Clarence Three Stars stood at his side as interpreter, a sign that the respected Carlisle student was sympathetic to the plan. The father of six children by that point, he seemed to be drawing closer to the idea of throwing open the county to white settlement. For ambitious men who had gained a glimpse of the wider world, the opportunity to make the land over, at least in a political sense, must have been tempting. On September 7, as McLaughlin cajoled various factions to approve the scheme, a petition was presented. Its signees, including Three Stars, declared "full confidence in Inspector James McLaughlin." The petition continued, "We are willing to leave the fixing of the boundaries of the portion, to be opened, to his judgment." The treaty provision requiring assent of three-fourths of adult males was ignored.

In December a companion bill was introduced in the House to dispose of unallotted land in Bennett County, and in May 1910 it was chiseled into law: once Indian allotments were complete, the government would offer surplus land to the highest bidder and use the revenue to finance the "education, support, and civilization" of the tribe—minus, to be sure, surveying and administrative costs. Once again, another wedge of earth had been pried from Lakota hands.[4]

Like many of his people, Clarence Three Stars was born to the land. He was old enough to remember the buffalo hunt, the moving camp with Lakota police scolding slackers, the winters full of firelight and stories, the nights under the stars, the rough and tumble games and cold dives into the river. His ancestors had been hunters, but he had had little taste for riding and tracking, not as a boy educated in the finer points of English grammar at the best of eastern boarding schools. Still, he had learned how to put up a four-wire fence around a small garden, how to make his own brand and take a hot iron to his herd in spring and fall. He wanted to work the land, not just live on it. But being bound to a square patch of earth by a mere piece of paper, the way it was with an allotment, was something a man had to think long and hard about.[5]

He had been of two minds about allotment. The idea of assigning land parcels to individual Indians, however lofty its promise to make prosperous farmers of them, was full of hazard. He voted for the 1889 agreement, which started the process of dividing common Lakota lands in severalty. But eight years later he was telling the U.S. Senate that the land was only fit for grazing, not planting and raising crops. He owned nearly a hundred head of cattle—he was a respectable rancher by century's end—but severalty, he had said in Washington, would cut back the land his cattle could graze on, force him to reduce his herd, and make a profitable ranching operation untenable.[6]

In fact, opposition to severalty, common among "full-bloods," was a lost cause. Market pressure for surplus land was relentless, and Oglalas had already voted, however suspect the ballot, in favor of subdividing their domain. Allotment on Pine Ridge thus began in the summer of 1904. Those who argued that breaking up their common lands would make paupers of them could do little but assent. For a Lakota family to refuse severalty, if such refusal were even possible, would have risked having the tribal land they lived and built on given over to someone else. Clarence waited his turn for the allotment process to march across the swells and bottomlands of Pine Ridge, a wagon load of surveyors toting compass and chain and sundry accoutrements of partition. There was only one thing worse than being land poor, it turned out, and that was having no land at all.[7]

In 1908, courtesy of the General Land Office and President Roosevelt, Three Stars was allotted 640 acres of restricted trust land about twelve miles northeast of Martin in what would soon become Bennett County. When Oglalas looked out over the sloping hills of cheat grass and buffalo grass those early years, they were far from the bustle of commerce and city; the nearest railhead was more than twenty miles distant. It was a place both remote and insulated, close to the heart of the land but as far from the edge of the country as one could get. Clarence's allotment was barely twenty miles from what geographers would later call the continental pole of inaccessibility—the place in North America farthest from any ocean—which made it, in one sense, the most centered patch of land on the continent. He knew that rainfall was scarce. In some places on Pine Ridge, as one agent later put it, "no living water is found." He knew that scratching out a living with a half dozen children would be a gamble. In March his daughter Louisa had died, and the loss of a life cut miserably short weighed heavily on the family. With allotment, though, came hope of something better. Now he had what white men like Wanamaker called an asset, even if it sagged under the load of Indian Office regulations that controlled what he could buy and sell, how he spent his money, and even the kind of food his family ate. He was deep in the world now but somehow on the edge of it, on the verge of finding a way beyond school and store if only he could get a grip on his piece of land and make use of the gift it somehow promised.[8]

The opening of Bennett County was controversial. Most "full-bloods" opposed it, but Three Stars wasn't just any "full-blood." He was a protégé of Pratt, spent a formative trial in the employ of Wanamaker, and had put in years running or working at trading posts on Pine Ridge. He was an up-and-coming man of commerce, and Bennett County was soon to be a place where a little entrepreneurship could help a man distinguish himself. Schooled and missionized, Clarence was already convinced of the advantages of "civilization," at least some of the more tangible ones. Perhaps he could be a man of standing in a fiefdom far removed from the red tape of the Indian Office. The birth of Bennett County might be the perfect opportunity for the blossoming of Clarence Three Stars.

Barely six months after the county was opened, Three Stars applied for a fee simple patent. With a patent the allotment would be his as private property, no longer subject to trust restrictions, and he would become a U.S. citizen. The Burke Act of 1906 had made this possible, allowing "competent" Indians—those no longer considered government wards—to forego the twenty-five-year waiting period required by the Dawes Act before patenting their section and owning the land free and clear. Clarence was nothing if not competent, as the agent, the day school inspectors, and his business associates would attest. But removing trust status exposed the land to the whims of the market: buying and selling and potential profits, yes. Yet the pitfalls were serious: taxation, mortgages and liens, defaulted loans, estate sales, and foreclosures. Once Clarence was ready to file for a patent, a public notice announced, "Any person acquainted with the applicant and knowing anything which in his judgment would tend to show that such patent ought not to be issued, is urgently requested to make it known to [the agent]." It sounded like marriage banns asking any doubting Thomases in the congregation to kindly speak up before it was too late. If anyone ever stepped forward to object to Clarence making his fortune from Section 13, Township 38 North, Range 36 West of the 6th prime meridian in South Dakota, they don't appear to have put up much of a fuss.[9]

Clarence and Jennie weren't exactly "marrying" their land, but a patent was a solemn vow in the eyes of the General Land Office. In fact, the application required more paperwork than a marriage license and eventually came with as much pageantry. Mr. and Mrs. Three Stars missed, by only a few years, the spectacle arranged for future patentees: the shooting-of-the-arrow citizenship ceremony instituted in 1916. In this ritual the new patentee would step out of a tipi and fire an arrow into the sky to symbolize the old way of life he was leaving. He then walked to a nearby plow and grabbed it with both hands to acknowledge the new labor of tilling the earth. Finally, he held up an American flag and swore, "[I] give my hands, my head, and my heart to the doing of all that will make me a true American citizen." Despite such vows some allottees had made plans to sell their land before they even grasped the plow, and Clarence wasn't far behind them. A man who had traveled to Washington to initiate damage claims for the taking of the Black Hills would soon be giving up his own piece of tribal real estate.[10]

The 640 acres allotted Clarence (Jennie was allotted 320 separately, and their six children 160 each) were assessed at ten dollars an acre. That it was "tillable" in the eyes of the boss farmer made it valuable by Pine Ridge standards, given the lack of regular rainfall. Clarence and Jennie had already improved the allotment with a house, a barn, a corral, fencing, horses, and cattle and had cleared forty acres of brush for a hay meadow. But the patent application took pains to weed out "bad" character. First, Clarence had to confirm he was free of debt, a detail that was essential for his emancipation from trust status and a principle that had been instilled in him early on at Carlisle. Second, he affirmed that while he'd been eligible to lease his land, it was a privilege he didn't exercise. Nor, Clarence vowed, had any speculators approached him to buy his patent, meaning he wasn't likely to "flip" the allotment as soon as the authorities signed off. All appearances suggested that Clarence was going to make one very fine American.[11]

His journey to get there had been a long one. "All was struggle with me for an independent manhood," he confided in his application. He had been absent from the ration rolls since 1901, he noted, a testament to his means and ambition. His previous life was a source of some embarrassment: "I would not yield to old barbarous activities but stick to the new life which was grafted into my soul." He outlined his work at Wanamaker's and Carlisle, at the boarding and day schools, and at his ranch full of horses and cattle. He was as American as any man by hope and habit. "I desire to be a citizen of the state," he declared. "I am willing to pay taxes, I think that is what makes a citizen." In his eagerness to join, even a grudge emerged: "In my associations with citizens in a business

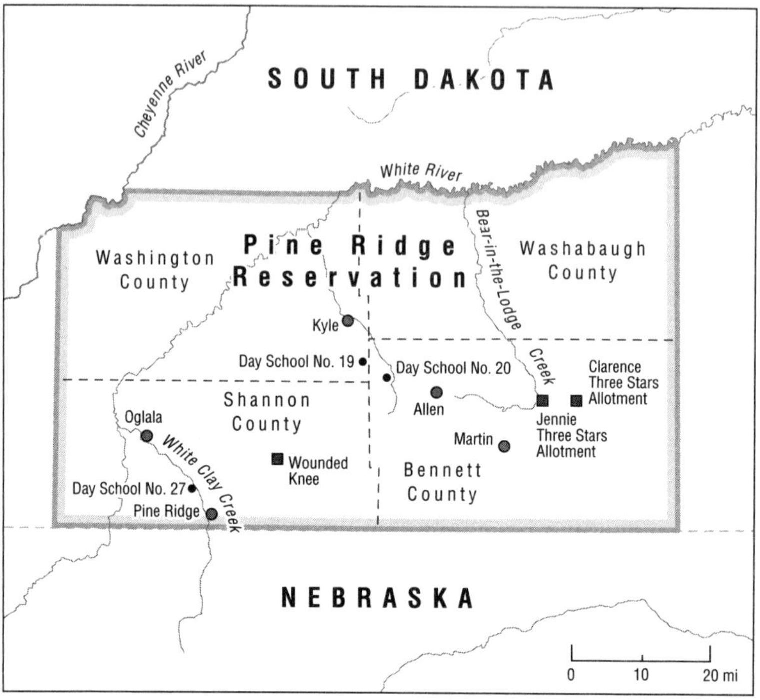

Map 3. Pine Ridge Reservation, 1910. Erin Greb Cartography.

capacity, I am sometimes [word obscured] just because I was not a citizen, yet I was capable!"[12]

Three Stars enlisted the cattle baron H. A. Dawson as a character reference. Clarence was "possessed of intelligence beyond the ordinary," Dawson wrote. "He is one of the few Indians who, after being educated, did not revert to his former condition." Further, he attested, "He is as well qualified in [business affairs] as a majority of white men." This was the same Dawson who, a dozen years previous, Clarence and colleagues had reproached in Washington for trespassing his cattle and making a personal fortune at Oglala expense. Like many things, including allotment, Clarence had changed his mind. He was going about the hard work now of remaking his life—and the still bigger task, perhaps, of making a fortune. In December 1910, with his last child, Mary, soon to arrive, the patent was approved.[13]

Now in his midforties, fee patent in hand, Three Stars had undergone a civic rite much like the sacrament he'd taken in a Carlisle church thirty years before. For the first time in his life, he was in a position to make real money. He had earned wages on his Carlisle outings, but most of them were diverted to Pratt. At Wanamaker's he delivered merchandise he could never have hoped to afford himself. As a rancher, his cattle herd was modest by most standards. Even as a teacher he didn't see more than sixty dollars a month. He had held a few dollars in his hands for a few days or weeks, even turned them over pensively in his pocket, but he never had anything more than what would get a family of eight to the next payday. Pratt had schooled them on the importance of saving, but how much could an Indian, even an educated one, really save? Now he had something that he could sell and buy back and sell again if it pleased him, a place where he could walk out the door and hike a full mile in any direction and still call the earth underfoot his own. He was a free man, his land unencumbered, beyond the meddlesome reach of Washington. At last he was *emancipated*, if that was the right word—but wasn't emancipation what they did to the slaves after the war? What did it mean for an Indian to be emancipated? What had he given up to get a piece of the earth, to get a sheaf of paper inscribed with his name and a government seal?

There before him, at long last, stood the civil trinity of democracy: owning land, acquiring the vote, getting an education. Becoming a citizen meant accepting one and all. The land was allotted piece by piece, man by man, apportioned even to children. Then came "political allotment," the practice of one man, one vote and the disappearance of tribal influence. All this was unthinkable without the schoolroom, where children were taught that success or failure rested solely in their own hands. Cheap land, free elections, public school—the great rallying cries of American history! But they could bear bitter fruit for tribal people. Enfranchisement (via allotment) could lead to foreclosure. Education could mean estrangement from family. Citizenship, the dream of many a slave and immigrant, was a double-edged sword in Indian country, even if Clarence Three Stars gladly welcomed it.

And so the 1,200 square miles of Bennett County, excluding lands already allotted, were opened as "surplus" to white settlement in 1910.

Two years later the county went a step further, formally organizing and electing a government independent of the Oglala Tribal Council. In political terms the county withdrew from the reservation, at least in the eyes of the mostly "mixed-blood" men who hoped to run it. The election that allowed them to organize was something of a rigged referendum itself, enfranchising as it did only "mixed-bloods" and "full-bloods" with a fee patent, as Three Stars had just become. It seemed the "mixed-blood" Oglalas had learned something about elections from the shrewd government commissions that had speechified their way through Lakota country for decades.[14]

Clarence straddled the gulf between the "mixed-blood" and "full-blood" worlds. Blood quantum was sometimes a useful measure for predicting beliefs and behavior, but not always. How could one even pigeonhole Three Stars in one camp or the other? He was fluent in both Lakota and English. He had spent years studying and working in white-run boarding schools, but he used Lakota means and methods to teach his own students. He sought to help George Sword recover tribal myths and legends—but was unalterably opposed to Indian dances. He decried allotment as divisive—but sold off his own parcel of land as soon as he was able. He was an enterprising "full-blood" in what was rapidly becoming a "mixed-blood" world.

For all its contentious origins, Bennett County *was* that world. White settlers drew lots to file claims on land assigned in 160-acre parcels, later expanded to 320. Given that a third of the county had already been allotted, the new tracts made Bennett a vast checkerboarded district where Indians and whites would farm and ranch cheek by jowl and attend the same schools and churches. This checkerboarding mirrored what was happening elsewhere on Pine Ridge, but in a more comprehensive way. And since the county had, by dubious election, "seceded" from the reservation and governed itself from the county seat of Martin, it wriggled out, at least in part, from under the thumb of the Indian Office. It was, on the borders and margins, contested ground. Native allotments were governed by federal law; white allotments, by state law—and everything depended on the patch of earth where you stood.[15]

Bennett County, in fact, would embody Clarence's interior struggle. His family ranched in a place where races, cultures, and jurisdictions mingled and competed. The parceling of the land was motley and varied—one law ran out at the end of a fence line, and a different one started on the other side. Clarence's life was checkerboarded much the same, marked by tipi and school, by pipe and sermon, and by the open prairie of his youth and the bustle and grime of central Philadelphia. His marriage to a "mixed-blood" wife twenty years before had turned out to be a symbol of the very place where they settled, zigzagged with white and Indian interests, an in-between place for a man whose education had marooned him halfway between cultures.[16]

In a figurative sense, Three Stars was an *iyeska*. An *iyeska* is, colloquially, a person of mixed racial blood. But *iyeska*, literally, means *translator*, someone with knowledge of two cultures. Schooling, teaching, and store tending had made of Clarence an interpreter who translated concepts from one world to the other. But for all the talk of being caught between worlds, as one often said of *iyeska*, perhaps there weren't two worlds at all. There was only the daily project of working and living, and only in one vast world, the one where the land of Lakotas was disappearing, a world in which Clarence walked a path while being watched from both sides as he struggled, in plain view of both, to be a father, a teacher, and a man who had even taken to reading the law, halfway through his life, and who had found some of its claims and remedies wanting.

Some of his own people might have said, "You are Lakota, look to the past for guidance." But wasn't it more Lakota to change direction when opportunity arrived rather than gather dust in the same place? Long ago his people had lived on lakes and harvested rice in canoes, and then they walked onto the plains and drove herds of thundering buffalo over a cliff before harnessing the power and speed of the holy dog that they could ride like a mad gale in the Moon When the Wind Shakes off Leaves. And when defeat came they had to wait for slabs of cow meat served on the block. Then they picked themselves up and learned to take the cattle, still living, and run them from pasture to field with an eye to butchering beef or fattening for market. They had learned to live off what the earth would give them, even if that land, for every family, had been cut down to a small square of ground a man could ride across in a few minutes if he was in a hurry to get somewhere.[17]

There was no model of the world they could follow, and little they confronted that their ancestors would have understood. There was no plan of the future, no system they could envision to show them the way forward. Those who had been to school would have to notch into the wood like a sculptor with no design or pare deeply into the stone and see just what kind of shape would emerge. The only way they could carve a niche from the world their parents made was by disfiguring it, at least on the surface, so they could hold on to it and keep it alive.

He was Clarence Three Stars, internal Lakota immigrant, who had never left his land. He hadn't moved very far in his life—from near Bear Butte, where he was born, to the center of Bennett County, all of 120 miles as the crow flies. He hadn't crossed an ocean or a national border. He still spoke the language he was first taught, even if it was the new Lakota and not the old one that Sword wrote down. But he had learned and taught another tongue. He had been to the city and survived. He knew something about how the law could steal and bestow. He was a pioneer of sorts, a new man of Pine Ridge, a Wanamaker dropout and day school doyen who kept breaking trail to follow the spirit of his ancestors and the barely visible track they left him.

He had discovered the real size of the world. And it awed him.

His old friend Edgar Fire Thunder came back from Carlisle too, like so many others educated but unprepared, disciplined but feckless. Edgar signed on as an army scout at Pine Ridge, following his white father's footsteps, and served in the Wounded Knee campaign. He worked as a railroad brakeman later and came to love the freedom and speed of riding on the freight cars—until the day he fell from his perch, suspended helplessly above the tracks from a single piece of iron, almost falling into the ties below where he would have been crushed were it not for his desperate shouts, which stopped the train and saved his skin just in time. Given his school training as a blacksmith, he got a job shoeing government mounts in Pine Ridge, only to be booted by a long-eared mule so far into the street one day that he readily agreed that working in the village smithy wasn't his destiny any more than hanging from a moving freight car was.[18]

For years he carried his money in his pockets, unsure about leaving his dollars to fester in someone else's house—what white people called a "bank." But he got used to the idea over the years and eventually became a man of means. He still held on to the old ways, like the healing plant his grandmother showed him as a boy, a weed, as he called it, that would bring down a fever and saved many a soul during the time when the Spanish flu raged. They say hardly anyone who made it to the Fire Thunder ranch perished that year.[19]

The son of a "mixed-race" union, Edgar didn't put much store in family trees. He liked to say his Indian ancestors wouldn't have been around to greet the Pilgrims when they got to America, since his people were probably out fishing on Lake Michigan, oblivious to it all and not even apprised of the event for a couple centuries. Like Clarence, Edgar was anchored to the reservation by work: he was assistant and boss farmer at Kyle and Allen, and an official interpreter at the agency for twenty years. They said you could set your watch by when Edgar rode up to work in the morning on his favorite horse. And like Clarence, he would eventually hold public office and make many trips to Washington as a tribal representative. The two men were close, especially that April day in 1888 when Edgar married Susan Weasel Bear and Clarence stood up as best man.[20]

Clarence's other friend Luther Standing Bear would steer a more worldly course. Much had happened since he and Three Stars parted ways at Wanamaker's. After returning from the East, Luther taught school at Rosebud agency, married early, and had his first child by 1887; like Clarence, he signed the 1889 agreement to divvy up the Great Sioux Reservation. As Luther told it, following the Wounded Knee massacre his father took the peace pipe to the Stronghold hideout in the Badlands and convinced the last of the ghost dancers to come in and surrender. Luther moved to Pine Ridge and applied to be postmaster, but he was flatly turned down by none other than John Wanamaker, his former employer, now Postmaster General, who decided an Indian just couldn't be eligible. In 1891 Standing Bear took charge of the day school at Allen and organized a debating club called the Oglala Council; he then clerked for the agent in Pine Ridge and managed a trader's store. In some ways his life story tracked the same course as that of his chum Clarence, returning students armed with near useless vocational skills, who eagerly sampled the few careers available to them on the reservation.[21]

Luther's life took a turn when he was recruited in 1902 to be an interpreter and chaperone for Lakotas riding in Buffalo Bill Cody's Wild West show. He crossed the ocean with his wife, reveled in his new surroundings, met and performed for the king of England, struggled as he could to keep Indian performers out of pubs, and, while he was at it, fathered a daughter, all in the course of a year or so. Soon after his return stateside, he was traveling by train to join the Cody show in New York when his train violently crashed, killing several of its Lakota passengers and injuring dozens of others, Standing Bear among them. Luther, who was initially listed among the dead, managed to survive the crash with only several broken bones and a heap of good fortune. He was made a ceremonial chief of the Oglalas not long after.[22]

Luther wasn't destined to grow old on Pine Ridge. He later recounted how Superintendent Brennan kept him from getting his allotment until Luther went to Washington and badgered bigwigs like General Nelson Miles to cut the red tape and give him his due. Allotted in 1907, he obtained a fee patent that gave him a freedom he had never known before, so much, he said, that he "began to feel that [he] had been raised higher than a chieftainship." Brennan opposed Standing Bear going back to Washington to represent the tribe, and Luther ended up selling his land and leaving Pine Ridge altogether, tired of trying to decide whether to "keep [his] mouth shut or fight the agent all the time."[23]

The bonds of old school ties sometimes weaken. In 1911 Clarence affirmed to the Indian Office that friend and classmate Luther Standing Bear owed a balance of a little more than $400 to trader H. A. Dawson, dating back to 1893. As a former (and perhaps current) employee of Dawson's, Three Stars noted, "This bill is still on the book unpaid up to this writing." The balance, which was suspended as long as Standing Bear was a government ward, became active once he was allotted. Three Stars swore out a complaint that accused Luther of forgery and lying, but it isn't clear how the affair was resolved. It must have been a painful break, for the two had been almost cultural twins—they attended Carlisle together, took first communion side by side, did their school outings at Wanamaker's, worked as reservation teachers, and became outspoken advocates for their people. Both settled in Bennett County, distinguished Lakota men fighting for respect in an era of cultural assimilation. By the time of their dispute, though, Luther had moved to Sioux City, Iowa, and would soon leave for California to seek his fortune as a Hollywood actor, working with the likes of silver-screen cowboys like Douglas Fairbanks Sr. and William S. Hart.[24]

Standing Bear had been, by all accounts, a "successful Indian," one of the best known Native people in the country. He had special privileges with Pratt and recruited for Carlisle on Rosebud. He earned the praise of the great John Wanamaker during his outing. He knew the incomparable Buffalo Bill, and after he moved to Los Angeles became a valued actor in the famous Thomas Ince Studio. He authored popular books about Lakota traditions, among them *My People the Sioux* and *Land of the Spotted Eagle*. Even his personal letterhead, stamped from Venice, California, named him the "True Authority on All Questions Concerning the Sioux Nation." Standing Bear knew, like Three Stars, the hard truths of reservation wardship. But Pine Ridge was no place for a man of big ambitions. "As long as I was on the reservation I was only a helpless Indian," Luther wrote. "If I tried to better the condition of my people, while on the reservation, I found it was an utter impossibility."[25]

Three Stars had once fled Philadelphia and earned Luther's scorn as a "quitter." Some thirty years later it was Standing Bear who gave up on Pine Ridge and moved to southern California, apparently with an unpaid invoice in his wake.

It was in 1913, the year after Bennett County organized, that Three Stars unofficially retired from teaching. It was the first time in memory he would be free from working for the Indian Office. Washington would no longer be his faraway father, the one who paid his wages and decided on his curriculum and had once told him that he couldn't even teach his own people. While his connection to the schools wasn't completely severed, he had a plan to become something more than a schoolmaster, more than the pudgy-faced young man who returned to Pine Ridge an eager Episcopalian, more even than an experienced interpreter who knew that most things in life had more than just one name. His entrepreneurial spirit had already been aroused. It was a decade earlier that he had spent his Saturday nights digging for coal in the Nebraska hills, sending rock samples to the governor to no avail. Now, in Bennett County, there was a chance to become a man of standing without even striking it rich.[26]

Cut loose from the Indian Office, Three Stars threw himself into a short but distinguished career in public service. Elected as a county commissioner in 1912, he was soon appointed the first Bennett County state's attorney. He arrived a week late for the bar exam in Pierre due to a misunderstanding about the test date, a mishap widely reported in the papers because of the novelty of an Indian even sitting such an exam, which he finally did in early 1913. Two years later he served as a county judge and justice of the peace at a salary almost double what he had made as a teacher. But he was restless. In 1916 he ran for county auditor and lost. His comings and goings in Martin, the county seat, are logged in local newspapers like the itinerary of a landed bigwig.[27]

Clarence's legal training, not to mention his Episcopalian catechism, may not have prepared him for everything he saw in the courtroom. As state's attorney he prosecuted a man for sodomizing his own stepdaughter: "Did he stoop some in his position?" Three Stars asked of a witness. "Was the girl's dress open?" "How far was the dress up?" As justice of the peace he imposed bail on a prankster who posted in the Martin pool hall "a certain obscene, indecent, lewd picture . . . the same being offensive to decency and being adapted to incite vicious or lewd thought or acts, and being filthy and vile." Some cases on his docket were more conventional, like the horse thief who betrayed a penchant for rescuing bay mares that didn't bear his brand. At times it is hard to distinguish things he did because they were his legal duties and those that were motivated by the litigious personality he had cultivated. On one occasion Three Stars prosecuted a fellow attorney for embezzling over $800 from a neighbor and later took out a personal affidavit against him on a similar count. The accused, it turns out, was a man of some distinction in Bennett County justice circles. The son of Yellow Knife was given to picking fights with his social equals and even with influential men above his station.[28]

It was during that time that Three Stars began dealing in Bennett County's most prized commodity—allotted sections of land—just as he had traded in harnesses and hats and hammers as a Corn Creek trader. In 1913 he became a leading incorporator of the Pine Ridge Townsite Company, capitalized at $6,000 ($160,000 in current exchange). He was a busy man by the look of county deed books, selling a quarter section of his own allotment to Etta Nash and the other 480 acres, already mortgaged, to an Omaha businessman. He and Jennie deeded a quarter section of their own to the Townsite Company, and three years later deeded it back to Clarence, by which time he was president of the operation. He bought another quarter section from Grace and John No Neck and became a land agent for the Bates-Foster Investment Company of Nebraska, off-reservation bankers who bought land and made loans in the heady first years of the county. In 1918 Clarence was still wheeling and dealing, selling 152 acres to John Red Wing and another 160 to Mary Volz, trading tracts of land the way his grandfathers would have swapped paints and palominos. His influence seemed to be gathering. A contemporary account lauded him with the made-up honorific of "Chief of the Pine Ridge Reservation." In Bennett County it had become feasible for entrepreneurial Lakotas to escape Indian Office restrictions—but it was freedom that came with a cost. In 1919 the Pine Ridge superintendent estimated that a quarter of patented allotments on Pine Ridge had been sold outright, the rest mortgaged to pay taxes and interest. Clarence's allotment, like hundreds of others, had gone out of Indian hands.[29]

The Three Stars clan, six children in tow after Louisa's death, settled on Jennie's allotment a few miles west on Bear-in-the-Lodge-Creek. All the horse trading in the world didn't seem to have made them wealthy, though they thrived enough to build a modest ranch and acquire a small herd of cattle. Their lives were embedded along the way with the institutions that held together neighbors on the short-grass prairie. In 1914 they deeded (or sold) land to Martin School District No. 2, which later bore the fruit of what came to be known as Three Stars School. To the Chapter of Calvary Cathedral in Sioux Falls, Clarence conveyed six acres and then eight more to the Episcopal Church for a building site; two more acres went to the school district and another half dozen to the church in short order. Clarence and Jennie had developed a civic sense of duty, derived from their Lakota training, the teachings of the church, and even the civilizing mission that had been forced on them at Carlisle.[30]

His father and his uncle had roamed the land, used the land, reaped what the land gave them, never owned it. But the world had changed.

They were Americans now. And the pull of war and politics, so intrinsic to the American grain, soon beckoned.

14

Politics and the War Years

In October 1918 Private Joseph Oklahombi, a Choctaw Indian from southern Oklahoma, was stationed in the Etienne sector of the Argonne Forest, where some of the most vicious fighting American doughboys encountered in the Great War took place. A member of Company D of the 141st Infantry Regiment of the Thirty-Sixth Division, Oklahombi, whose name meant "man killer" in Choctaw, raced two hundred yards through a mess of barbed wire emplacements under heavy German machine gun fire. The Choctaw soldier, along with two dozen of his companions, overran the German position, found in it more than fifty machine guns and artillery pieces, and turned the guns on enemy positions while defending their ground for several days. In the melee he helped capture 171 German prisoners and was awarded the French Croix de Guerre by Marshal Henri-Philippe Pétain. The press regaled Oklahombi as a veritable Alvin York, famed Medal of Honor winner and one of the most decorated of American doughboys. Few Indian soldiers could match his legendary success, but many more would prove their mettle beyond dispute, no matter the dire consequences that would befall Indian country as a result of the war.[1]

Clarence Three Stars was in his early fifties, safely beyond fighting age, when Congress declared war on Germany in the spring of 1917. In some ways one would expect him to have been an avid supporter of the war to defeat the kaiser. Having spent the better part of five years at Carlisle, Three Stars had been immersed in a military world of uniforms, mass drilling, shorn hair, corporal punishment, and barracks-style boarding. Carlisle was where the key manners and relationships of his life were formed: it is where he reached his majority, where he (probably) met his future wife, where he learned how to read and write and speak English, and where he developed friendships that would last, if not for a lifetime, at least for the better part of one. But for all that he may have owed the school, Three Stars didn't view the Great War as sanguinely as did many of Captain Pratt's schoolboys.

The army meant other things to the ambitious son of Yellow Knife. It reminded him of Red Cloud Agency, the frontier compound where his family had been confined in the months following the Little Bighorn Battle, a place where they had to stand in line to submit ration tickets for a bad cut of beef. When he thought of the military he would have remembered how the Oglala Boarding School, his employer of many years, closed up like a tomb with guards posted around its barbed-wire perimeter in the aftermath of Wounded Knee. So too was the army mingled with the memory of his grandfather High Forehead, the warrior who had antagonized an army lieutenant and lured an entire detachment of soldiers to their doom by doing nothing more than shooting a lame cow out of season. The army was there to protect civilians and boldly ride among the enemy, his Carlisle chums may have avowed, but sometimes it was a force of fury, his people knew only too well, that no man or tribe could restrain.

The army that would fight the "Hun" at Chateau Thierry hardly resembled the frontier force of volunteers Pratt served with during the Indian Wars. Rather than face some of the finest light cavalry in the world, as the army boasted of its Indian foes, it would now encounter millions of German troops, raised in the rigid spirit of Prussian militarism and deeply entrenched in the muck and mire of places as dark and hazardous to navigate as the Argonne Forest and Belleau Wood. The American Expeditionary Force (AEF) required nothing less than the conscription of millions of American males, a number that led to a heated debate when the Selective Service Act was passed in 1917. Registering men en masse for combat had last happened in the Civil War, leading to riots in New York City and providing the North with not even 6 percent of its fighting men in the end. What the Wilson administration now envisioned was without precedent in American history, a mass mobilization that ran counter to the American credo of individual autonomy and freedom from government coercion.[2]

Enacted in May of 1917, the military draft was unpopular in some places and often wielded with ham-fisted inconsistency. Congressional resistance was considerable, especially among Democrats in the west. Exemptions for noncitizen immigrants were widely contested. People complained that draft boards were inconsistent in handing out deferments for men with dependents. While 36 percent of African American registrants were accepted for service, only 25 percent of whites were so classified. Some twenty thousand conscientious objectors, most of whom eventually chose to fight in the war rather than submit to hazing and ridicule, were inducted and sent to camps pending alternative service arrangements. Public raids looking for "slackers" who failed to register rounded up fifty thousand men in one dragnet alone that swept cities and towns across New York and New Jersey.[3]

Pockets of Indian resistance to the war sprouted all over. Hundreds of eastern Cherokees, uncertain about their citizenship status, resisted induction and service. Goshute tribal members refused as a group to register for the draft, not understanding that the Selective Service Act required everyone to register, even if noncitizens were released from service. Similar disputes occurred with the Creeks of northeastern Oklahoma, the Chippewas of Tower, Minnesota, and the Navajos of Arizona, some of whom resented becoming cannon fodder as replacements for white recruits. Even so, deferments were claimed by only about 1 percent of Indians who registered for the draft, an indication of general Native solidarity regarding the war.[4]

Such was the extent of evasion and noncompliance among the public that, by August 1918, the government raised the age limit for draft eligibility to forty-five, not high enough to include Clarence, though a little too close for comfort. By the summer of that year, nearly ten thousand men per day were embarking on ship transports bound for Europe until, by war's end, America had four million doughboys in service to fight the kaiser. It was a massive mobilization that would have seemed impossible only a few years before, a reverse migration to the Old World that would mix men of different faiths and races and ages, not least of them Native Americans.[5]

Indian country was fertile ground for army recruiters. Near and far from Three Stars—in Bennett County, across all of Pine Ridge, throughout America—the warrior tradition stirred men of many tribes to answer the call of duty. Many had heard stories of their ancestors' military exploits and burned to revive them. In a more pragmatic light, army pay was attractive on reservations where jobs were scarce or low wage. Then, too, the prospect of going overseas appealed to those who may have never ventured out of the county where they were born. Though some in the army questioned the discipline of potential Indian units, and the lack of English skills put some Indian recruits at a disadvantage, military service could be an attractive alternative to life on a remote reservation where money and work were hard to come by.[6]

Many white officials welcomed Indian service, if for different reasons. The draft was, in the largest sense, the culmination of the assimilationist philosophy that Pratt established at Carlisle. The army, like many boarding schools, taught basic lessons about discipline, order, punctuality, and obedience, all valued virtues in the larger civic life of a citizen. Military service would culturally separate men from their reservations, Indian commissioner Cato Sells believed, and "detribalize" them the way that allotment and tribal schools had long intended. The army was the best taskmaster for turning a stubborn or "backward" Indian into a fervent patriot, the thinking went, whether the initiation took place in a domestic cantonment or a shell-pocked French bivouac.[7]

Tribal participation in the Great War—as in many wars to follow—was enthusiastic and widespread. Though more than one-third of Indians weren't even considered citizens in 1917, Native people served in numbers far beyond the size of their population. About 25 percent of Indian males, if not more, wore a service uniform during the war—compared to 15 percent of American men in general. At least half of those Native men were volunteers, including 90 percent of eligible off-reservation boarding school students. Over two hundred scholars from Carlisle wore the doughboy helmet because, in the words of President Wilson, "The world must be made safe for democracy." One of Clarence and Jennie's own boys would be swept up in the furor.[8]

No matter how fervent the support for war in Indian country, the toll in human life was severe. The casualty rate for Indians, 5 percent, was five times greater than for American forces overall. Lakota men and their Sioux cousins were in some of the heaviest action of the war, and many would have done their ancestors proud. Joe Young Hawk was captured by the Germans as a sentry at Soissons, at which point he killed three of his captors with his bare hands and captured two more that he marched back to camp in spite of wounds to both legs. Chester Armstrong Four Bear from Cheyenne River, a sniper and messenger, survived a gas attack and rescued a French messenger who, in gratitude, gave him his Croix de Guerre.[9]

Casualty rates among Pine Ridge soldiers were greater still: a staggering 12 percent. The fighting tradition of Red Cloud and Crazy Horse was well served by men from Kyle and Wounded Knee who spent their days slogging through mud and dodging exploding ordnance after going "over the top" through a mesh of barbed-wire fence and a blaze of machine-gun fire. The pain of the war didn't end with the armistice, either. Sioux veteran Felix Renvielle received multiple shrapnel wounds in the Argonne Forest. He was given up for dead, and his parents were sent a death certificate. When a burial detail discovered he was still alive, he was rehabbed and returned home but disabled for life. Even the Choctaw hero Joseph Oklahombi would return stateside to battle alcoholism, unemployment, and poverty, like so many other Indian doughboys, including Paul Three Stars. Some Lakotas remembered veterans returning with newly acquired habits like drinking spirits, the first step in turning alcohol on Pine Ridge from a nagging problem into a full-blown epidemic.[10]

Sacrifices were common on the home front too. Sells estimated that ten thousand Indian women volunteered their services to the Red Cross. Women served in many ways: planting Victory Gardens, knitting clothes, selling crafts, entertaining troops, and serving as nurses at home and in Europe. Native investment in Liberty bonds tallied $25 million, an average of $75 per buyer, after extensive encouragement from the Indian Office. Sells believed that even the bond market would aid the goal of assimilation by encouraging Indian families to save for the future.[11]

But the war effort often hurt Indians at home. Many tribes stepped up agricultural production by more than half during the first year of the war; Indian-owned cattle herds increased by almost 20 percent, and livestock prices soared. But as prices climbed, Washington and white cattlemen encouraged Indian ranchers to sell their herds and reap big profits. A few years later the cash windfall ran out, by which time Pine Ridge ranchers had sold away their breeding stock and gutted the local economy. The stock selloff, some have reckoned, was a disaster for the Oglalas, second only to the disappearance of the buffalo a few decades before. In fact, every contribution to the war effort had a consequence, often unpleasant. The Interior Department might temporarily refuse to cash Liberty Bonds for Indians who were still government wards, claiming they didn't know how to use the money properly when they got it, and sometimes even denied "competent" Indians from cashing in for the same reason.[12]

Already established before the war came to America, the competency commissions continued to do considerable damage. "Mixed-blood" Indians and graduates of government schools were their first convenient targets—and then the trouble began. Many of those deemed "competent" during the war years couldn't pay property taxes, and so their land was repossessed. Between 1917 and 1919 the Indian Office issued more than ten thousand patents nationwide, more than during the previous ten years. The war had relied on Indian volunteerism at the same time the government clawed back tribal land at home and rendered thousands landless. Unlike Clarence and Jennie, many were those who had the status of citizenship clamped on them like an unwelcome yoke.[13]

Leasing of Indian land, also started before the war, became a big business thereafter. The Indian Office urged Native ranchers to lease allotments to white cattlemen and produce more beef and wool for the war effort. The result transformed the economic base of Oglala life. Nearly a million acres on Pine Ridge were leased in 1918, and 75 percent of the reservation was feeding the cattle of white ranchers by war's end. Little by little, restrictions on leasing meant to protect Native ranchers were lifted. The condition that lessees make improvements to the land was often waived during the war, and in a few years leasing was even foisted on allottees against their will.[14]

Eventually, the war fanned a controversy in Bennett County, where Clarence Three Stars became spokesman for a protest regarding noncitizen Indians. Aided by county officials, he argued that Indian men who had not patented their allotments were not yet U.S. citizens and thus exempt from conscription. The position was unpopular during wartime, especially on Pine Ridge where the patriotism of Oglalas ran deep. That Three Stars was arguing, in effect, against the induction of his own son Paul made him suspicious in some eyes. "I personally believe that [Three Stars's] efforts have not been patriotic or in the interest of his people," noted Pine Ridge Superintendent Henry Tidwell in 1918, "so much as for his personal gain."[15]

But which Indians were citizens, and which were not? Anyone taking out an allotment before 1906 was granted immediate citizenship by the Dawes Act; after that, only those who had received a fee patent, as Three Stars did in 1912, attained the same status. Grants of citizenship were also made through tribal treaties and agreements, but many people had fallen through the cracks. Though estimates vary, about a third of American Indians had to wait until 1924 to gain citizenship status and federal voting rights, the last large demographic block to be enfranchised before the voting age was extended to eighteen-year-olds in 1971.[16]

Tidwell complained that Three Stars discouraged Indian recruits from reporting for service to army cantonments. "There is a feeling so great against Mr. Three Stars . . . and one or two others who seem to be the principle agitators against the young men going into the military service, that I would not be surprised at any time to see the citizens of that County prefer charges against these persons for interfering with the selective draft." He then offered an assertion that he admitted was lacking in hard evidence: "agitators" like Three Stars were either being secretly paid for their efforts or seeking attention to secure public office in future. For Superintendent Tidwell, who just happened to be an ardent advocate of leasing Oglala land for the war effort, Clarence Three Stars was a reckless nuisance and, perhaps worse, a candidate for jail.[17]

There was more fine print about drafting Indians than the shrewdest Washington attorney could parse. In fact, there were so many riders against noncitizenship exceptions that it was hard for Native men to claim an exemption at all. If the recruit didn't state that he was a noncitizen when he filled out a questionnaire, Indian commissioner E. B. Meritt asserted, then he waived his exemption. Or if a recruit's parent had become a citizen, as was the case with Clarence, his children might also be considered citizens, depending on when they came of age. Outlying interpretations of the law went even further. The District Board of South Dakota ruled that any Indian living on a reservation who had adopted white clothing and habits, including "full-bloods," was subject to service even if he hadn't patented his allotment. Since Three Stars and other Lakotas were voters in Bennett County, their citizenship—and by extension that of their children—was undeniable. "I feel sure that none of these Indians would of ever complained," Tidwell wrote the Indian commissioner, "and would have been proud and glad to serve their country if it had not been for the efforts of one Clarence Three Stars, who, unfortunately in my opinion, is president of the Oglala Council of this reservation."[18]

Tidwell had no one but himself to blame that Clarence was president. Upon taking the superintendent's job, he made it his business to singlehandedly reorganize Oglala political life—with unforeseen consequences. The old Oglala Council dated from the nineteenth century and had a membership of several hundred older, traditional men. They discussed treaty obligations like the Black Hills, debated government regulations, questioned jurisdictional matters, and fielded an array of administrative complaints. In fact, the Indian Office didn't officially recognize the council, and there was even talk of abolishing it. Previous superintendent Brennan preferred to demur from such an extreme until the allotment process was finished and "as long as the society does not interfere with Department supervision." Besides, he conceded, you couldn't really stop them from meeting anyway.[19]

Tidwell couldn't stop them either, but he moved to make them obsolete. He petitioned Washington for an election to replace the traditional council, and soon after he recounted in a public bulletin to Oglalas that the "holding of election was left to [his] discretion" by the commissioner. The subsequent election, held in March 1918, was limited to male voters twenty-one and older. Each of seven districts was to elect three delegates for the tribal council, who would then elect the president and secretary from among their number. Delegates and officers were to serve a term of two years, pending reelection, without pay. On March 19, of over a thousand ballots cast in all districts, Three Stars was named as a delegate from Pass Creek with more district-wide votes (sixty-one) than any other candidate. The twenty-one delegates then elected him president of the council, a move that Tidwell would come to regret. His special election had put the "wrong" man in office.[20]

In early May Three Stars submitted, on behalf of the council, a draft for a new tribal constitution and bylaws. Tidwell saw in the draft a philosophy that competed with his own vision of what Lakota politics should resemble, at which point he rejected the document out of hand and refused to even make copies available. Among other issues, he snubbed the council's request to call their own meetings without the superintendent's approval; to receive payment for their service; to require that council members be at least thirty years of age; and to mandate that meetings be held in various districts rather than only at the agency. Tidwell eliminated the position of treasurer, proposed in the constitution, arguing that if the council had no money, they wouldn't need a treasurer anyway. "Such [council] members should have the interest of the tribe at heart and should be willing to serve without any money consideration," he argued, expressing an altruistic urge he didn't apply to his own government job as superintendent. Three Stars may have been president of the council, but Tidwell could block almost anything he did.[21]

The politics of war, family, and tribal council were tightly braided. At about the time Tidwell rejected the constitution, Three Stars had allegedly arranged for affidavits declaring certain draft-age Lakotas to be noncitizens, promising them deferments within days. In fact, the draft touched the Three Stars family directly. In a letter to Tidwell, Clarence argued of his eldest son, Paul, "Under the law he is not a citizen of the United States, because I was not a citizen of the United States at the time he was born [in 1894]." Judge Ray's former correspondence student cited chapter and verse to make his case, as one might expect from a former state's attorney. "I am anxious that he should be a citizen," he noted, "but regulation and Rulings would not permit it." The Carlisle man from Pass Creek district was starting to sound like an uppity Indian lawyer.[22]

The Indian Office was having none of it. When Paul Three Stars claimed exemption as a noncitizen, perhaps at his father's urging, the local draft board overruled him. Tidwell, for his part, wasn't sure Paul had ever voted—which would have demonstrated citizen status—but the superintendent argued he was eligible anyway because he had "adopted the ways of civilization." His opinion of Clarence was even more unfavorable. A month before the war ended, Tidwell alleged that Three Stars had claimed in his election campaign that "he would get all of the Indian boys of [the] reservation out of the army and have the others exempted." Such a promise would have been imprudent given enthusiasm for the war on Pine Ridge, and Clarence was too cagey for that.[23]

Paul appealed his case to the District Board, and again he was trumped. The committee argued that, since he had adopted the ways of the majority culture, he should be subject to the draft that defended it—and off he went to serve in Company C of the 351st Infantry. Clarence's objection to Paul's service, in fact, had deep roots. His grandfather had once been menaced by the military in an episode that ended as a deadly fiasco. As a boy, Packs the Dog had been virtually imprisoned at the agencies, guarded by bluecoats, before going off to school. And school itself, while cultivating useful skills, was based on an oppressive regimen that didn't always suit his contrarian instincts. Three Stars had gone from being a (largely) obedient student in a military-style school to an "unpatriotic" radical in a time of national emergency. From where Woodrow Wilson and John Pershing stood, he may have seemed more an Indian agitator than an American patriot.[24]

Clarence's nemesis remained the man in charge on Pine Ridge. Like Brennan before him, Henry Tidwell encouraged leasing on the reservation. He thought the arrival of white farmers and ranchers would only enrich the experience of the Oglalas. He didn't think Indians with money in hand could be trusted. He complained of a tendency toward immorality, what with peyote use, divorce, adultery, bastardy, gambling, and family abandonment said to be on the rise. But it was his attitude toward Oglala self-government and Indian military service that led to clashes with Clarence and others, a corrosive influence achieved in a few short years.[25]

The erstwhile state's attorney for Bennett County struck back against Tidwell the next summer at a public meeting on grazing and leasing complaints. First to be aired was a litany of grievances from his fellow

Oglalas over how their property was being abused by outsiders. Then Clarence stepped forward to dismiss them with a wave of his hand: "I stand my own grounds," said Three Stars, president of the tribal council. "If I were to have charge of these proceedings I would throw everything out. These individual complaints do not amount to anything. If we have the right kind of administrative affairs at Pine Ridge Agency now, trouble would not exist today." It was a radical position and a slap in the face at everyone attending, including Red Cloud's grandson James, who had just outlined the many injustices of the Indian Office. Clarence was speaking like a leader who had been pushed to the back of the room to make way for a clamorous gripe session. There to do more than just grumble about details, he was opposed to the entire premise of how the Oglalas were governed.[26]

That's when he faced the attendees and read aloud from a resolution signed by members of the council and approved by a vote of fifty-eight to seven: "A majority of the leading Sioux Indians of the Pine Ridge Reservation . . . petition the honorable Commissioner of Indian Affairs, Washington, D.C., to have all troubles remedied by removing or transferring the superintendent, H.M. Tidwell, to another agency, a smaller agency that fits his caliber." The insult of the last phrase was unmistakable. But the petition didn't change anything. Three Stars appears to have become a marginalized figure by this point—whether by tribal factions or the superintendent's own doing—and the meeting continued as though the resolution had never been read. Despite Clarence's misgivings, Tidwell would continue in his role as superintendent for years.[27]

The prairie lawyer and progressive teacher took a courageous stand against the draft. Whether or not he was trying to shield his own son from combat, he took an enormous risk by incurring the antagonism of Tidwell, the annoyance of the Indian Office, and the prospect of potential imprisonment. The Espionage Act of 1917, and the Sedition Act of the following year, made it a crime to disrupt the war effort or even speak out against it. The government prosecuted more than two thousand Americans for protesting the war—and a good half of them were convicted.[28]

Three Stars was flanked on every side. The Society of American Indians actively supported the mobilization and condemned all who flinched from rallying to the flag: “Anyone who voices treason to the United States Government should be reported to the nearest United States Marshal,” the SAI’s quarterly journal hectored. “Tell on the traitor, tell on the spy, tell on the draft evader, tell on the man who spreads false rumors and evil stories about the Government.” His own professional “family” had staked out a position that made Three Stars seem like an agent of Kaiser Wilhelm. He had crossed over a bridge in this, the crisis year of his political calling. By this time Clarence hadn’t just exceeded the expectations of Richard Henry Pratt, a career army man who swore fealty to flag and country—now he was defying them.[29]

Tidwell’s suggestion that Clarence be investigated was no idle threat. Thousands of Americans were silenced by fear of imprisonment. None other than Richard Pettigrew, former U.S. senator, was charged under the Espionage Act for opposing American involvement in Europe. Ably defended by Clarence Darrow, however, he managed to stay out of prison. Pettigrew, of course, was known to Three Stars as the senator who had borne the brunt of Clarence’s complaints on behalf of the Committee on Indian Affairs in 1897. This time petitioner and petitioned were ranged on the same side; politics bred strange bedfellows—even, or perhaps especially, in wartime.[30]

The Great War left a divided legacy in Indian country. Military service spurred returning veterans to ask for new rights at home. But the benefits—and drawbacks—of citizenship were hard to untangle. Conscription, though a step toward becoming American, went hand in hand with allotment. For reluctant volunteers, fighting for democracy—even voting for it—was just another way to assimilate Native men into a body politic that rarely had their best interests at heart. While groups like the Society for American Indians clamored for integration, others saw it as a way for the government to terminate tribal sovereignty. The fundamental question never went away: Was the reservation a prison to break out of, or a homeland to protect? Clarence decided that Bennett County offered a refuge somewhere between the two extremes, a compromise that avoided terminating the tribes, on one hand, and leaving them trapped in traditional ways, on the other. It was hard to be a flag-waving patriot—or an unyielding outcast—when one’s loyalties were so mixed. As it turned out, citizenship was granted to World War I Native veterans, but only if they applied for it. A few years later, the Indian Citizenship Act (1924) extended this status to all American-born Native people, their desires notwithstanding. The ultimate goal of many immigrants from Calabria or Krakow was foisted on the children of the oldest Americans, whether they wanted it or not.[31]

By now Three Stars had planted hayfields and strung fence; tendered belts and bonnets in the dry goods trade; marched boarding-school students to class in rank and file; taught young ones how to recite poems about the Pilgrim fathers; and studied trial law and brought cases as a state's attorney, hearing others as a judge. But everywhere he was dogged by the shadow of the Indian Office, telling him which reader he should use in class, whether he could slaughter a steer or sell a stand of timber, and when he could meet with his own elected council when he became tribal president. So he followed the rules at the same time that he pushed back against them—or looked the other way—but the struggle came with a cost. He had argued that noncitizen Indian men shouldn't be draft fodder for Kaiser Wilhelm's War, but the Great Father only scowled, and the agent maligned him as a conspirator.

So Clarence had left the classroom and entered public life. His business was no longer teaching times tables or fables in the day schools but fighting over turf in the contentious and grudging world of adults—"full-blood," "mixed-blood," and white. In swift succession he had become attorney, judge, delegate, tribal president—and troublemaker at-large. By 1918 he was the owner of a small Ford Touring Car, a prestigious acquisition for Pine Ridge. He was ambitious but rooted to the land his people had been allotted. He was a father who had lost a child, and a husband who would soon be a widower. He saw both the promise and duplicity of the America he aspired to be part of and worked to make the gap between them bearable. He was still interpreting the world for himself, making sense of the educations he had survived, first endured as an uncertain gift, and then blazed as a path of his own making. He had, in fact, been interpreting since his first day on the steamer to Carlisle, taking stock of the passing shore as best he could while the world he had known disappeared behind him, his life fixed on a boat running forward into the future, his image a dim reflection in the waters of the Big Muddy.[32]

With war came plague. The beginning of the Spanish flu probably dates to 1917, but its spread intensified in the war's final month, due to the movement of soldiers, both within the trenches and returning home, that allowed the blight to sweep the world with a fury. From October 1918 to March 1919 the contagion struck Indian country like a thunderbolt. In a six-month span, one in every four American Indians in the country was infected by the Spanish flu virus. Some 6,000 Indian people died, including between 350 and 400 on Pine Ridge alone, accounting for half the Native flu deaths in all of South Dakota. Altogether, more than 2 percent of America's Native population died in the contagion, a loss reminiscent of earlier plagues like smallpox, measles, and tuberculosis that had burned through Native communities for four centuries. Many tribes, still in disarray from the displacements of the nineteenth century, were vulnerable. The lack of adequate nutrition; crowded housing; preexisting conditions like tuberculosis; and scarcity of doctors—all endemic problems on most reservations—contributed to the astonishing death rate.[33]

Even comparatively speaking, Indian people were hard hit. Philadelphia, where Three Stars had once lived, witnessed one of the worst urban outbreaks in the nation. The virus struck in October of 1918, and the death toll climbed to over four hundred people a day. The gravediggers were sick or dying. There weren't enough coffins to go around, or even to steal, if one were so inclined. The corpses were stacked on porches, hidden away in homes, and overflowing in the city morgues. There they sat, foul and decomposing, turning a vile hue of black. Nurses and doctors were away serving in the military—or had been stricken with the infection themselves. People wore masks when they ventured out, if they dared go out at all. Had Clarence walked the same route after the Armistice that he had ridden on a streetcar from the far side of the Schuylkill to Market Street thirty-five years before, he would not have recognized the city where people once gathered in the aisles of the Wanamaker emporium to buy their silks and linens and chat about summer homes on the developing Main Line. Eerily quiet and deserted, the city bore no resemblance to a burg of a million and a half citizens. Philadelphia, in fact, lost as many as sixteen thousand people during the crisis, suffering the highest mortality rate of any American city. But per capita Native numbers rivaled even that, reaching a rate four times greater than the toll for large American cities as a whole.[34]

Pine Ridge was a mess. Railroad cars stacked with coffins lined up in border towns to hold the Oglala dead. The flu mowed down Indians in the potato-field camps near Allen; so many died in the towns and on the roads that the Indian agent had to call out special burial details to handle the volume. Some of the afflicted wandered away from the reservation looking for help, while others who had once left the area came back to care for their families. Doctors were scarce, but they had been scarce even in the best of times.[35]

Experts disagree over how many people the 1918 flu killed. Current estimates suggest fifty million deaths worldwide, though some historians call for a number close to twice that. Over 90 percent of those infected eventually recovered. But many who survived were left to battle serious problems like depression, chronic fatigue, sleeping sickness, and schizophrenia. One of those survivors was Sophia Three Stars, the eldest child of Clarence and Jennie, whose life was spared but may have been unalterably changed by the flu. If so, this altered existence would doom her to years of confinement, far from home and family, not many years after the war had finished.[36]

15

Canton

On August 25, 1922, a young and troubled Sophia Three Stars was admitted to the Hiawatha Indian Asylum in Canton, South Dakota. As she looked up at the main building after her long journey from Pine Ridge, she must have been impressed by a structure that made the schoolhouses her father taught in seem insignificant. It was an imposing brick and stone edifice topped with dormers, high chimneys, and a steep-pitched roof. A pillared porch embellished the front entry. Sophia was led inside to find offices for asylum officials facing the front windows and a hallway that led to the dining room, kitchen, and pantry in the rear. Both the first and second floors had two wings, each of which housed a residential ward with a dozen patients—males on the right side, females on the left. This was to be her home for the next eleven years.[1]

The admitting official described her as "subject to periods of excitement during which she [was] dangerous to others" and capable of violence. She was diagnosed with "dementia precox," or schizophrenia, and displayed additional symptoms over time, including indifference, laziness, taciturnity, and susceptibility to outbursts of profanity. She was about twenty-nine when she arrived at the asylum, unmarried and stricken with a severe infestation of head lice. Authorities confiscated her valuables, if indeed she had any. Then she was stripped, bathed, deloused, and had her hair cropped short, a grueling admission ritual that her father would have recognized from his first days at Carlisle. She was humiliated, far from family, cast among strangers, and about to begin a confinement that had no precise end in sight.[2]

The Canton Asylum for Insane Indians opened in 1902, only the second federal institution for the insane, after St. Elizabeths Hospital in Washington DC. The asylum was promoted by Senator Richard Pettigrew, chairman of the Committee on Indian Affairs, who saw an opportunity to spur economic growth in the Canton area by bringing dozens, if not hundreds, of inmates, attendants, and tradespeople to the region. It was the only asylum specifically dedicated to Native patients, although the superintendent of St. Elizabeths doubted there were enough of them to justify a separate institution. It was a common act of segregation in an era that had grown comfortable with the idea of separating races in every setting—from train carriages to toilets, from bars to ballfields, from restaurants to schools to swimming pools. What came to pass at Canton for the next three decades would become yet another source of heartache in Indian country.[3]

Locally known as "Hiawatha," the asylum stood two miles east of Canton, a mile from the Big Sioux River in southeastern South Dakota. The visitor was met by tall gates adorned with the words "Hiawatha Asylum," and the grounds, planted with a variety of hardwoods and shrubbery, were enclosed by a seven-foot steel fence. The main building was two stories of brick and stone, divided into four wings where everyone—patients, attendants, and officials—lived under the same roof during the early years. Amply supplied with well water, the building was heated with a coal boiler and radiators and outfitted with a sewage system, bathrooms, and water closets. The institution grew from one building to an entire campus, and by 1909 there were barns for horses and cows, cribs for poultry and pigs, and a laundry building. In 1916 the addition of a residential hospital introduced a hydrotherapy unit and solarium. Like Carlisle Industrial School, Canton was a "total institution" whose residents worked, ate, slept, and, in some cases, died on a campus run with strict hierarchical command and martial efficiency.[4]

Over the course of its existence, Canton was the home of almost four hundred Indian patients, among them Sophia. She was born in 1893, a year after her parents married; by 1915 she was declared as a head of household in the annual Indian census. Three years later, by then in her midtwenties, she was stricken with the Spanish flu, an affliction that medical authorities later said, with some suggestion of causation, left her depressed and indifferent. Among influenza survivors the connection between flu and subsequent psychiatric conditions, especially schizophrenia, was established before the epidemic had even run its course. The two illnesses may or may not have been linked in Sophia; that she was living by herself before 1918 suggests that she was then capable of normal adult independence. Surviving a case of the deadly influenza, though, didn't necessarily mean that suffering had passed; in fact, Sophia's journey through chronic silence and confinement would last long into the future.[5]

In just the year before her commitment, Sophia's mother, Jennie—Rosebud-bred and Carlisle-schooled—succumbed to heart and kidney disease; she passed away on October 15, 1921. Her death left her husband as the sole guardian of a large brood of dependents. The previous year Clarence had been cited as head of household for five sons and daughters (Sophia, Paul, Guy, Thomas, and Mary), a daughter-in-law (Sarah), and a grandchild (Ruth); this was a considerable burden for a man in his midfifties. Without Jennie, Clarence's companion in marriage for thirty years, at his side, Sophia's remoteness challenged him now as never before.[6]

At Jennie's death, the Three Stars family was living on her allotment. Assigned 323 acres that she patented in 1912, Jennie retained all or part of the land until she died. She also had six horses valued at $90 and an interest in the $4,000 estate of her father, Antoine—a 2⁄45 share worth only $177 and change. But the value of her land had withered. Her allotment was appraised at $7,900 when patented, but less than a decade later its worth was estimated between $250 and $1,000, the result of either the sale of part of the estate, the collapse in land prices after the war, or both. As she had written in her patent application, "I have been making my own living and at this period I feel I am able to care for my affairs and I should be released from wardship entirely." In response to her submission, Superintendent Brennan described Clarence as "first class" and "one of the most forward men of this reservation." Further, Brennan said, he was "not likely to desert his wife." Now the widower Three Stars, retired from his government job in the day schools, had to keep his burgeoning family together in a gathering storm of bad circumstances.[7]

Sophia was committed to Canton the next year, 1922, at the request of Superintendent Tidwell, her father's nemesis in the controversy over both the tribal constitution and the military draft. Because Tidwell had dismissed Three Stars as unpatriotic, perhaps even worthy of prosecution, his recommendation to commit Sophia may have been influenced by personal animosity. Whatever his role in the decision, the committal was ultimately made by the commissioner of Indian Affairs, who was the approval authority for any referral to Canton.[8]

In the early days of the asylum, conditions were fairly good. The wards weren't overcrowded. The grounds and facilities were new. The cultural practices of the tribal patients were given consideration. Staff did what they could to keep the days from being long and dreary. Outdoor games like basketball, horseshoes, and croquet were popular in good weather, and indoor pursuits included checkers, dominoes, basket weaving, and beading. In 1913 six swing sets, a giant slide, and a seesaw were installed on the grounds, giving the Hiawatha estate the innocuous appearance of a large grade school. But conditions deteriorated over the years. What had once been run almost like an Indian boarding school came to be a muddle of disorder and repression that was amplified with the arrival of Superintendent Harry R. Hummer, who had been running the asylum for some fifteen years before Sophia arrived.[9]

Hummer described Sophia on admission as "an insane female, ward of the federal government." Both her predicament and his blunt description were telling. She was, in fact, a dependent three times over in the eyes of the Interior Department and the larger world: she was Indian, she was a (single) woman, and in the assessment of the authorities, she was "insane." From the perspective of an early twentieth-century bureaucrat—or even a doctor—Sophia was on the wrong side of race, gender, and genetics, at least insofar as genetics were commonly understood at the time.[10]

The 1920 federal census noted that Clarence's eldest daughter could read and write. In the next census, ten years later, she was counted as illiterate. The turnaround is mysterious, if not astonishing. Confinement at Canton for most of that interval had reversed the typical path of learning and literacy. While it may have been a shocking turnabout, it echoed the fate of many Indian children in the early reservation period.

When Native youth went off to school, they were usually fluent in their mother tongue but clueless in English. Suddenly they were cast as "slow" and "ignorant," a judgment that would take years to overcome, if ever. As Clarence had lamented to his lost daughter, Louisa, "You and I long for education," a clue to what literacy would have meant to Sophia's family. She could read and write by the age of seven, which means that she attended Pine Ridge day schools and probably learned the alphabet at the knee of a man who first studied English from a book written for the deaf and dumb.[11]

Life at Hiawatha rested on the baleful legacy of American asylums. The nineteenth century saw the number of asylum patients explode in both America and Europe. This rising tide crushed many of the therapeutic inclinations of asylums until, by the 1880s, the belief was widespread that such institutions had a merely custodial purpose. One reason for increasing numbers was insanity caused by alcoholism. Another was that the family was changing from a property-based role to one of domestic sentiment, and the prospect of protecting family by sending away a disturbed relative was growing more attractive. Some historians even suggest that schizophrenia emerged as an identifiable condition only in the nineteenth century. The result, by century's end, was overcrowding in many institutions and a diminished reputation for psychiatrists. Harry Hummer and Hiawatha weren't so much glaring exceptions to common practice as they were relics of an era soon to undergo serious and widespread reform.[12]

A government inspector, Dr. Samuel Silk, visited the asylum in 1929, near the end of Sophia's stay. His observations of the state of the asylum under Hummer's direction are sobering today.

The wards were fifty-two by sixty-four feet large, had eleven-foot ceilings, and were lit by electric lights and heated with steam radiators, noted Silk. Each had an eight-bed dormitory, three additional rooms (one with two beds), and a toilet room and bathroom. The wards were full. Forty-eight patients lived, ate, and slept in the building, many under vigorous restraints.

The door opened to the first floor of the men's ward, wrote Silk. Most patients were sitting on the floor or perched on their beds. There were no chairs. Three patients had been removed to be padlocked in separate rooms. One of these had a brain tumor. Another was a boy strapped in a strait jacket. (An open chamber pot sat near him, though Silk believed he'd be hard-pressed to use it with his arms bound.) On the second floor, another man had been padlocked in a room for almost three years. He was thought to be epileptic, though no one had ever seen him taken with a fit. He complained of "too much bad breathing" and was allowed out of the room an hour a day.[13]

Furnishings were like something out of a medieval castle. As the wards were supplied with nothing but iron beds and uncovered chamber pots, patients had little choice but to sit on their beds or the floor. Restraints included straitjackets, metal wristlets, and shackles that might confine a patient for months at a time. While primitive restraints were common in other institutions of the day, inspectors described their severity and routine usage at Canton as unusual. Something as simple as a toothbrush was unavailable, not to mention basic dental care.[14]

The asylum was understaffed, and employees typically worked seventy-two-hour weeks. Turnover was high, which increased the workload whenever a vacancy occurred. Most staff had no experience working in a psychiatric ward and were given inadequate training before they started. They likely had little if any knowledge of American Indian lifeways—many asylum records didn't even refer to tribal affiliation. Inmates were frequently subjected to racial taunts, beatings, and sexual harassment. And staff were poorly paid—in most hospitals, salaries accounted for three-quarters of maintenance appropriations, but at Canton it was barely half. Tight-fisted budgets, administrative neglect, and marginal staff personalities all conspired to make Hiawatha a distressing netherworld for its residents.[15]

In the women's wards, Silk described in his report, the occupants were confined to the main area, which had no sitting room. There was no space to keep clothing. A paraplegic and hemiplegic were fed on one ward, and their dishes, made of rusty enamel, were washed in the bathroom. The female wards in the main building were watched over by a single attendant, frequently an old nurse whose hand trembled, perhaps a victim of Parkinson's disease.

The female wards were locked, noted Silk. An attendant was stationed to let patients out in case of an emergency. In the main building, a half-naked girl was sleeping on a mattress in the bathroom, confined there by an attendant, observed Silk, who considered her "disturbed."[16]

There was little encouragement to develop or learn. Occupational therapy was absent. Many patients didn't speak English, and no interpreters were provided. The lack of educational materials and books must have been keenly felt by a schoolteacher's daughter who had fallen backward into the dark hole of illiteracy during her stay. Canton would provide Sophia with no tools to mediate or deflect its influence over her when the day finally came for her to leave, a stark contrast to her father's experience at Carlisle.

Next door, in the hospital building, Silk observed that females resided on the first floor, males on the second. The sheets in the sleeping wards, for both men and women, were almost black because of soot from the coal furnace in winter, difficult to clean in hard water. The corridors, floors unfinished, were almost empty of benches, tables, or chairs.

The solarium on each floor was stifling and sultry, unbearable in summer, wrote Silk. The windows were closed and barred, and there were no shades. A blind man reclined on the floor on a mattress. A tubercular boy was lying in a bed, but the windows were shut and no fresh air was circulating.[17]

Canton patients were introduced to a strict eating regimen—breakfast at 7:30, lunch at 1:30, dinner at 5:30. Silk explained that patients ate pork, boiled potatoes, gravy, bread, and spinach at noon. For dinner they had peas, potatoes, apple sauce, and bread. Milk and tea were served at both. Plates were badly chipped. Knives, forks, and spoons were provided, the knives with a blunt edge. No one counted the cutlery at meal's end.[18]

Able-bodied patients were expected to perform manual labor that included hoeing weeds, picking vegetables, cleaning walls, and scrubbing and varnishing floors. The unpaid labor allowed the asylum to run on a shoestring budget as was done in asylums across the country, and as boarding schools like Carlisle even did. Though inmates were remunerated for their beadwork, if they did any, the real work at Canton was unpaid, whether that work took the form of the stoop labor of garden weeding or the backbreaking grind of cleaning floors and washing laundry. No doubt, the work provided needed physical activity and a time-consuming occupation during the dreary winter months indoors. But the cogs and gears of Canton turned on the daily toil of many an epileptic and schizophrenic—and of others who had even less reason to be confined—who received little more for their trouble than rudimentary self-satisfaction and the prospect of killing extended periods of time.[19]

For diversion from work, Silk noticed, many patients liked to smoke, but the fire extinguisher in the main building was kept locked in a second-floor closet. The radiators until recently were unregulated, and patients were sometimes burned by touching them. The operating room had no equipment. There was no laboratory for testing. The hydrotherapy room was unused.

To get some air, even a little, opening the main windows in the wards required unlocking three padlocks and removing the window blind. They couldn't be opened from the top, and from the bottom they had to be forced with a lever to raise them an inch or two. They stayed closed, mostly, wrote Silk. The frames were dirty, and the air was stale and stuffy, almost intolerable at night with eight reeking chamber pots. The more Silk wrote, the more desperate the place appeared.[20]

Once Sophia was lodged at Canton, she had virtually no legal rights. The state couldn't intervene in an Indian Bureau institution, where "wardship" was the dominant paradigm and inmates were regarded as either dependent or utterly helpless. Many patients were committed at a young age, some before they reached their majority. Some were wrongly committed for infractions such as fighting at school or arguing with a spouse. Several were intellectually deficient in minor ways but showed no signs of a psychosis, while others had conditions such as epilepsy that could have been supervised in a home environment. A St. Elizabeths doctor later reckoned that barely one-third of the ninety patients needed the supervised environment of a mental institution. In many ways, then, Hiawatha functioned as a holding pen rather than a hospital. One could argue that Sophia was less Dr. Hummer's patient than his medical prisoner, confined without legal recourse or hope of removal. Hummer himself agreed that many of his patients weren't insane, but he demurred at releasing them to return home because he eventually hoped to sterilize them—though he didn't yet have the means to do so. It was fitting that, when the asylum closed in 1934, it was converted by the state into a penitentiary for first offenders.[21]

Hummer wasn't alone in his desire to render the Hiawatha patients childless. Involuntary sterilization of mental patients was common by the time of World War I. A mental hygiene movement based on a belief in eugenics developed in the late nineteenth century at the same time that surgical procedures for male and female sterilization were improved. By 1940 a majority of states had passed legislation calling for sterilization of mental patients, and over eighteen thousand such surgeries were performed nationwide before World War II. In South Dakota alone over five hundred "feebleminded" (noninstitutionalized) persons submitted to the procedure. Hundreds of doctors subscribed to the procedures that Hummer envisioned for Canton.[22]

Though it would seem unlikely, the asylum became a popular showplace. Just as Pratt courted Washington politicians to visit his industrial classrooms, so did Hummer invite local dignitaries, tourists, and schoolchildren to traipse through the grim halls of Hiawatha. Over one thousand visitors called at the asylum in 1913 alone. A small cottage industry at the hospital sold patient beadwork and whittled art, and evidence suggests postcards, pictures, teacups, and commemorative cutlery were sold in town. Canton was a worthy subject of study for elementary-school students, advanced medical students, and everything in between; the premises were accessible to them all, provided they inquired from 1:00 to 5:00 on Wednesday and Friday afternoons. Meanwhile, the local press fawned over Hummer's extraordinary oversight.[23]

But Dr. Silk knew better. Unseen to casual visitors were the chamber pots he saw scattered across the wards. The male urinals didn't flush. A barefoot one-eyed boy, who lost a fight with another patient, emptied his own chamber pot of excreta and retired to his bed with filthy feet. A sick boy was padlocked in a separate room so others couldn't bother him, and another was sequestered with a strait jacket because he tore his clothing. The doors to the wards were padlocked as an extra defense against escape.

At night, offered Silk, the male wards were completely dark, an attempt to save money. The corridors, bathrooms, and toilets were unlit but for a lantern carried by a strolling attendant. In the morning, the smell from the wards was revolting.[24]

Silk may not have realized that not all visitors were even welcome, however. Dr. Hummer discouraged personal visits because he believed, like many professionals of the day, that family could be harmful to the healing process. One theory held that the home environment itself was the cause of the illness; another said that family visits might inspire high anxiety in patients who weren't allowed to leave with their relatives. It's quite possible that Clarence never—or only rarely—saw his daughter during the decade she was interned at Canton. If he ever did hazard a visit, he would have found it a dark and haunted manor that would have discouraged most first-time callers from ever passing through the iron gates of Hiawatha again.[25]

Harry Hummer's temperament wasn't well suited to lead an institution like Canton. His attitude could be defensive, insular, and even secretive. The holder of a psychiatric degree from Georgetown University who had practiced medicine for seven years at St. Elizabeths, the doctor was no novice when he became Canton superintendent in 1908. It was his approach to recordkeeping that alarmed inspectors. While the daily regimen at Canton was well documented, much of it by Hummer himself, little analytical information was kept about inmates. There were no family records for patients. Clinical histories were vague and generic. Physical exams included minimal data. Summaries for death or discharge were missing. Most patients were still classified as having the same illness they were diagnosed with at admission, even when years had elapsed and early symptoms were no longer observed. Neglect at Canton, in fact, had many forms. Tuberculosis and syphilis took a heavy toll on patients, the former accounting for 50 percent of inmate deaths. But Dr. Hummer did little if anything to test for such maladies, nor did he quarantine or treat those likely to be infected.[26]

It's not clear why Hummer sought a transfer to Canton in the first place. Born and educated in the nation's capital, he evinced little interest in the West during his studies at Georgetown and employment at St. Elizabeths. In fact, he had been responsible for more patients in Washington than he ever would be at Canton. He may have grown disenchanted with working the night shift in the capital. He may have felt overshadowed by his superior, Dr. William Alanson White, a popular lecturer and author of a classic text on clinical psychiatry. Or he may have been attracted to the idea of heading a novel institution like an Indian asylum where research opportunities were unique. Whatever his motives, several personal shortcomings were on display well before he moved to South Dakota, among them obstinance, pettiness, and a disposition to angry outbursts. Canton may have signified Hummer's dream of professional independence, but it was a dark abode for a man who sought to illuminate his greatest talents.[27]

In fairness to Hummer, he was the only doctor at the asylum. Much of his time was taken up reading and typing daily ward reports. Another doctor to assist with rounds, not to mention a stenographer, would have alleviated his administrative load. But during his long tenure at Hiawatha, the profession had been transformed. Diagnosis and extensive record-keeping had become part of standard medical procedure. An asylum was no longer considered a custodial environment, as the old paradigm had it, but a place where patients should be thoroughly analyzed, carefully treated, and eventually released. All this seems to have passed Hummer by in what became, over the course of his twenty-five years as superintendent, a ghostly place that one could have called, with little fear of exaggeration, "the Asylum Where Time Stood Still."[28]

In the end, there were few good ways out of Hiawatha. Escapes were common, but runaways were usually caught after returning to their home reservations and sent back to the asylum. Hummer estimated at one point that about ten patients were discharged from Canton every year—nine of them through death. By the end of his administration, the cemetery had 121 graves, their occupants ranging in age from two months (a babe born to a woman who was pregnant before her committal) to ninety-five years. As at Carlisle, which had its own dedicated burial ground, scores of Indian residents walked onto the campus at Canton never to depart again, even when the gates closed for the final time.[29]

There was one other way out of Canton, as proven by Charles Hawk, a Lakota from Pine Ridge. On January 18, 1929, while confined alone to the men's ward during a motion picture showing in the patients' dining room, Hawk hanged himself. He had been isolated as punishment for having run away from the institution two years before. When apprehended after his escape, he was forced by Canton authorities to pay for his own recapture, forfeiting $7.30 from his individual money account. By the time of his last night, Hawk had been an inmate at Canton for nine years; six of those years had been spent waiting for his first physical exam. The combination of neglect, arbitrariness, and repression was too much for some patients to endure.[30]

Hiawatha was "a place of padlocks and chamber pots," concluded Dr. Silk. "The Canton Asylum does not meet in any of its major departments the very minimum standards required of an institution for the care and treatment of mentally ill people . . . It is only because of the isolated location and the fact that it is rarely being visited by patients' relatives that the Institution could escape serious criticism for its conduct."[31]

Silk made extensive recommendations for improvement, most of them ignored by Dr. Hummer. His diagnosis, however, was only the first act in closing down the asylum. It would take years of lobbying the Indian Office to make his charges stick.[32]

Sophia's father, hundreds of miles and a world removed from Canton, had moved on after the loss of Jennie. In 1923, the year after Sophia's committal, he had married Mary McLane (a.k.a. Mary Emery), who was fourteen years his junior and, like Clarence's mother, enrolled at Rosebud agency. Mary had a mixed educational background, having been schooled at St. Francis by Jesuits as well as at St. Mary's Episcopal Mission School. In 1925 the couple was living with two of Clarence's children: Thomas, who was nineteen, and Mary, who was thirteen. When government surveyors came for a visit that year, their job was to make a tally of every reservation family and their material well-being. They rather grimly described the Three Stars abode on Jennie's allotment as a log house with a dirt roof and root cellar on Bear-in-the-Lodge Creek. But their photo of the site shows a bigger place than just a homesteader's hut: it was a plastered log house with narrow, double-hung windows, a pitched shingled roof, and two brick chimneys, all awash in bright April sunlight. In the photo a chicken strolls in the yard and a horseless buggy or two are parked out back. The scene conveyed a faintly prosperous aura, if indeed the photo is actually of the Three Stars spread as archived.[33]

The family was described as in good health. They had a log barn and plenty to store in it, including a passel of mowers, rakes, plows, a breaker and harrow, and three wagons scattered about the property. Clarence ran a dozen head of cattle, a small herd compared to thirty years before when he had been a semiprosperous rancher, but he was older now, and much of Pine Ridge had been invaded by leasing cattlemen in the interlude. The survey also counted sixty-five horses and two dozen chickens—all the wealth they had had probably been walking around the farm. The agents noted that Clarence and Mary had put thirteen acres under cultivation the previous year. The time of Dust Bowl drought wasn't yet nigh, but it wouldn't be long before the agent described many Pine Ridge allotments as impossible to lease or sell. Some grazing land had been plowed under and planted and would be unusable for years after the sod had blown away. By the time of the Depression, already looming on the horizon, parts of Pine Ridge would be uninhabitable.[34]

Clarence had come so far, from a teenager who had never opened a book to a teacher who had explained the deeper mysteries of John Greenleaf Whittier and the ancient Aesop, from a ward of the government to a man who read legal briefs and settled cases. He had also seen his share of failure; there had been things he had put his hand to but still come up wanting. He had fled Philadelphia like a man escaping a fire. He had run for county auditor and lost. His translations for Walker had been unwelcome. The government wouldn't have him as special agent for liquor traffic. He couldn't keep Paul out of the draft, Louisa from the grave, or Sophia from her wretched detention. They were indignities, some petty and others enormous, borne by a man who attempted so much but never got so far as his star had beckoned.

The 1920s brought a levelling in his fortunes. Paul had more acres under cultivation than his father did; his old Carlisle friend Edgar Fire Thunder had more chickens and more horses and three houses to boot. The survey revealed a land-poor but educated Lakota elder who had survived the war and numerous recessions with not much more to his name than his dignity, his book learning, and the farm tools he had gathered to make a bare-knuckle subsistence living. The census men didn't take all that well to Clarence either, characterizing him in their notes as "an agitator." One can imagine the earful they probably got from a Carlisle boy and prairie lawyer who had been to Washington on business and seen the workings of the Great Father for himself. Probate records show Clarence and Mary were divorced by Indian custom a year later. His bid to replace Jennie had been unsuccessful and short-lived.[35]

The family losses may not have been unusual for the time, especially on a reservation. But the family's suffering was still considerable. Jennie was gone. Clarence had remarried but to little avail. And the Three Stars family had now lost two daughters to plague: Louisa to consumption, buried on a plot in the Episcopalian cemetery of Pine Ridge, and Sophia to mental illness, locked away from her family after she contracted the Spanish flu, destined to linger for decades in a twentieth-century house of Bedlam.

16

The Black Hills

The wars and epidemics and family tragedies came and went in Lakota country. What never seemed to end was a controversy from Clarence's childhood whose repercussions spanned his lifetime and continue to follow his people even today. Standing watch in the wake of every triumph and hardship for his tribe were the Black Hills, He Sapa or Paha Sapa, as they are known in Clarence's mother tongue, that loom in the background of any important story about Lakotas from the Civil War to the era of civil rights and beyond. Any portrait of the modern Oglalas must grapple with what the Black Hills have represented for generations of Lakotas—the beating heart of a historical claim that binds them to ancestors long since disappeared. Young Packs the Dog wasn't even in his teens when a handful of his people purportedly agreed to sell He Sapa to the U.S. government. But Clarence Three Stars would become a leader in the early fight to compensate the tribe for an illegal taking that has come to be synonymous with the very notion of government duplicity. For Lakotas, the Black Hills became the mother of all land grabs.

Paha Sapa was central to Lakota life for almost a century before the discovery of gold by a government expedition in 1874. Not only Lakotas but Cheyennes, Arikaras, Kiowas, and Crows believed certain places in the region to be sacred. Rock inscriptions suggest that the area had religious significance dating back thousands of years. When Lakotas reached the Black Hills in their westward migration at about the time of the American Revolution, their ties to the land merged with sacred stories told by many of their neighbors and perhaps their own ancestors. As with a holy place like modern-day Jerusalem, sacred space can be affirmed by different peoples and even occupied through force without diminishing the claims of any. And so Lakotas dominated the region with military muscle and expelled their tribal rivals during the decades around the turn of the nineteenth century.[1]

But Lakota ancestors likely had known of the Black Hills far longer than a century before the gold strike. The constellations that Lakotas mapped in the sky mirrored the geography of that same land in their legends and stories. Paha Sapa functioned as a vertical axis, linking the sky with underground places like Wind Cave, the nearby site where Lakota belief says the first human beings emerged into this world long ago. Some have argued that a Lakota connection to the Black Hills goes back more than a thousand years, even if the area hasn't been continuously occupied by the tribe.[2]

Paha Sapa climb to four thousand feet above the surrounding prairie, an impressive, forested ridge of granite and limestone whose shades seem to change from dark black to deep green the nearer one approaches them. The land had, and still has, a powerful hold on Lakotas, especially such places as Wind Cave, Black Elk Peak, and nearby Bear Butte, where Three Stars was born. But the Black Hills had more than religious significance. In more material terms, they harbored enormous plant and animal resources and were commonly called the "meatpack" by Lakotas for the herds of deer, elk, bison, and antelope that grazed there; the bison were so thick they were said to be herded by the tribe. Even when the herds began to dwindle, the diversity of food, including fish, was extraordinary. The bounty of the area was proof of the favor Wakan Tanka had bestowed on Lakotas. The spiritual and material significance of Paha Sapa were inseparable.[3]

That the Black Hills were possessed of prodigious wealth was well known in Washington by the 1870s. With prospectors pouring into the area after the gold strike, the government dispatched a commission to lease or buy the Black Hills region, which had been promised to the Lakotas only seven years before at Fort Laramie. Led by U.S. senator William B. Allison in 1875, the commission was rebuffed by a confederation of Lakota subtribes who angrily challenged the right of Washington to alter an official agreement that had been affirmed by all parties. Though soundly rejected, the commissioners left some chilling advice for the next delegation: "If they do not consent, the Government should withhold all supplies not required by the treaty of 1868," the envoys advised. "If the government will interpose its power and authority, they are not in condition to resist." It wasn't the last time that a land commission failed to achieve its goal in Lakota country, only to spawn a successor more practiced in the finer arts of arm-twisting and irresistible rhetoric.[4]

Several events intervened to make the next government mission more urgent. In November President Grant ordered that miners sneaking into the Black Hills, their trespass notwithstanding, should no longer be challenged or arrested. The following June George Armstrong Custer and some 260 of his troopers were killed by Lakotas and Cheyennes at Little Bighorn, creating a rash of yellow journalism and public demands for revenge. Finally, in August 1876 the U.S. Congress placed a rider on the Indian appropriations bill that would cut off rations unless the Lakotas agreed to sell Paha Sapa. The way toward dispossession was clear. The government prepared to dispatch yet another troupe of emissaries, this time armed with something even the cavalry couldn't provide—the warhead of a congressional mandate.[5]

Their first agency stop was Red Cloud. Uncle Three Stars and family, the boy Packs the Dog in tow, were almost surely there. The leader of the Kiyuksa band, Little Wound, knowing the enormous sacrifice they were being forced to make, called for everything he could think of in return: annuities, ammunition, rations, wagons, domestic animals. "The country upon which I am standing is the country upon which I was born, and upon which I heard it was the wish of the Great Father and of the Great Council [commissioners] that I should be like a man without a country." The threat of withholding rations—or even physical removal from the region—was too great to bear. Little Wound signed. So did Red Cloud. Fire Thunder, too, the man who had adopted Clarence's Carlisle friend Edgar. It was said that Fire Thunder held a blanket in front of him when he signed, signifying that Lakotas were working blind under the harsh pressures of the commission. The "meatpack" of their ancestors was being sold to a bunch of hungry white men.[6]

From Red Cloud the commissioners rode to other agencies to obtain what signatures they could. They threatened Lakotas with removal to

Indian Territory (now known as Oklahoma) if they wouldn't sign, a gloomy prospect of exile to a land far distant and different from their own. Finally relenting, tribal leaders ceded seven million acres of their reservation, including the Black Hills, and gave up hunting rights in much of their unceded lands. Not many Lakota men signed the completed agreement, far fewer than the supermajority of three-quarters of adult males required by treaty. That the Lakotas were thus cheated out of the area soon became a part of tribal, and even national, lore.[7]

Grumbling about the loss of the Black Hills never subsided, often bubbling to the surface in Oglala Council meetings. In 1897 the Washington delegation that included Red Cloud and Three Stars carried with it a catalog of grievances that included the seizure of Paha Sapa. Three Stars acknowledged the value of the Black Hills when he told Senator Pettigrew, "We only know that the land was not sold to the Government by three-fourths of our nation. We know that now, but we do not know how much is coming to us out of the Hills." What he meant by "how much is coming to us" is ambiguous on the face of it, one of the earliest recorded acknowledgments that Lakotas expected a settlement for the taking. It looked like their sacred land was becoming monetized. Once it had been appropriated from the tribe, the value of the land was transformed from "the heart of everything that is," as Lakotas reverently put it, to a property with a rising sticker price. It was a translation that a man with significant time in the non-Indian world, under the tutelage of men like Wanamaker, Pratt, and Dawson, would have instantly understood.[8]

In later years Red Cloud recounted, with Three Stars as his interpreter, just how the Black Hills had been lost. As the old man looked back on their loss thirty years later, he recalled telling the commissioners in 1875 that he would only lease the Black Hills if they gave his people sufficient money and provisions for seven generations, a way to quantify the foreseeable future, a demand confirmed by many eyewitnesses. When the commissioners rebuffed their offer, the Lakotas resolved not to sell the area at all. After learning the specific terms of the proposed agreement, Red Cloud believed that a misunderstanding had occurred. "The interpreters at that council were not good," he said through Clarence, "and I believe they made the mistake of interpreting my proposition for seven generations to seven millions." The latter was an estimated value of rations and annuities issued to Lakotas by the treaty. It was, if true, a shocking blunder. Like the mishap at the Grattan battle some twenty years before, their words had been mangled, Red Cloud believed, beyond recognition. As the old man later insisted, "We never sold the Black Hills to the government." Three Stars could see, standing before him, how a prodigious warrior could fight on for the land long after retiring from the field of battle.[9]

In 1892 hundreds of Lakotas had signed a petition asking for $10 million as restitution for the forced sale, early evidence that monetary compensation was on the minds of many. But when Three Stars spoke with Senator Pettigrew in Washington five years later, his delegation had been assigned the task of finding a lawyer and perhaps reclaiming at least some of the land itself: "The Indians claim they have a right to the Black Hills country," the press reported. This was one of the earliest signals that Lakotas wanted more than just greenbacks or treaty commodities and foreshadowed the emerging sentiment that the land, and only the land, would be enough to satisfy them. Still, during the next quarter century there would be little if any public mention of reacquiring the Black Hills themselves, if only to avoid alarming their white neighbors.[10]

Lakotas faced daunting obstacles in their campaign to get something for what they had lost. In the early 1900s the Interior Department denied them the right to hire their own attorney, a privilege reserved for the Indian Office, which considered the Black Hills claim unwinnable. Even more disturbing was the policy, established in 1873, that no tribe had the right to sue the U.S. government because of the legal concept of sovereign immunity. Instead, Congress had to pass a special jurisdictional act before the case could be taken up by the Court of Claims. What had been seized with a few weeks of clumsy maneuvering in 1876 would take decades to restore, and only then by means of a settlement deemed unsatisfactory by future generations.[11]

The former law school student was eager to bring his legal training to bear on the Paha Sapa dispute. In 1913, then working as state's attorney, Clarence was serving on the Black Hills Council executive committee, which was based in the newly minted Bennett County. Devoted to settling the Black Hills claim, the council represented itself cautiously in public releases, choosing patriotic rhetoric over combative bluster: "The light of education that has been brought to us by the paternal arms of Government opens our mind to the fuller life in store for the Indians who will listen to and progressively learn the teachings of the white mans civilization," they intoned. Deferential in tenor, the council promised to use what boarding schools like Carlisle had taught them—the estimable tools of a new language and literacy—so they could carve out a better life for their people. "We hereby renew our declaration of allegiance to the flag of this glorious Republic of the United States," the committee gushed, although their real motive was obvious enough. Their letterhead motto was "Justice to All," and justice meant something more than what Lakotas got in 1876.[12]

It was only in 1914 that the Indian Office agreed to support an act challenging the Black Hills taking, along with other grievances. Three Stars coauthored a letter from the Black Hills Council thanking the Indian commissioner for his decision. But Lakotas didn't speak with a single voice. Disagreements between progressive and traditional elements over the claim intensified on Lakota reservations, and the bill for a special act stalled. Three Stars himself stood at the crossroads of this schism. He had been, in his youth, an adolescent forced to don a military uniform. He was indeed a returned student and certifiable progressive. But his identity was blended. As a "full-blood," he had been raised in the Lakota way and clung to many of its traditions. In fact, he was a casebook study in acculturation. And there were many like him—men and women, chiefs and ranchers, medicine men and day laborers and expectant mothers—all caught in the dilemma of not knowing who to turn to in illness, or whether their children would learn the right things at school, or whether the rancher waving the lease papers in the air was a dependable man or even honest.[13]

As long as the Great War tied up the congressional budget, the Sioux bill limped along in Washington. In 1918 Three Stars was elected president of the Crow Creek Agency meeting for the Black Hills Council, representing Lakotas, Northern Cheyennes, and Arapahos. The council petitioned to the Indian commissioner that the seizure of the Black Hills was a violation of the 1868 treaty in several specifics: the agreement wasn't fully explained to the Lakotas; fewer than three-fourths of the required adult Lakota males signed the agreement, some of them under duress; and the leaders who did sign weren't qualified to represent the entire tribe. They concluded, simply, "The Black Hills country has not been legally ceded to the United States." Even the names of Red Cloud and Spotted Tail, at best reluctant signers of the original agreement, weren't good enough for a new generation raised with different expectations of their leaders, people like Clarence Three Stars and Henry Standing Bear and Charles Turning Hawk in this longest of legal battles. While the Black Hills Council struggled to unify its constituents, the Homestake Mining Company was taking $10 million of ore every year out of Paha Sapa.[14]

Finally, in 1920, Congress passed the Sioux Jurisdictional Act, a law that allowed Lakotas to advance with claims that included annuities, education benefits, and compensation for the loss of the Black Hills. Even then consensus on how to move forward was lacking. The several Lakota reservations were first required to choose different lawyers to represent them, each with a disparate notion of how best to proceed. Once that condition was lifted, the attorney that Lakotas finally settled on was Ralph Case, a white man born in Sioux country the same year Clarence went off to Carlisle. Case filed a formal claim for Lakota grievances in the form of a hand-delivered petition to the Court of Claims in the spring of 1923. The next month he set off for South Dakota to begin interviewing elders who still remembered the Black Hills commissions from almost fifty years before. Three Stars interpreted for him on Pine Ridge in what had become, for Clarence, a familiar and even honorable role.[15]

Getting from there to a just verdict, or even to a semblance of one, was an arduous journey. It would take years to complete an audit of what the government had spent on Lakotas during the nineteenth century in order to determine offsets to the claim. Not until 1932 was the audit completed, and two years later Case filed an amended claim that sued the government for land takings, undelivered annuities, inadequate education, rations, and clothing, plus interest—a sum amounting to nearly $1 billion. And so Washington stiffened. In 1942 the Court of Claims dismissed the Black Hills case after deciding it had no jurisdiction over questions of compensation. The next year the Supreme Court refused to intervene. The Indian Claims Commission (ICC) Act of 1946 created a panel that could award monetary compensation for wrongful takings. But there was an increasing sentiment among Lakotas that money would be neither sufficient nor appropriate to satisfy their festering grievance.[16]

A generation passed, full of contention, and the case remained in judicial limbo. In 1974 the ICC ruled that the Black Hills were taken unconstitutionally and recommended a monetary settlement, a decision the Court of Claims dismissed the following year. Back and forth went plaintiff and defendant, tossing to and fro a legal bombshell that bounced from government commission to high court until a hundred years had come and gone since the 1877 act that codified the taking. Tribal lawyer Mario Gonzalez would eventually argue that any monetary settlement was an immoral form of restitution for land that had been wrested from Lakotas without the consent of three-fourths of adult males, a stipulation of the 1868 treaty, not to mention a violation of the Fifth Amendment, he reasoned, which states that land takings be for public use only.[17]

The saga of getting justice for the Black Hills taking has outlasted many a generation. In Clarence's time on earth, it had taken Lakotas three decades of internal debate and organized lobbying just to get the full claim filed. It would take far longer to get it resolved by the Supreme Court, by which time Clarence Three Stars and many of his descendants would be long in their graves.

17

The End of It All

The year he died Three Stars was still mired in the lengthy political controversy over the tribal council. For years, Oglalas had struggled over how best to constitute a representative body to administer the tribe. In 1921, just as they had under the Three Stars administration, the tribe developed a written constitution that, once again, was rejected by Superintendent Tidwell and never approved by the Indian Office. Stymied a second time, the Oglalas revised the constitution until it was finally approved by the commissioner in 1928. The new Business Council, known as the Committee of 21, opened participation and voting to a wider and younger constituency with a set of constitutional by-laws. The Indian Citizenship Act of 1924, which made citizens of all Native Americans, was stirring a strong desire for widening the franchise and wresting power from traditional leaders.[1]

The movement met stiff resistance when, in 1931, a group of chiefs and their descendants, Three Stars among them, challenged the legitimacy of the Business Council. Clarence's collateral descent from headmen Three Stars and Black Bear was his ticket of admission to stand with these "traditionals," notwithstanding his English proficiency and status as a returned student. But it wasn't simply a skirmish between "full-bloods" and "mixed-bloods," between traditionals and progressives; a disputed 1929 election had caused several supporters of the council to rethink their loyalties and switch sides. Led by the likes of James Red Cloud, descendant of the great warrior, and Charles Turning Hawk, a leading voice in the Black Hills legal action, the new group assembled at the Episcopal Church in Porcupine and declared the Business Council discontinued.

In its place they elected new delegates on the authority, they said, of three-fourths of adult Oglalas, a provision that echoed the supermajority provision of the 1868 treaty. The old men of Pine Ridge had, on paper at least, pulled off a political coup.[2]

The takeover was ridiculed by younger, school-educated Lakotas. The chiefs were "ignorant and illiterate," wrote one partisan. "The only emotion they seem to have developed was a sense of self-importance and cheap ostentation." The description hardly seemed apt for Clarence, a Carlisle man with a more than passing knowledge of trial law. "Even now, some of these noble sons of chieftains stand accused of insidious and questionable conduct in tribal affairs," he continued. "All that the old fellows like to do is feast and sleep." Another said their haphazard meetings were conducted "to the disgust and embarrassment of the civilized members of the Tribe," what may have been overheated rhetoric but spoke to the political brawl that was gathering. Clarence was the first signee at the top of one petition page to reorganize the council; in another entreaty he was described, with his fellow signers, as a "chief." The returned Carlisle scholar had traveled a long way back to find his roots.[3]

That summer the opposing camps came together in a joint session and, by a landslide vote, formally overturned the Business Council and created a new body loosely based on the old assembly of elders so often maligned by government agents and tribal progressives. This Tribal Council, as it came to be known, eventually included both "full-" and "mixed-bloods" and provided for an Executive Board that was solely responsible for negotiating land issues with the government, and only then with three-quarters approval of adult males.[4]

For the time being, the elders had won back their council. But the grandson of High Forehead wouldn't live long enough to see what would happen to it.

In August of 1931, his body covered with severe burns, Clarence lay huddled in a government hospital bed in Pine Ridge. Days before, he had tried to start a fire with gasoline, a strange errand that went unexplained in the papers. The dubious venture, perhaps nothing more than a careless attempt to light a stove, ended with a gas explosion that put him on the brink of death. On August 24 he was visited by a state examiner to draw up a will. A man of no small sophistication, Clarence would have realized the risk of having his estate, for want of a bequest, land as an ungainly mess in probate court where it would probably linger for years. Shopkeeper, land speculator, lawyer, teacher—his callings fell away like layers of old skin as he struggled to move or sit up in bed, his body no doubt racked by blinding flashes of pain.[5]

Three Stars confirmed the lands he had sold, those he retained from his deceased children's allotments (Louisa and Guy), and how he wanted to dispose of his estate. His estrangement from some of his children was evident. He gave everything he owned, an estate initially valued at some $1,300, to Clarence Jr., neither his eldest child nor the eldest of his sons. He willed the legacy on condition that Clarence provide a home for his youngest siblings, Thomas and Mary, who still lived with their father. Paul, the World War I draftee, was given nothing because his father said he had already received property. Sophia, the Canton inmate, wasn't mentioned at all. Clarence's legacy would be passed through the boy he had himself taught at Day School No. 27, the police officer and secretary in his model student government, the man who shared the name bestowed on his father during his first disorienting days at Carlisle.[6]

In his final hours, Clarence Sr. was sentient, comprehending, able to speak. The man who had once translated for Red Cloud and James McLaughlin and the secretary of the interior hardly needed an interpreter. He dictated what he wanted in English, and the examiner, Mr. Thompson, wrote it out before reading it back, word for word. Clarence assented. He was anxious to sign the statement but afraid his nerves were bad and didn't feel "his signature would be such as he would want," he said to Thompson, his hand visibly trembling. So the veteran state's attorney settled on a method unlettered Indians used when writing an X was no longer deemed sufficient for signing official papers: he inked his thumb, pressed it down on the paper, and was done with it.[7]

His final reckoning was at hand. The boy from Carlisle hadn't known the terror of ambush or the exhilaration of the hunt, as his ancestors had, but instead signed the council petition, contemplated the case study, wrote out the invoice, and worked up the school lesson plan. He had stood, in his final years, gnarled and formidable, like an old cottonwood tree with three or four different rippled trunks, perhaps one of them dead, another with a few limbs sawed off. He had stood out in the wind and rain and darkness, through land loss and plague and world war, and had still put forth leaves when the spring came. He was an agitator, some said, who knew the deep acceptance of the Psalms but had read widely in the commentaries of Blackstone, too, in case he needed to prepare a brief or make an objection or just plain raise any Cain.

The Depression had put eight million people out of work. Herbert Hoover was president. Prohibition had outlawed the production and sale of alcohol. And the August moon was full. Or one might call it the Moon of Black Cherries, because that was another way to measure the passage of time—one he had learned as a boy. His people had painted winter counts on animal hides, a chronicle of years told not with numbers but pictures tied to important events. He was born in the Year They Were Fighting with the White Man. He went away to Carlisle the Year Spotted Coyote Was Killed. He ran away from Wanamaker's the Year White Buffalo Shot a Woman. He was married the Year Covered Face Was Run Over by a Wagon and Was Killed. He gave his commencement speech at Carlisle the First Time the Government Took the Hides Back, and he went back to teaching the Year They Had Small Pox. His daughter Louisa succumbed to tuberculosis the Year the Keeper of the Winter Count Died. It was a modest history, at once spare and sober and powerful, not about epic events, perhaps, but about the critical ones through which life, for a small group of people, is made and unmade, incidents done and undone. It was the Year They Issued Out Blankets when Clarence passed away, a reminder that the reach of the Great Father was rarely far from their thoughts.[8]

The man formerly known as Packs the Dog lingered in the hospital for ten days, almost immobile. His agony came to an end on August 28. The burns that covered his body were acute. The attending doctor identified the proximal cause of death as toxemia, the spread of bacteria in the bloodstream, a common diagnosis for burn victims. He was buried, an Episcopalian, in the Inestimable Gift Cemetery next to Jennie Three Stars, just down the road from where he had once set up shop in Corn Creek.[9]

The week after Clarence passed, the Martin schools opened for the new academic year, and the evening curfew for children went into place. The former state superintendent of banks, convicted of embezzlement, began work on the rockpile at the Sioux Falls penitentiary. The Entsminger Lumber Company in Martin was burgled, but the thieves found nothing except the company books in the safe and a grand total of only fifty-five cents, which they left, perhaps disgusted, in a drawer. Hogs and hay were plentiful in the Wanblee region, though the corn harvest had been small because of drought. The world wheat crop was projected to be three hundred thousand bushels below the previous year, a good bit of news for wheat farmers since the scarcity would boost prices. Mortgage foreclosures were up. The usual advertisements for Indian land sales, cash or deferred payment, appeared. An editorial in the Martin paper wrote, "The opinion is growing that the cardinal issue in 1932 will be prosperity instead of prohibition. But how can it be, seeing that in reality we have neither?" Thirty Indians left Pine Ridge to tour Europe with the Circessni circus at the same time that the state fair opened a new women's exhibit that displayed home appliances and practical kitchens. A Winchester Model 97 shotgun went for $28.50, a large can of Heinz spaghetti for 20 cents, and coffee was 37 cents a pound. Life went on as always and as ever, and the seasons did their turn as planned.[10]

Clarence Sr.'s passing wasn't quite the end of it. What he handed down to his family didn't sit well with the children. Clarence Jr. wouldn't accept being the sole heir and said as much in a probate hearing three years later. He offered, to the admiration of the court, to split the estate evenly with his four siblings, Sophia, Paul, Thomas, and Mary. Possessed of a landed estate worth $1,300, Clarence Sr. had had an additional $184 on account in Individual Indian Money. But once his creditors had come calling, the legacy was carved away: a debt of $634 with a storekeeper in Martin halved the estate, a liability his children seemed to know nothing about. Buying and selling and singing and teaching and interpreting were among his many skills, but husbanding money had never been a particular talent.[11]

Clarence Three Stars was dead at sixty-seven, a respected elder if not yet an ancient one. His life, by census accounts, had begun during the Civil

War and ended in the Great Depression. He had lost a daughter, a son, a wife, an election or two, an allotment, and another daughter to illness and confinement. In some ways the son of Yellow Knife was ahead of his time: a member of the first class at Carlisle, an innovative classroom teacher, a lawyer by correspondence, an early advocate of rectifying the Black Hills holdup. Then too, he was a man of tradition when tradition was under fire, an advocate for the old tribal council and a keeper of the Lakota tongue.

It wasn't long before the dreams of that council were dashed. The Indian Reorganization Act of 1934 fundamentally altered tribal political life and would end up eroding Oglala sovereignty. A new tribal constitution would include "limiting clauses" requiring approval of the Indian commissioner or secretary of the interior for important tribal resolutions. Soon, the secret ballot, female franchise, and rule by elected officials were standard features in Oglala government, but at the cost of resorting to a form of indirect rule managed from faraway Washington. It was not what Clarence Three Stars—a man of considerable experience and reckoning—would have wanted.[12]

At the heart of the man was a thicket of contradictions. His people taught him the Lakota way as a boy and then sent him to a school where his language and culture were forbidden. He walked away from a good job at Wanamaker's only to remake himself at a tiny reservation store. He signed the 1889 agreement confirming allotment—and then vigorously opposed it. He was drilled with soldierly discipline, though much of his career consisted of defying authority. He was said to have resented faraway boarding schools but later sent his own daughter to one. He had spoken at a Carlisle commencement like the most eager American convert and then fought to keep noncitizen Indian boys out of a foreign war. He may not have been a well-educated man, but he was a man of many educations.

He had learned and unlearned, often and willing. His education had happened so many times that the word had almost lost its sense, and what it meant at the end was perhaps no clearer than the day he had boarded the train, draped in a blanket, bound for Pennsylvania. Would his students follow the same path? Would their learning become a ragged part of something that never fit together? Would they ever find the spirit of the real lessons he taught, that sense of discovering the world with mind and hand together, unspoken but palpable, a feeling that dwelt in the air and everywhere around them but could never be found written down exactly right on any page, in any language, or in any book?

Three Stars chafed at the lessons of school—the long hours of memorization and writing and recital—at the same time he transformed them into something he could use in the service of his people. For the grandson of High Forehead and the protégé of Richard Henry Pratt, education had been a long and difficult journey in the course of becoming a husband and father, a U.S. citizen, and in the Lakota way, an *ikce wicasa*, a common man or man of the people, a worthy distinction he never shunned.[13]

A couple years later the school named in Clarence's honor suffered its own demise. The Three Stars School had been built on land he and Jennie donated in 1914 near Bear-in-the-Lodge Creek, a public school that enrolled Lakota and white children in Martin School District No. 2. One day "the building just seemed to explode," a former pupil later recalled, after a crack of lightning struck and burned the prairie school to the ground. It burned the way Clarence had been scorched in the gasoline fire two years earlier, the way the electric current crackled and shocked the Carlisle students at the long-ago lecture on lightning, burned like the deaths at Lightning Creek so many decades before. The course of his life straddled the arc from candlepower to the incandescent bulb, only to have his school char and smolder in a hot flash from the thunderbirds, the unruly *wakinyan* spirits who ruled the sky. Fire and light were written in the very name of Three Stars, and so they illuminated his way until the very end of his life and after.[14]

About the time the school burned, in 1933, Dr. Samuel Silk returned to the Canton asylum for another assessment, only to find conditions largely unchanged from his earlier visit. New Indian commissioner John Collier charged director Harry Hummer with malfeasance, and Secretary of the Interior Harold Ickes dismissed the doctor in October. Meanwhile, the South Dakota congressional delegation and the Canton Chamber of Commerce lobbied the Interior Department to keep the asylum open, arguing that closing Hiawatha would cause severe economic hardship for town residents. An injunction was passed to prevent authorities from moving patients out of Canton, its supporters claiming it would do irreparable harm to withdraw them far from their families. But the failures of Canton had been too well documented. The injunction was soon quashed, and the patients prepared for removal.[15]

In December 1933 Sophia Three Stars boarded a train for Washington DC, more than fifty years after her father had embarked on Maza Canku for the long journey east to Carlisle. She was one of seventy-one patients being transferred to St. Elizabeths Hospital. Dr. Silk had noted in his reports that dozens of these patients were feebleminded, rather than psychotic, and capable of living on a reservation with family supervision. Research published before Sophia ever left Canton revealed that two-thirds of flu patients diagnosed with dementia praecox recovered within five years—an opportunity, if such was the causal connection in her own illness, that she was never given. Referring to Canton patients whose abnormalities had long since disappeared or receded, Silk concluded that "if all such patients were released it would almost empty the place." Empty the place they did, though only a couple dozen patients were released outright; the remainder were remanded to a facility 1,500 miles from Pine Ridge, more than half a continent from home and family for most of them. In early 1934 Hiawatha closed its doors.[16]

Sophia weighed 154 pounds on admission to St. Elizabeths. She stood five feet, five and a half inches and walked with a steady gait. Her blood pressure was 132/90. During her admission interview, she bowed her head and refused to look up or answer questions. She appeared apathetic, her facial expression blank. At one point she turned her back to the examiners. "She does not appear interested in her surroundings," the admitting authority noted.[17]

By then forty years old, she would spend the next twenty-eight years at St. Elizabeths, a residential stay pocked with pain and violence. A fight with another patient yielded an injured hand. In a second encounter she was bitten and in yet another, received a cut on her right arm. An abdominal disorder sent her to the Medical and Surgical Building in 1941, and attacks of nausea and vomiting followed the next year. In 1938 her brother Thomas was admitted to the hospital, suffering from depression.[18]

St. Elizabeths would be a far different abode than Canton. The patient population numbered in the thousands. The institution was strictly segregated, and moderate attempts at integration wouldn't take hold until the 1950s. By 1957 mixed-race dancing among patients was banned over the protests of some and in spite of attempts to integrate the wards. The most advanced psychiatric methods were employed, including groundbreaking drug regimens and electric shock therapy. In March of 1962, at almost seventy years of age, Sophia Three Stars, the firstborn of an accomplished Carlisle couple, was finally discharged, her condition said to be "improved."[19]

After forty years of detention, she was still alive.

Epilogue

A Hundred Years After

Only scraps of Clarence's life remain—archived letters, probate and census papers, a handful of obscure photos. The most candid picture is the one from 1925, an image of an older man dressed in overalls, hands thrust in his pockets with a shock of hair falling over his forehead, a few friends or family milling about the yard. They seem indifferent to the attention of a census taker's camera, which sets it apart from the other photos we have of Clarence: the lone dark-skinned teacher at a summer institute, a young man pinched between Oglala diplomats in the back row of a Washington delegation, a boy in buckskins in an early Carlisle print. The only personal portrait we have is an oval-framed shot from a school album, and so the group photos contribute even more to the sense that we know him not so much as an individual but as the member of a family, a class, a congregation, a tribe. One is tempted to say that Clarence was almost forgotten by history. The fact is, like so many others, he was barely remembered in the first place.

Though he likely encountered photographers as a boy in Nebraska, his introduction to the formal photograph took place at Carlisle, a home of the notorious publicity tool of boarding-school portraits taken before and after students began their studies. The "before" shots were taken soon after students arrived on campus, clad in blankets and buckskins that their hosts discarded or destroyed. Authorities would then frame a desk mate for that shot with an "after" print, one that showed a boy posed in military attire, hair shorn, face set in a deadpan stare or a girl in a high-collar dress with buttons and bows and bearing her own inscrutable expression. Side by side, the photos tell an antiquated, if romantic, tale of unlettered Indians who had become the stuff of civilized young adults. As bookends these portrait pairs make for good symmetry, but they were never enough to tell a whole story. To a modern eye they feel something like the ancient masks of comedy and tragedy, flat and vacant looking, each one blinkered and intolerant of its mate. It's no wonder they come up short: their subjects had the rest of their lives before them.

Clarence's Carlisle portraits, if taken at all, have never surfaced. It took years before he ripened to his place in the world. What would a third portrait of Three Stars have looked like? One can see a middle-aged man, a pudgy face crowned with a crop of short hair, a wrinkled forehead and bright, dark, intense eyes, perhaps holding a prop in hand like a book or chalkboard pointer, pausing for a moment to see if his words have taken. It would have to be a picture that showed the grit he used to question the system that trained him. It would have to show the way Carlisle groomed him—quietly, if unwittingly—inspiring him to undermine its own lessons. For the school had taught him to obey, not protest; to speak in English, not Lakota; to accept what the government gave him, not quibble about the fine print. But it had also trained him to read books, write letters, speak before an audience, and make his way in a city of a million people.

No photograph could put the terms of his dilemma just so: Did his education stunt his growth as a Lakota man? Or did it succeed beyond all measure?

A small patch of land is all that remains of the sacred Black Hills in Lakota hands. After the early advocacy of leaders like Three Stars, compensation claims for the Black Hills crept on for decades. In 1980 the Supreme Court awarded the Sioux tribes more than $100 million in compensation for the taking. The tribes refused the award and asked for the return of the land itself, an option that would have seemed unlikely, but not impossible, to Clarence's generation. Compound interest has swelled the award to over $1 billion today, but the tribes will neither take the money nor budge from their claim for reversion of the land. Neither the courts nor the government seem anxious to entertain their demands.

Most, if not all, of the original day schools on Pine Ridge have been razed or abandoned. The old Oglala boarding school, once it burned to the ground, was rebuilt in 1894 on the west side of Pine Ridge village, and its renovated campus, operated by the Bureau of Indian Affairs, still serves Oglala students K–12. The Indian school Louisa attended continues to operate as an off-reservation boarding school known as the Pierre Indian Learning Center. Pratt's famous Carlisle campus reverted long ago to its original function as a U.S. Army barracks. The Canton Asylum closed its doors in 1934; the original asylum building was razed a dozen or so years later. St. Elizabeths, where Sophia was transferred, still provides care for patients with serious mental illness, though on a smaller campus. And the Episcopal church where Clarence catechized as a young man was uprooted from Pine Ridge village and towed out to a field on BIA Route 41, where it sits like a fallen aircraft or a missing chapel out of time.

Clarence's allotment, a strip of rolling prairie, lies a dozen or so miles northeast of Martin. The biggest markers on the land, just west of Highway 73, are bales of hay, an occasional stand of corn, a copse of trees every mile or so that track the old section lines and shelter many a house along the road in their copious shade. The earth gently slopes upward as one looks west, a hill or two on the horizon. To the east, a ridge of pines ambles off toward the Rosebud Reservation. Some would call it drab country, a range of sandy hues in a dry season, broken by the rare splotch of green. It is made up of rough grass, purple wildflowers, invasive thistle weed, and a carpet of short-grass prairie as far as the eye can see. Bear-in-the-Lodge Creek, like an arterial vein, runs through Jennie's old tract five miles to the west. Dry farming is a difficult ask, though some still do it. Long ago allotted, long ago sold, Clarence's land seems quietly alive a hundred years later.

A few miles up the paved road to Allen from Highway 18 is a holy place known as Inestimable Gift. A country graveyard flanks a small-spired church covered with aluminum siding and metal roof. There is a hayfield to one side and a deep gulley on the other. A barbed-wire fence surrounds the cemetery. "Jennie Three Stars, 1870–1921," says one stone. "Clarence Three Stars, 1864–August 22, 1931," says another. The Three Stars markers are simple white crosses, more modest than the cut stones of granite and marble that surround them. They are made of painted concrete, the names are lettered in black capitals, and the crosses are badly chipped, vandalized by inclement weather or the ugly hand of boredom. Other markers stand for Guy and Paul and Thomas and the generations that followed. The marker for Paul's wife, Sarah, has been turned over, a medicine wheel draped over it. Around them the field is filled with Whirlwind Horses, Iron Clouds, Bad Wounds, Turning Hawks, Standing Bears, Conquering Bears, and Last Horses, a lively menagerie of Oglala clans. The Three Stars crosses, solid but spare, stand tall among all the others, something in them stubborn and strange.

The church next door no longer holds Sunday services. The nearest house of worship, the Pass Creek Church of God, in Allen, is a few miles back down the road, a stone's throw from where Clarence once set up his general store. It's a nondenominational congregation of Indian and non-Indian, fitting for the "mixed-blood" blend of Bennett County. In the sanctuary two colorful star quilts hang next to a painted mural of Christ strapped to the cross. Children, mostly Indian, sit in the front row for a sing-along. Adults intone the melody of "Fly to Jesus, Fly," the lyrics flashed across a video screen above the pulpit. The service is casual and vernacular, no high-church formality that Clarence would have known as a catechist at the Good Shepherd Station—no candles, vestments, or *Book of Common Prayer*. No Bible thumping, either. People at the church are today dressed like they've come in off the tractor or are on their way to the feedstore. Communion consists of an oyster cracker and tiny plastic cup of grape juice.

They teach Lakota in the rez schools. At Little Wound in Kyle kids get the Lakota K–12 treatment, a fact that would have pleased the former teacher of Day School No. 27. In one middle-school classroom, students pull out Chromebook laptops to work on PowerPoint presentations about Lakota history. The teacher calls out words in English—*blue*, *red*, *white*, *autumn*, *How are you today?*—and students respond, hesitant and somewhat muffled, in Lakota. If they need the bathroom key, they can't ask for it in English. Down the hall, another teacher has set up a tabletop lab of local plants and herbs—sage, bear root, dried turnips. They burn a strand of sweetgrass every morning. The teacher, Dorothy Thunder Bull, says she didn't know any English when she first went to school, and now she finds herself teaching kids who hardly know any Lakota. It was that way with English for Clarence, too, though she aims now to revive a Lakota in danger of passing away. Over the intercom the principal's voice is almost pleading, "No hoodies in the classroom!"

On a summer's night when the sun goes down, the sky changes color from yellow to orange and then from blue to deep blue and black, until the stars blink across the firmament against the smoky cloud of the Milky Way. The points of light swarm across the night sky, dispersed as in *oglala* (meaning "to scatter one's own"), stars strewn far and wide, turning as on a wheel around the celestial year, the far-off ones staked to the pattern as much as those close to the center. Clarence heard stories about the stars as a boy, about how Skan made the star people and told them to hide when the sun was above and to watch the earth at night and tell him what they saw. Who scattered them? How did three stars become more than a million?

God, you might say. The Great Spirit. The Divinity. Wakan Tanka. Taku Skanskan. The Great Holy.

Clarence had learned that there was more than one way to say everything.

Notes

Prologue

1. Clarence Three Stars heard the story of High Forehead, his grandfather, from the mouth of his own father, Yellow Knife, and others, including Red Cloud. For Clarence's brief account of the Grattan event, see Ricker, *Indian Interviews*, 347. The prologue is a composite reconstruction, based on historical sources, of how he might have heard the story as told from a Lakota point of view. The main primary source is U.S. House of Representatives, *Engagement*. A collection of eyewitness accounts that also contributed valuable details to my recounting is McDermott, Paul, and Lowry, *All Because of a Mormon Cow*. The framing of the story at beginning and end is a dramatization, but the quotes are otherwise historical ones: "hoped to God he would have a fight" was a statement of Mr. Obridge Allen (U.S. House of Representatives, *Engagement*, 20); "you tell the Bear I have come down here" was also stated by Allen (U.S. House of Representatives, *Engagement*, 21); "would eat their hearts raw" comes from a journal extract from James Carrey (U.S. House of Representatives, *Engagement*, 16); "massacre" is in the report of Lieutenant Fleming (U.S. House of Representatives, *Engagement*, 19); and "murder" is from the *New York Daily Times*, October 24, 1854, 2. For the size of the Indian encampment, see Hämäläinen, *Lakota America*, 225. Many sources disagree over who fired the first shot, not to mention over myriad other details of the battle and what precipitated it. While a number of army reports defended Grattan's performance, others described him as impetuous, aggressive, and irresponsible; see, for example, U.S. Senate, *Report of the Secretary*, 1–2.

1. The Iron Road

1. We're fortunate to have two very different sources that describe the long journey to Carlisle by Lakota young people in 1879. The school founder's account of the trip can be found in Pratt, *Battlefield and Classroom*. Standing Bear chronicles, in fascinating detail, the same episode through the eyes of a Lakota boy in *My People the Sioux*. Together the two offer a remarkable blend of perspectives, often starkly

opposed, that speaks to the cultural conflict of the moment. See Standing Bear, *My People the Sioux*, 125–26, for early details of the journey.

2. Standing Bear, *My People the Sioux*, 123–24; Pratt, *Battlefield and Classroom*, 222–26. Both recount only what happened at Rosebud agency, but it's a fair assumption that the process was repeated at Pine Ridge with Packs the Dog's family.
3. Pratt, *Battlefield and Classroom*, 226–27; Standing Bear, *My People the Sioux*, 126.
4. Pratt, *Battlefield and Classroom*, 228; Standing Bear, *My People the Sioux*, 127.
5. Clarence (formerly Packs the Dog) gives his birth year as 1864 in almost all the annual Indian censuses, making him likely fifteen when he left for Carlisle; see, for example, Indian Census Roll, Pine Ridge, 1886, roll M595_362, p. 97, National Archives and Records Administration, Washington DC (NARA-W). But ages can be hard to determine in record-keeping for Indians: he is listed as sixteen in "Descriptive Statement of Indian Children Sent to Carlisle Penn From Pine Ridge Agency Dakota September 23, 1879," Pine Ridge, 1154489, "Descriptive Statement of Children Sent to Schools," 1879–1887, National Archives and Records Administration, Kansas City, Missouri (NARA-KC); and also as sixteen in Clarence Three Stars (Packs the Dog) student file, Carlisle Indian School Digital Resource Center, Dickinson College (CISDRC), https://carlisleindian.dickinson.edu/sites/default/files/docs-ephemera/NARA_1327_b038_f1876_0.pdf. See Standing Bear, *My People the Sioux*, xxiii, 3, and 149, for some confusion regarding Luther's age. Luther is listed as fifteen on his Carlisle student information card, CISDRC, though by his own account he was born in 1868, making him eleven, at most, when he arrived. As such, Indian ages from this period are educated guesswork. All CISDRC sources cited throughout were copied and digitized from the National Archives in Washington DC, Record Group 75, by students and staff of Dickinson College. Student files can be searched and downloaded from the Carlisle Indian School Digital Resource Center, Dickinson College website: https://carlisleindian.dickinson.edu/. For more on the Lakota translator, see Pratt, *Battlefield and Classroom*, 227–28.
6. Pratt, *Battlefield and Classroom*, 228–29. For Clarence's smoking, see Statement Concerning Applicant for Appointment in the U.S. Indian School Service, R. H. Pratt, May 17, 1892, file 21328, "Letters Received by the Office of Indian Affairs, 1881–1907," entry 91, RG 75, NARA-W.
7. Pratt, *Battlefield and Classroom*, 228.
8. Standing Bear, *My People the Sioux*, 128–29.
9. Standing Bear, *My People the Sioux*, 129–31.
10. Standing Bear, *My People the Sioux*, 131–32.
11. For discussion and accounts of *hanbleciya*, the vision quest, see Walker, *Lakota Belief and Ritual*, 129–32; Hassrick, *The Sioux*, 271–76; and Mails, *Fools Crow*, 49–50.
12. Standing Bear, *My People the Sioux*, 133; Pratt, *Battlefield and Classroom*, 229. Lakota dress in the earliest days at Carlisle is described in the *Morning Star*, *Eadle Keatah Toh*, January 1880 (1, 1), 1, Cumberland County Historical Society (CCHS).

13. Pratt, *Battlefield and Classroom*, 228; Standing Bear, *My People the Sioux*, 133–34, 140–41.
14. Standing Bear, *My People the Sioux*, 135–36, 140–41.
15. Standing Bear, *My People the Sioux*, 137–38. Luther's description of how he received his name is presumably the same way Clarence received his.
16. For Lakota naming, see Hassrick, *The Sioux*, 312–13; and Mails, *Fools Crow*, 40. For an amusing account of how accidental a name could be, see Lame Deer and Erdoes, *Lame Deer*, 22.

2. Agency Boy

1. For Clarence's birthplace and father's name, see U.S. Senate, *Statements of a Delegation*, 15; for Lakota calendars, see Walker, *Lakota Society*, 144. For Big Woman, see Clarence Three Stars, South Dakota Certificate of Death, 139578, November 19, 1931, South Dakota Department of Health (SDDH). For naming, see W. Powers, *Oglala Religion*, 38; and Clarence Three Stars (Packs the Dog) student file, CISDRC. Almost all Indian censuses report Clarence's age based on a birth year of 1864; federal decennial censuses show more variability. In one job application, Clarence gives his birth state as Wyoming, but the congressional testimony seems more reliable; see Application for Appointment, February 1, 1892, file 21328, "Letters Received by the Office of Indian Affairs, 1881–1907," entry 91, RG 75, NARA-W.
2. For wives of Three Stars, whose names sometimes vary in the census, see, for example, Indian Census Roll, Pine Ridge, 1895, roll M595_366, 14, NARA-W. Eli S. Ricker mentions the elder Three Stars in *Settler and Soldier Interviews*, 219. Catherine Price discusses Black Bear in *Oglala People*, 106–8.
3. For a calendar, see Karol, *Red Horse Owner's Winter Count*, 60. An interview with Elton Three Stars Sr. (great-grandson of Clarence Three Stars) suggested that Miles was the inspiration for Clarence's surname. Elton Three Stars Sr., in discussion with the author, Martin, South Dakota, July 13, 2017.
4. Most of these Lakota practices were compiled from Standing Bear, *Spotted Eagle*, 11, 13–16, 21–22, 33–35, 50, 70. For moon and rainbow, see Powers, *Oglala Women*, 92.
5. For movements in and out of the agency, see Buecker and Paul, *Crazy Horse Surrender Ledger*, 5–6. For a sampling of massacre reporting in the press, see the *Chicago Tribune*, July 7, 1876, 1; the *New York Daily Herald*, July 7, 1876, 4; and the *Sioux City Daily Journal*, September 8, 1876, 1.
6. Life at Red Cloud Agency is well documented in Buecker and Paul, *Crazy Horse Surrender Ledger*, 24, 124, 13. There is some evidence, though weak, that Little Wound may have been at the Little Bighorn Battle. But it seems clear that his band, the Kiyuksa, were not there. See Wagner, *Participants in the Battle*, 160. Wagner logs neither Three Stars nor Packs the Dog as present at the battle.
7. For a detailed description of life at the agency, see Buecker, *Last Days*. The expanse of land estimate is from Haämäläinen, *Lakota America*, 83.

8. For ration day details, I rely on Buecker, *Last Days*, 101–3.
9. Buecker, *Last Days*, 33, 115, 141.
10. For derivation of "Kiyuksa," see Powers, *Oglala Religion*, 31. Collective *tiyospaye* numbers are taken from *Report of the Commission Appointed*, 19. For a description of changing customs, see Buecker, *Last Days*, 133, 147, 211.
11. For a riveting description of Crazy Horse's demise, see Powers, *Killing of Crazy Horse*, 420–26.
12. The exodus to the Missouri is described in moving detail in Hyde, *Red Cloud's Folk*, 299–303. For a full text of the 1868 treaty and creation of the Great Sioux Reservation, see *Treaty with the Sioux*. For a more recent transcription of the treaty and other key documents in Oglala history, see Reinhardt, *Oglala Nation*, 60–67.
13. Pratt, *Battlefield and Classroom*, 222–23. There is some doubt among colleagues at the Carlisle Indian School Digital Research Center whether he made this speech before a large crowd, as he suggests in his memoir, but the argument he makes for educating young Indian people was one Pratt commonly espoused.
14. Pratt, *Battlefield and Classroom*, 225–26.
15. For mixing tribes and taking hostages, see Pratt, *Battlefield and Classroom*, 227, 220.

3. School Days

1. For the story of Clarence's classroom disruption, see Pratt, *Battlefield and Classroom*, 243–44. It seems odd that Pratt, who was Carlisle superintendent, would narrate the encounter with Clarence in the third person, referring as he does in the memoir to "the superintendent." As such, it may have been assistant superintendent Alfred Standing who actually delivered the tongue-lashing. In any case, Pratt clearly approved of the way the matter was handled and recalled it with satisfaction, years later, in his memoirs.
2. For the original campus map I rely on "Maps of the Carlisle Indian School," CISDRC, https://carlisleindian.dickinson.edu/sites/default/files/docs-resources/CIS-Resources_Maps-Powwow2000_Fear-Segal.pdf. For student repairs, see Pratt, *Battlefield and Classroom*, 234; and Bell, "Telling Stories," 60–61.
3. The literature on Indian boarding schools is huge. Two extremely detailed and engrossing accounts are David Wallace Adams's *Education for Extinction* and Michael C. Coleman's *American Indian Children at School, 1850–1930*. For enrollment and budget figures, see *Annual Report of the Commissioner of Indian Affairs* (ARCIA), 1888, xi, 276.
4. For segregation of campus and cemetery, see Fear-Segal, *White Man's Club*, 170, 182; for a physical description of campus and military organization, see Bell, "Telling Stories," 62, 128–29; for information on the church, see Standing Bear, *My People the Sioux*, 144–45.
5. Dorm conditions are well described in Bell, "Telling Stories," 129, 134; for sleeping

arrangements, see *Eadle Keatah Toh*, May 1884, 1, CCHS; and for inspections and possessions, see Standing Bear, *My People the Sioux*, 145, 156.

6. The daily schedule for girls and the newspaper quote are found in *Eadle Keatah Toh*, August 1881, 3–4, CCHS. The Dubray name is spelled with a lower case *b* in Carlisle records but an uppercase *B* in many Indian Office documents; I use the former throughout the book.
7. Standing Bear describes their clothing in humorous detail. See *My People the Sioux*, 142–44, 156.
8. For examples of the role of hair in Lakota culture, see Hassrick, *The Sioux*, 90, 228; Brown, *Sacred Pipe*, 10–12; and Lars Krutak, "Treasures of the IACB: Oglala Lakota Leader Shirt, ca. 1890–95," Indian Arts and Crafts Board, U.S. Department of the Interior, November 26, 2019, https://www.doi.gov/iacb/treasures-iacb-oglala-lakota-leader-shirt-ca-1890-95. For the Mrs. Pratt incident, see Pratt, *Battlefield and Classroom*, 232.
9. The military organization of Carlisle is frequently noted in the school newspapers, a rich source for understanding daily life at the school; more than one paper was frequently published at the same time, and occasionally they changed their names. See *Eadle Keatah Toh*, November 1880 (1, 7), 4; March 1880 (1, 9), 3; October 1881 (2, 3), 4, CCHS. For sentences and punishment, see Bell, "Telling Stories," 249–50, 286; for corporal punishment, see ARCIA, 1880, 302; for whipping, see *Eadle Keatah Toh*, August 1880 (1, 5), 3, CCHS. For an analysis of how Pratt used the Carlisle school papers to advance his assimilationist objectives, see Matthews, "Killing a Culture," 46–106.
10. Standing Bear, *My People the Sioux*, 139–40. For dining hall and tribal rivalries, see *Eadle Keatah Toh*, May 1880 (1, 3), 2, CCHS. Genevieve Bell notes segregation in "Telling Stories," 139.
11. Fortunately, the HathiTrust Digital Library (www.hathitrust.org) has given us access to school textbooks used during much of American history. The quotes in this section are from John R. Keep's *First Lessons for the Deaf and Dumb*, which was used at Carlisle in the early years, as noted by Pratt in ARCIA, 1880, 301. Quotations are from the second edition, published in 1875, the version most contemporaneous with the events described. I have used the most contemporaneous editions for all school textbooks cited. Apparently, there were few if any texts on the market for teaching second-language learners; Carlisle teachers resorted to using a book for teaching disabled children instead.
12. Keep, *First Lessons*, 14.
13. Keep, *First Lessons*, 20.
14. Keep, *First Lessons*, 69.
15. Keep, *First Lessons*, 76.
16. Keep, *First Lessons*, 76.

17. Keep, *First Lessons*, 76.
18. Keep, *First Lessons*, 80–81; for letter-writing expectations, see *Eadle Keatah Toh*, May 1880 (1, 3), 1, CCHS.
19. Pratt attests that Swinton's geography was a standard text at the school. See ARCIA, 1881, 243; also see *Eadle Keatah Toh*, October 1881 (2, 3), 1, CCHS. For what the students read about Africa and elephants, see Swinton, *Primary Geography*, 25, 78. For the eclipse and the shape and rotation of the earth, see Standing Bear, *My People the Sioux*, 155. The Ponca quotation is from *Eadle Keatah Toh*, January 1882 (2, 6), 4, CCHS.
20. *Eadle Keatah Toh*, April 1880 (1, 2), 3, CCHS, describes the lightning lecture in detail. One of the students at the lecture was named High Forehead, Clarence's grandfather's name, although no High Forehead was ever recorded at the school. If unlikely, it's still conceivable that this may have been the name that Clarence, an older boy at the time and possibly a member of the group, gave to the reporter.
21. For theories about sleeping and waking up to speak English, see Standing Bear, *My People the Sioux*, 155.
22. *Eadle Keatah Toh*'s issues from October 1881 (vol. 2, no. 3, 1) and January 1880 (vol. 1, no. 1, 1–2), CCHS, note the importance of music and singing, an interest that guided Three Stars throughout his teaching career.
23. Indian boarding schools used student labor to become as economically self-sufficient as possible. Many vocational skills in the curriculum were put to active use and allowed schools to survive, if not thrive, financially. For rate of pay and for general merchandise, see *Eadle Keatah Toh*, October 1881 (2, 3), 3 and November 1881 (2, 4), 2, CCHS, respectively. The tailor shop and laundry are described in *Morning Star*, May 1884 (4, 10), 1, CCHS.
24. *Eadle Keatah Toh*, August 1880 (1, 5), 2, CCHS. For the tailor shop, see Champney, "Another Indian Invasion," 949. For details on Clarence, see *Morning Star*, May 1883, 3, CCHS. For underwear, see Sydney, "Carlisle School," 233.
25. Clarence's letter can be found in "Home Letter," *School News*, November 1881, 2, CCHS.
26. For the number of those baptized, I rely on an email communication with Jim Gerencser, CISDRC, May 11, 2021. We have church records that designate the days the boys were baptized and confirmed and took their first communion. St. Johns church, where these events took place, still stands in downtown Carlisle. Using the most contemporary edition of the *Book of Common Prayer* and existing records, I reconstruct what the baptismal ceremony would have looked and sounded like. Historical details of the church are provided in *Spire on the Square*, esp. 63–64.
27. Quotes are from the 1871 Standard edition of the *Book of Common Prayer*, 242–44.
28. Church records provide details about the boys and their names; for baptisms, see *St. John's Church Parish Register*, 1879–81, February 8, 1880, 138–39, CCHS.

29. For the symbolism of four offerings and four as a sacred number in Lakota thought, see W. Powers, *Oglala Religion*, 48–49.
30. For communicants, see St. John's *Church Parish Register*, 1881–86, January 3, 1882, 252–53; for confirmations, see St. John's *Church Parish Register*, 1881–86, April 9, 1882, 86–87, both in CCHS.
31. For Sunday school, see *The Spire on the Square*, 71.
32. *Spire on the Square*, 70–71.
33. Luther Standing Bear describes Paul Black Bear in *My People the Sioux*, 145–46, 156; Genevieve Bell describes the orphan strategy in "Telling Stories Out of School," 126–27.
34. Biographical details about Fire Thunder come from Bennett County Historical Society, *70 Years*, 423; and Lewis, *Wo'Wakita Reservation Recollections*, 93. Three Stars is described as the adoptive son of Fire Thunder in his obituary. See "Indian Educator Burned in Gas Explosion," *Martin Messenger*, September 3, 1931. Standing Bear describes Fire Thunder in *My People the Sioux*, 140. For information on Edgar's name and band, see Edgar Fire Thunder (White Man) student file, CISDRC; for Edgar's drawing, see Witmer, *Changing Images*.
35. Standing Bear's *My People the Sioux* gives a broad and fascinating chronicle of his life (149, 161–63, 167–68, 171, 178, 180).
36. For the first letter to Luther's father, see *Eadle Keatah Toh*, July 1881 (1, 12), 4; his letter criticizing his father is in the *Morning Star*, February 1883 (3, 7), 3, both from CCHS.
37. Luther's prize-winning translation is in Champney, "Another Indian Invasion," 948.
38. For diversions, see *Eadle Keatah Toh*, June 1881 (1, 11), 3, CCHS; Bell, "Telling Stories," 151; and Standing Bear, *My People the Sioux*, 153–55. The story of the eel is recounted in the *Morning Star*, August 1883 (4, 1), 3, CCHS.
39. Student quote is from the *Morning Star*, September 1883 (4, 2), 3, CCHS.
40. Pratt, *Battlefield and Classroom*, 80–82.
41. Pratt, *Battlefield and Classroom*, 152–53, 163, 190.
42. Pratt, *Battlefield and Classroom*, 215–16. Fetterman's boast, widely quoted in various forms, may well be apocryphal, as recent debunking scholarship suggests. See John H. Monnett, "The Falsehoods of Fetterman's Fight," HistoryNet, October 1, 2010, https://www.historynet.com/the-falsehoods-of-fettermans-fight.htm. For Grattan, see Charles Days to Lieutenant Colonel William Hoffman, May 28, 1855, "Letters Received by the Office of the Adjutant General" (Main Series), 1822–1860, roll 546, frame 589, M567, NARA-W.
43. Pratt, *Battlefield and Classroom*, 223.
44. For scarce details on Pratt's home life, see Eastman, *Pratt*, 59, 79, 218. For the man in the bandstand, see, for example, *Indian Helper*, October 25, 1889 (5, 10), 2, CCHS. "Captain" is the rank Pratt held for most of his time at Carlisle.

45. David Wallace Adams gives a useful and succinct summary of Pratt's philosophy and motto in *Education for Extinction*, 51–55.
46. Edgar's embarrassing episode is told in Sydney, "Carlisle School," 232–33.
47. For background on Daklugie, see Ball, *Indeh*, xv, 32, 86, 101, 144, 146. For measurements, see Asa Daklugie student file, CISDRC.
48. Daklugie recounts his encounter with Pratt in Ball, *Indeh*, 150–51.
49. See Asa Daklugie student file, CISDRC; and ARCIA, 1895, 5.
50. *School News*, August 1882 (3, 3), 4, CCHS.
51. For outing background, see "History of the Outing," WA MSS S-1174, box 30, folder 814, 1–2, Richard Henry Pratt Papers, Beinecke Library (BL).
52. For planting out, see ARCIA, 1884, 15. For extent of practice, see ARCIA, 1881, 245. For pay, see ARCIA, 1882, 29; and Bell, "Telling Stories," 66–67. For Pratt quote, see ARCIA, 1881, 246; for outing rationale, see ARCIA, 1884, 230; for family influence, see White, "White Power," 108.
53. For details on how outings both succeeded and failed, see Bell, "Telling Stories," 171, 173, 188.
54. A very good overall summary of the outing program can be found in Adams, *Education for Extinction*, 156–63; the later outing requirements (1900) and the Pratt quote are laid out by the Captain in "Outing Rules," WA MSS S-1174, box 30, folder 815, BL.
55. For the Schall incident and lesson quote, see R. H. Pratt to M. Schall, December 30, 1882, WA MSS S-1174, box 10, folder 6, frame 72, BL; the English quotation is in R. H. Pratt to Michael Schall, June 2, 1883, WA MSS S-1174, box 10, folder 6, frame 455, BL.
56. Standing Bear recounts this story in *My People the Sioux*, 174–75.
57. For letter to Three Stars, see R. H. Pratt to Three Stars, May 9, 1883, WA MSS S-1174, box 10, folder 6, BL.
58. For some of the attractions of boarding school, see Coleman, *American Indian Children*, 65, 70–71; Adams, *Education for Extinction*, 260; and Child, *Boarding School Seasons*, 16.
59. On attendance, see ARCIA, 1884, 18; and ARCIA, 1891, 67. For denying rations, foiling officials, and parental consent, see Adams, *Education for Extinction*, 63, 211, 65.
60. For gangs, see Lomawaima, *They Called It Prairie Light*, 98, 114; for chronic runners and arsonists, see Adams, *Education for Extinction*, 225, 229–30.
61. Carlisle runaways are thoroughly treated in Bell, "Telling Stories," 210, 212, 214, 219, 410. The advertisement for Thomas is quoted in "Telling Stories," 240.
62. On accommodation, see Adams, *Education for Extinction*, 255–57. Richard Henry Pratt recounts political and practical advantages of learning English in *Battlefield and Classroom*, 223.

63. On those who rejected school but later regretted it, on valuing discipline and earning honors, and on the value of literacy for preserving culture, see Coleman, *American Indian Children*, 170–73, 107, and 184, respectively.

64. See *Eadle Keatah Toh*, January 1880 (1, 1), 3, CCHS, for death announcement. Also see Abraham Lincoln student information card, CISDRC. For his father's standing, see "Report on First Three Parties of Students Brought to the Carlisle Indian School," November 13, 1879, CISDRC, https://carlisleindian.dickinson.edu/node/19290.

65. For Lakota children, see *Eadle Keatah Toh*, December 1880 (1, 8), 3, CCHS; for measles and scarlet fever, see ARCIA, 1881, 242; on the death of six children in 1884, see ARCIA, 1884, 231; for tuberculosis (consumption) deaths, see ARCIA, 1887, 341; for Apache deaths and Pratt quote, see ARCIA, 1888, 278.

66. For more on communicable diseases and Haskell, see Child, *Boarding School Seasons*, 55–56, 66.

67. See R. H. Pratt to Chief Big Bull, September 22, 1880, WA MSS S-1174, box 10, folder 4, frame 129, Richard Henry Pratt Papers, BL; John Bull student file, CISDRC, recounts the future life of Bull, described as the "grandson" of Chief Big Bull.

68. See R. H. Pratt to Chief White Thunder, December 15, 1880, WA MSS S-1174, box 10, folder 4, frames 199–202, Richard Henry Pratt Papers, BL.

69. See R. H. Pratt to Road Traveller, December 22, 1883, WA MSS S-1174, box 10, folder 7, frames 452–53, Richard Henry Pratt Papers, BL.

70. For mortality numbers, see Bell, "Telling Stories," 399–400; for a more recent estimate of overall mortality numbers, see Vitale, "Counting Carlisle's Casualties."

4. Philadelphia

1. News stories are from the *Philadelphia Inquirer*: April 18, 1884, 8 (white elephant); March 19, 1884, 8 (weather); March 18, 1884, 4 (St. Patrick's Day); March 18, 1884, 1 (Episcopal Church); March 18, 1884, 2 (police department); March 18, 1884, 3 (Trenwith); March 18, 1884, 3 (Mack). For the Improved Order of Redmen, see "Timeline of Philadelphia History, 1646–1899," Independence Hall Association, accessed September 14, 2023, www.ushistory.org/philadelphia/timeline/.
2. Standing Bear, *My People the Sioux*, 178–79.
3. Standing Bear, *My People the Sioux*, 180–81.
4. For numbers, see Waring, *Report on the Social Statistics*, 813–14; for city hall, see Burt and Davies, "Iron Age," 506.
5. For description of historical Philadelphia, see Burt and Davies, "Iron Age," 471, 479, 483–85.
6. Burt and Davies, "Iron Age," 492–93.
7. On city epidemics, see Geffen, "Industrial Development," 318. For reports on streets, animal carcasses and water, and burials and smallpox, see Waring, *Report*

on the Social Statistics, 812, 833, 832. For remedies, see *Philadelphia Inquirer*, March 11, 1884.

8. For specific fires, see "Timeline of Philadelphia History," Independence Hall Association, accessed September 14, 2023, www.ushistory.org/philadelphia/timeline/; for fire alarm system, see Waring, *Report on the Social Statistics of Cities*, 835.
9. Standing Bear, *My People the Sioux*, 181.
10. For pay rates and textile production, see Burt and Davies, "Iron Age," 495, 481.
11. Standing Bear, *My People the Sioux*, 182.
12. Biographical and store details from "John Wanamaker Firsts," 2188, box 91-B-2, folder 11, John Wanamaker Collection, Pennsylvania Historical Society (PHS).
13. Timeline and Grant quote from "John Wanamaker Firsts," 2188, box 91-B-2, folder 11, John Wanamaker Collection, PHS.
14. This depiction of the store is based on an undated illustration of the depot interior, 2188, box 120, folders 9–10; and "Wanamaker's Catalogue: Fall and Winter 1887–88," 2188, box 70, folder 8, John Wanamaker Collection, PHS.
15. Merchandise details compiled from "Wanamaker's Catalogue: Fall and Winter 1887–88," 2188, box 70, folder 8; and "What Is the Best Way to Wait on a Customer?" 5, 2188, box 73, folder 1, John Wanamaker Collection, PHS.
16. Wanamaker, "A Short History of the United States," 25–28, 2188, box 72, folder 2, John Wanamaker Collection, PHS.
17. For Wanamaker business practices, see "A Short History of the United States," 23–29, 2188, box 72, folder 2, John Wanamaker Collection, PHS; for quotation, see the *Weekly News* (Frederick MD), July 3, 1884, 2.
18. For clothing, see John Wanamaker to R. H. Pratt, October 14, 1879; and for the quotation, see John Wanamaker to R. H. Pratt, June 30, 1913, in WA MSS S-1174, box 9, folder 313, Richard Henry Pratt Papers, BL.
19. "History of the Outing at Carlisle, Pa.," 25, WA MSS S-1174, box 30, folder 814, Richard Henry Pratt Papers, BL.
20. Standing Bear, *My People the Sioux*, 182–83.
21. In some official correspondence the Lincoln Institute is also known as the Lincoln Institution. The history of the school is recounted in "The Lincoln Indian School," 1886, in *Eighteenth Annual Report of the Board of Indian Commissioners*, 84.
22. The school report can be found in "Boys' Educational Home," October 27, 1884, in *Fifteenth Annual Report of the Board of Commissioners of Public Charities*, 118–19.
23. "Boys' Educational Home," October 27, 1884, in *Fifteenth Annual Report of the Board of Commissioners of Public Charities*, 119.
24. "Boys' Educational Home," October 27, 1884, in *Fifteenth Annual Report of the Board of Commissioners of Public Charities*, 119; "The Educational Home," in the *Seventeenth Annual Report of the Executive Committee of the Indian Rights Association*, 15–21; LaFrance, *An Indian Boy's Story*, 1784; *Washington Post*, January 19, 1900, 3; for graduate status, see Clarence Three Stars, employment application No. 27 Day School, May 22,

1911, Personal Record of Clarence Three Stars, Official Personnel Folders (OPF), National Archives and Records Administration, St. Louis, Missouri (NARA-STL).

25. See R. H. Pratt to Clarence Three Stars, September 29, 1884, WA MSS S-1174, box 10, folder 9, frame 200, Richard Henry Pratt Papers, BL; Standing Bear, *My People the Sioux*, 183; R. H. Pratt to V. T. McGillycuddy, December 5, 1884, WA MSS S-1174, box 10, folder 9, frame 417, Richard Henry Pratt Papers, BL.

5. Coming Home

1. For Clarence's roll number, see Indian Census Roll, Pine Ridge, 1886, roll M595_362, 97, NARA-W. The census number changed every year.
2. For buildings and guns, see McGillycuddy, *Blood on the Moon*, 4, 135, 159–60; the water tank is described in ARCIA, 1880, 164; for construction of the boarding school, see ARCIA, 1882, 98, and ARCIA, 1884, 83.
3. Clarence's obituary in the *Martin Messenger*, September 3, 1931, 1, notes his "civilized" attire upon returning from school.
4. Clarence's grandmother is named Smoke in Indian Census Roll, Pine Ridge, 1886, roll M595_362, 97, and Tobacco Smoke in 1887, roll M595_363, 226, NARA-W; for the letter to the agent, see R. H. Pratt to V. T. McGillycuddy, December 5, 1884, WA MSS S-1174, box 10, folder 9, frame 418, Richard Henry Pratt Papers, BL.
5. Clarence notes his position as assistant in Clarence Three Stars, employment application No. 27 Day School, May 22, 1911, Personal Record of Clarence Three Stars, OPF, NARA-STL; oddly, no Indian hires at the school are listed in Annual Report for Pine Ridge Boarding School, 1885, Pine Ridge, 598936, "Letters Sent by the Agent, 1876–1914," NARA-KC.
6. For the construction of the boarding school and a description of physical premises, see Morgan, "Reminiscences of My Days," 23–24; for windows, see Eastman, *Sister to the Sioux*, 128.
7. For furnishings and initiation, see Morgan, "Reminiscences of My Days," 23–24, 26.
8. For braiding, see Morgan, "Reminiscences of My Days," 26; the story of the boys' haircuts, perhaps apocryphal, is from McGillycuddy, *Blood on the Moon*, 205–6.
9. For chores and farm details, see ARCIA, 1893, 288–89; for the children's diet, see ARCIA, 1884, 84.
10. Morgan, "Reminiscences of My Days," 26, 28–29.
11. The duties of a disciplinarian are outlined in ARCIA, 1890, cl, and ARCIA, 1903, 311; for Clarence's reluctance, see Clarence Three Stars, employment application No. 27 Day School, May 22, 1911, Personal Record of Clarence Three Stars, OPF, NARA-STL.
12. *Indian Helper*, May 3, 1889 (4, 37), 1, 4, CCHS.
13. Clarence Three Stars to Indian Commissioner, October 5, 1889, file 28657, "Letters Received by the Office of Indian Affairs, 1881–1907," entry 91, RG 75, NARA-W.

14. Clarence notes his disability in Clarence Three Stars, employment application No. 27 Day School, May 22, 1911, Personal Record of Clarence Three Stars, OPF, NARA-STL; see Child, *Boarding School Seasons*, 58; and Walker, "Trachoma: A Dangerous Disease," *Oglala Light*, undated, Zc 16 O25 + Og4 f. 13_3, BL, for methods of spreading. Shannen K. Allen and Richard D. Semba provide an excellent historical discussion of the ailment in "The Trachoma 'Menace' in the United States, 1897–1960." In his February 1, 1892, application for appointment, Clarence writes that he has no vision disability, which means the infirmity likely surfaced later in life. See file 21328, "Letters Received by the Office of Indian Affairs, 1881–1907," entry 91, RG 75, NARA-W.
15. Methods of treatment are noted in Walker, "Trachoma: A Dangerous Disease," *Oglala Light*, undated, Zc 16 O25 + Og4 f. 13_3, BL; for tarsectomy and grattage, see Allen and Semba, "The Trachoma 'Menace,'" 507.
16. For survey numbers, see Allen and Semba, "The Trachoma 'Menace,'" 501, 504; for rate of affliction, see Child, *Boarding School Seasons*, 57.
17. For enrollment issue, see ARCIA, 1890, 53; and ARCIA, 1892, 176.
18. Indian Bureau policy regarding withholding of rations as coercion for school attendance can be found in ARCIA, 1884, 18, and ARCIA, 1893, 10; for runaways at Oglala and end of term, see ARCIA, 1892, 457–58; for Lame Deer, see Lame Deer and Erdoes, *Lame Deer*, 27.
19. McGillycuddy's quote is from ARCIA, 1884, 83. For white day-school teachers, see ARCIA, 1888, 51.
20. Pratt's quote is in ARCIA, 1884, 231; the explicit argument for educating rather than fighting Indians was frequently made, and appears in ARCIA, 1885, 14; for English-language only, see ARCIA, 1887, 20–21.

6. A Dubious Deal and Wounded Knee

1. The role of Lakota boys signing their names in 1883 is ably detailed in Hyde, *A Sioux Chronicle*, 138–39. For a primary source of the commission and its tactics, see U.S. Senate, *To Examine into the Condition*, esp. 138 and 140, for eyewitness accounts of the children from William Garnett and George Sword, respectively (the boys who signed and the ages of some are listed by Sword on 299). For the warrior story of Sword, see Morgan, "Reminiscences of My Days," 34–35.
2. George E. Hyde bears out the number of boys in *A Sioux Chronicle*, 139, as does Sword's list noted above.
3. Samuel Hinman and Valentine McGillycuddy offered their defense for collecting the signatures in U.S. Senate, *To Examine into the Condition*, 202, 385; George E. Hyde discusses the honor motive in *A Sioux Chronicle*, 138.
4. For a discussion of Hayes and various nineteenth-century election practices, see Lepore, *Story of America*, 250–51, 385.

5. For a discussion of the seventh generation and the Black Hills treaty, which predated the Sioux Agreement of 1889, see DeMallie, *Sixth Grandfather*, 168–69.
6. For the signature of Three Stars ("Wicahhpi-yamin") and for Red Cloud's regret, see U.S. Senate, *To Examine into the Condition*, 355, 134–35; George E. Hyde summarizes Lakota complaints in *A Sioux Chronicle*, 118–19.
7. In *The Plains Sioux and U.S. Colonialism from Lewis and Clark to Wounded Knee*, Jeffrey Ostler explains in detail the color symbolism (224–26); John Grass repudiates the colored paper ballots, and voting certificates are shown in U.S. Senate, *Report Relative to Opening*, 79, 286–287. (The voting certificates can be found between pages 286 and 287.)
8. The interpreter exchange is noted in U.S. Senate, *Report Relative to Opening*, 77.
9. For the quotation on the commission's recounting of its defeat, see U.S. Senate, *Report Relative to Opening*, 23.
10. For the quotation on the commission's recommendation, see U.S. Senate, *Report Relative to Opening*, 20.
11. Jeffrey Ostler describes these tactics in *Plains Sioux*, 230–37; George E. Hyde recounts the Pine Ridge meetings in detail in *A Sioux Chronicle*, 213–20. For the supermajority as applied to each band, see Gonzalez and Cook-Lynn, *Politics of Hallowed Ground*, 251.
12. For consensus governing, see Walker, *Lakota Society*, 30.
13. See U.S. Senate, *Reports Relative to the Proposed Division*, 85. For more on the quitclaim and a list of dissenters, see U.S. Senate, *Reports Relative to the Proposed Division*, 71, 85.
14. See U.S. Senate, *Reports Relative to the Proposed Division*, 99, 110.
15. Elaine Goodale Eastman discusses the misleading nature of Great Father rhetoric in *Sister to the Sioux*, 90; for the difference between Great Father, on the one hand, and the apocryphal Great White Father, apparently an invention of dime novelists, see Viola, *Diplomats in Buckskins*, 94. Also, see DeMallie, "Touching the Pen," 50–51. I occasionally use Great Father in the text because of its acceptance among some Indians, many government officials, and numerous scholars such as Francis Paul Prucha. See Prucha, *The Great Father*, x.
16. For signatures, late voting, and dimensions of reservation and ceded land, see U.S. Senate, *Reports Relative to the Proposed Division*, 242, 254, 270, 115, 41.
17. U.S. Senate, *Reports Relative to the Proposed Division*, 114.
18. Elaine Goodale Eastman describes the school lock down in *Sister to the Sioux*, 156; Robert M. Utley describes Sitting Bull's demise in detail in *The Last Days of the Sioux Nation*, 146–60.
19. Many are the accounts of Wounded Knee. For a sampling, see David Humphreys Miller's *Ghost Dance*, an early narrative sympathetic to the Lakota perspective; Robert M. Utley's *The Last Days of the Sioux Nation*, which provides a broad and detailed

scholarly version; Jerome A. Greene's *American Carnage*, which is a fine recent interpretation; and William S. E. Coleman's *Voices of Wounded Knee*, which gives contemporaneous and eyewitness accounts. Conditions at the boarding school can be found in Morgan, "Reminiscences of My Days," 50–56; for Clarence's early work in the church, see *Spirit of Missions*, 112; for Fire Thunder's military service, see Bennett County Historical Society, *70 Years*, 423, and "Declaration for Survivor's Pension—Indian Wars," January 12, 1928, Personal Record of Edgar Fire Thunder, OPF, NARA-STL; and for Clarence's intervention with Little Wound, see *Boston Evening Transcript*, March 9, 1894, 3.

20. A good place to start on Eastman's career is with A. LaVonne Brown Ruoff's historical introduction to Eastman, *From the Deep Woods*, xix–lviii. The autobiography itself is an engaging and thoughtful account of much of Eastman's life; also see Wilson, "Writings of Ohiyesa," 55–73, on his voluminous works; Eastman is quoted on the Indian Bureau in Wilson, "Writings of Ohiyesa," 70. On the project of renaming Indian people, see Littlefield and Underhill, "Renaming the American Indian."
21. Eastman, *From the Deep Woods*, 219, 248–49. Eastman mentions a Charles Three Stars (219), but he doesn't appear in census records, so he may have confused the names Clarence and Charles. For Eastman's departure from Pine Ridge, see Wilson, "The Writings of Ohiyesa," 69.
22. The fates of various Carlisle returned students at Pine Ridge are enumerated in the *Red Man*, February–March, 1891 (10, 10), 8, CCHS.
23. The 1891 delegations were covered by several eastern newspapers. For composition of delegations, see the *Washington Evening Star*, February 3, 1891, 5, and February 5, 1891, 5; and the *Philadelphia Times*, February 6, 1891, 4.
24. An excellent general source for Indian delegations to Washington is Viola, *Diplomats in Buckskins*, esp. 11, 25, 28–29, 34, 137 for diplomatic motives.
25. See Viola, *Diplomats in Buckskins*, 56, 70, 92, 104. (Little Wound is quoted on 104.) Luther Standing Bear tells the story of his father's visit in *My People the Sioux*, 69–70.
26. For problems with interpreters, see Viola, *Diplomats in Buckskins*, 74–76, 78.
27. The meeting with Secretary Noble in described in the *Washington Evening Star*, February 7, 1891, 5.
28. The visit to Philadelphia is chronicled in the *Philadelphia Times*, February 6, 1891, 4; an article in the *Baltimore Sun* mentions the Lincoln Institute as Clarence's alma mater (February 6, 1891, 1).
29. An article in the *Philadelphia Times* recounts the second delegation trip to Baltimore (February 14, 1891, 2); Young Man Afraid of His Horses is quoted in Viola, *Diplomats in Buckskins*, 92.
30. *Baltimore Sun*, February 6, 1891, 1.

7. Family and Tribe

1. Many details of Antoine Dubray's life were provided to me by Darryl Kooiman and Rose Bordeaux, the great-granddaughter of Jennie's sister Mary. The information about Antoine is from a personal email communication with Darryl Kooiman, July 12, 2016. For details on Jennie, see Jennie Dubray student file, CISDRC; Jennie Three Stars, South Dakota Certificate of Death, 79491, October 16, 1921, SDDH; Jennie Three Stars probate, Central Classified Files (CCF) 07-39, E121, 36457-29-Pine Ridge—350, RG 75, Pine Ridge, NARA-W; and Antoine DuBray probate, May 26, 1921, document 39394-21, Rosebud Sioux 2337, 6 (copy provided by Darryl Kooiman), which suggests that Julia Moran was Jennie's mother. Kooiman believes, after close study, that her mother was named Louise Robinson, which further complicates the matter.
2. Personal email communications with Darryl Kooiman, July 12, 2016, and August 21, 2016.
3. Darryl Kooiman, personal communication, July 12, 2016; Antoine Dubray probate, 9. For the Little Raven story, see Coel, *Chief Left Hand*, 87. For more on Dubray, see Carter, "Chat Dubray," 143–46. For fractionation of Indian land, see Lawson, "Fractionated Estate."
4. Jennie Dubray student file, CISDRC; Jennie Three Stars probate, NARA-W. The quotation is from the *Indian Helper*, August 19, 1892 (7, 49), 2, CCHS.
5. Jennie's accomplishments are mentioned in a number of Carlisle school papers: *Indian Helper*, December 31, 1886 (2, 21), 4; *Red Man*, March 1890 (10, 2), 8; *Indian Helper*, March 1, 1889 (4, 28), 2; *Indian Helper*, October 4, 1889 (5, 7), 3; and *Red Man*, November–December 1892 (11, 9), 1, all CCHS.
6. George Brown to Indian Commissioner, March 11, 1892, file 9881; statement concerning applicant, R. H. Pratt, May 17, 1892, file 21328; George Brown to Indian Commissioner, May 4, 1893, file 17158; Charles Penney to Indian Commissioner, June 25, 1895, file 26798, all in "Letters Received by the Office of Indian Affairs, 1881–1907," entry 91, RG 75, NARA-W. For clothing promise, see R. H. Pratt to Clarence Three Stars, November 14, 1892, WA MSS S-1174, box 10, folder 22, frame 374, Richard Henry Pratt Papers, BL.
7. *Superintendent's Annual Narrative and Statistical Reports, Pine Ridge, 1910–1929*, 1921, frame 0403, M1011, roll 106, NARA-W.
8. For Oglala boarding school fire, see ARCIA, 1894, 288; the arsonist stories are from Adams, *Education for Extinction*, 229–31.
9. For early correspondence on transfer and the Three Stars quote, see Clarence Three Stars to Indian Commissioner, September 7, 1896, file 34844; Clarence Three Stars to Indian Commissioner, September 14, 1896, file 35682, both in "Letters Received by the Office of Indian Affairs, 1881–1907," entry 91, RG 75, NARA-W. For Pratt's opinion, see R. H. Pratt to Clarence Three Stars, December

28, 1896, WA MSS S-1174, box 10, folder 31, frame 400, Richard Henry Pratt Papers, BL.

10. The agent's quotation and explanation of transfer is found in W. H. Clapp to Commissioner of Indian Affairs, April 24, 1897, M1282, "Letters Sent to Office of Indian Affairs by Pine Ridge," roll 27, vol. 26, March 30, 1897–March 1, 1898, frames 47–50, NARA-W; Clarence's side of the story can be found in U.S. Senate, *Memorial of Sioux Indians*, 2–3.
11. Clapp mentions the store in W. H. Clapp to Commissioner of Indian Affairs, April 24, 1897; see also the *St. Louis Post Dispatch*, July 26, 1891, 6; U.S. Senate, *Statements of a Delegation*, 16; and the *Rapid City Daily Journal*, July 1, 1951, 7. See Pratt, *Battlefield and Classroom*, 243, for more on Clarence and arithmetic. For Eastman's intervention, see Charles Eastman to Indian Commissioner, January 26, 1899, file 4555, and Clarence Three Stars to Indian Commissioner, January 1, 1900, file 2424, "Letters Received by the Office of Indian Affairs, 1881–1907," entry 91, RG 75, NARA-W; for Pratt's intervention, see R. H. Pratt to Clarence Three Stars, July 18, 1891, WA MSS S-1174, box 10, folder 19, frame 261, Richard Henry Pratt Papers, BL.
12. A good description of a Pine Ridge store from the same period can be found in Kneale, *Indian Agent*, 38; other details are from Sears Roebuck Catalogue, no. 104 (Chicago, 1897), available at Gordon Hurst's Mr. Hurst's History Website, accessed September 15, 2023, https://www.hursthistory.org/uploads/1/0/7/0/107013873/sears_catalog_ppt.pdf. The exit of the former trader is explained in the *St. Louis Post Dispatch*, July 26, 1891.
13. For details on Dawson, see *Rapid City Daily Journal*, August 5, 1903, 1; *Weekly Pioneer Times*, April 18, 1901, 5; *Black Hills Weekly Journal*, May 16, 1902, 4. For Carlisle budget, see ARCIA, 1902, 623. Paul Robertson notes trespassing in *The Power of the Land*, 104.
14. For Brennan, see *Rapid City Journal*, September 1, 1925, 6; for Tidwell and the Wounded Knee contract, see Robertson, *Power of the Land*, 149, 104; see the *Oglala Light*, March 1, 1908, for the Dawson ad.
15. For the Three Stars herd and brand, see U.S. Senate, *Statements of a Delegation*, 18; and *Cody Cow Boy*, January 10, 1901, 1.
16. See the *Chicago Inter-Ocean*, February 12, 1896, 2, on early plans for trip; the primary source for their audience in Washington is U.S. Senate, *Statements of a Delegation*; for McKinley, see *Washington Times*, May 4, 1897, 3.
17. For Red Cloud's unique place in history, see Red Cloud, *Autobiography*, 6; for exploits, see Larson, *Red Cloud*, 41; see the *Washington Times*, May 10, 1897, 2, for a description of his visit to the capital.
18. For 1868 and 1851 treaties, see Larson, *Red Cloud*, 124, 66–67.
19. Larson, *Red Cloud*, 43–44, 58–60, 129. There is some dispute over who killed Bull Bear, but Red Cloud insisted he was responsible.

20. For Walker's stories and Red Cloud's humiliation, see Ricker, *Settler and Soldier Interviews*, 26, 316–17. Three Stars confirms the story of Red Cloud's humiliation in Ricker, *Indian Interviews*, 349.
21. U.S. Senate, *Statements of a Delegation*, 1[illegible]. A description of Red Cloud is available in the *Los Angeles Times*, June 17, 1897, 5.
22. U.S. Senate, *Statements of a Delegation*, 16.
23. Three Stars discusses the problem of white men marrying into the tribe in U.S. Senate, *Statements of a Delegation*, 17–18.
24. See U.S. Senate, *Statements of a Delegation*, 18 (for allotment and Three Stars quotation), 24–25 (for difficulties of planting).
25. See U.S. Senate, *Statements of a Delegation*, 21–22 (for problems with beef ration), 23 (for Three Stars quotation).
26. See U.S. Senate, *Statements of a Delegation*, 27 (for story of bull), 28 (for salting food and peeing on beef), 31–33 (for various unethical practices with reservation cattle), 20 (for Three Stars quotation).
27. U.S. Senate, *Statements of a Delegation*, 20.
28. U.S. Senate, *Statements of a Delegation*, 19.
29. U.S. House of Representatives, *Complaint*, 36–39.
30. For the hunting story, see Larson, *Red Cloud*, 295–96.
31. For Red Cloud's legacy, see Larson, *Red Cloud*, 286, 304; and Red Cloud, *Autobiography*, 7–8.
32. See Larson, *Red Cloud*, 292–93; and Red Cloud, *Autobiography*, 70, 211n5.

8. The Teaching Life

1. Clarence's Day School No. 27 is described in Phenix, "Day School No. 27," 145–48.
2. George P. Phenix describes the children and classroom in "Day School No. 27," 146–47; for recitations, see "Report of the 10th Annual Institute of Pine Ridge Agency," 11, 1154511, Day School Lessons 1908–1918, "Essays and Reports on Indian Education, cc. 1905," NARA-KC; for portraits, see the *Oglala Light*, May 1906 (7, 2), 1. For Columbus Day, see Columbus Day Programme, No. 19 Day School, file 39406, "Letters Received by the Office of Indian Affairs, 1881–1907," entry 91, RG 75, NARA-W. The Columbus Day reference is from earlier in Clarence's teaching career, 1892, but such ceremonies continued throughout his time as a teacher.
3. Smith, "Teaching on the Reservation," MS1, Jeanne Smith Collection, 51, Oglala Lakota College Archives (OLCA).
4. The "wonderful" exercise and the reference to Lincoln can be found in "Report of the 10th Annual Institute of Pine Ridge Agency," 6, 1154511, Day School Lessons 1908–1918, "Essays and Reports on Indian Education, cc. 1905," NARA-KC.
5. The text of "The Boy and the River" is from Arnold and Gilbert, *Stepping Stones to Literature*, 44–45; Clarence's use of the story is described in "Report of the 10th

Annual Institute of Pine Ridge Agency," 6, 1154511, Day School Lessons 1908–1918, "Essays and Reports on Indian Education, cc. 1905," NARA-KC.

6. Combining Clarence's teaching methods, as he described them, and a specific story they studied in school, this is a reconstruction of how a class discussion might have unfolded in a Three Stars schoolroom.
7. The piper story and the Twenty-Third Psalm are from Baldwin, *School Reading by Grades*, 193–206, 192; the fables and the Pilgrims are from Arnold and Gilbert, *Stepping Stones to Literature*, 30, 37, 90. The readings may or may not have been assigned, but they were included in texts that Day School No. 27 students were using on a daily basis.
8. For school busy work, see Arnold and Gilbert, *Stepping Stones to Literature*, 53; the moccasin debate is described in Three Stars, "Teaching Indian Pupils to Speak English in the Day School Work," 2, Pine Ridge, Day School Lessons, 1154511, "Essays and Reports on Indian Education," NARA-KC.
9. The Iktomi story is from Three Stars, "The Spider and the Fat Ducks," *Oglala Light*, March 1, 1909, 24.
10. We know about Clarence's accent from Efficiency Record, May 8, 1912, Personal Record of Clarence Three Stars, OPF, NARA-STL.
11. The daily schedule is described in Phenix, "Day School No. 27," 146–47.
12. For student ages, see ARCIA, 1898, 279; for Pine Ridge wages, see Ahern, "An Experiment Aborted," 274; ARCIA, 1896, 296, and Efficiency Record, October 23, 1911, Personal Record of Clarence Three Stars, OPF, NARA-STL; for wages in other states, see *Annual Reports of the Department of Interior*, 1902, vol. 1, lxxxi.
13. For the domestic life and gender roles of married teachers, see Cahill, *Federal Fathers and Mothers*, 87, 93–95; for red schoolhouses, see ARCIA, 1904, 333.
14. ARCIA, 1901, 365; *Oglala Light*, June 1901 (2, 3); a good overview of the schools can be found in "The Oglala Light," Zc16 O25 + Og4f.2_3, 1–2, BL; reasons for absenteeism are cited in ARCIA, 1898, 279.
15. For a description of buildings, see the *Oglala Light*, June 1901 (2, 3), 1; and *Superintendent's Annual Narrative and Statistical Reports, Pine Ridge, 1910–1929*, 1910, frame 0031, M1011, roll 106, NARA-W; the history and amenities of Day School No. 27 are described in detail in Pine Ridge, 1154521, "School Histories," Day School No. 27, NARA-KC.
16. The book of designs is described in Smith, "Teaching on the Reservation," MS1, Jeanne Smith Collection, 51, OLCA; the examples are all from the text that Clarence taught his advanced students: Baldwin, *School Reading by Grades*, 52, 9, 115–16, 157–58. All textbook examples are taken from editions that would have been current at the time Three Stars was teaching.
17. The entire inventory for Day School No. 27 in 1911 is listed in Pine Ridge, 1145593, Property Inventories, "Inventory List, 6–30–1911," NARA-KC.
18. The quotations "study your pupils" and "keep them busy" are from "Teaching

Beginners to Talk English," *Oglala Light*, April 1907, 6–9, in "The Oglala Light," Zc16 O25+Og4 f.8_1, BL; the quotation "they like any lesson" is from "Teaching Indian Pupils," NARA-KC. Three Stars explains or models his teaching methods in several sources: "Teaching Beginners to Talk English"; "Teaching Indian Pupils"; and "Report of the 10th Annual Institute of Pine Ridge Agency," Pine Ridge, Day School Lessons, 1154511, "Essays and Reports on Indian Education," NARA-KC.

19. Three Stars was evaluated in the classroom on a semiannual basis. Quotations are from the following efficiency reports: May 2, 1912; October 23, 1911; October 11, 1912; May 10, 1910; and December 17, 1910, Personal Record of Clarence Three Stars, OPF, NARA-STL. For English as a technology, see the incisive essay by Thomas Andrews, "Turning the Tables on Assimilation," esp. 422, 424, which analyzes Clarence's teaching style. Quotation on Native teachers is from John Brennan to Indian Commissioner, September 28, 1901, file 54527, "Letters Received by the Office of Indian Affairs, 1881–1907," entry 91, RG 75, NARA-W.
20. See Cahill, *Federal Fathers and Mothers*, 111 (for exams), 110 (for teachers), 121 (for teaching on home reservation). For the difficulties of Indian teachers, see Ahern, "An Experiment Aborted," 284–85.
21. See Spack, *America's Second Tongue*, 51 (for monolingual instruction), 42 (for difference between immigrant and Native languages). Albert Kneale recounts his surprise at the existence of multiple Native languages in *Indian Agent*, 48.
22. Phenix, "Day School No. 27," 148. For assimilation, communities, and schools, see Cahill, *Federal Fathers and Mothers*, 116.
23. For nineteenth-century teaching methods, see Finkelstein, *Governing the Young*, 41–48.
24. The missionary quote is from ARCIA, 1896, 13. For domestic visits, see ARCIA, 1892, 457; and ARCIA, 1901, 370. For sociological study, see ARCIA, 1903, 312.
25. The Three Stars republic, constitution, and enrollment details are described in Pine Ridge, 1154476, Day School Correspondence, "Day School Correspondence, #27," NARA-KC.
26. For Three Stars's manual skills, see J. J. Duncan to Day School Teachers, January 31, 1911, Pine Ridge, 1154476, Day School Correspondence, "Day School Correspondence, #27," NARA-KC; for topics of instruction, see ARCIA, 1899, 12; for "full-bloods," see ARCIA, 1901, 369; for Nebraska, see *Superintendent's Annual Narrative and Statistical Reports, Pine Ridge, 1910–1929*, 1915, frame 0153, M1011, roll 106, NARA-W.
27. For day school enrollments, see *Superintendent's Annual Narrative*, 1910, frame 0016; and 1927, frame 0856, M1011, roll 106, NARA-W.
28. For food, see ARCIA, 1904, 333; for bean and soup, see ARCIA, 1901, 369; for rations, see ARCIA, 1902, 340; for clothing, see ARCIA, 1898, 280, and ARCIA, 1897, 273. Three Stars's opinion is from the *Oglala Light*, May 1909 (10, 5), 14–15.

29. See *Superintendent's Annual Narrative*, 1920, frame 0296, M1011, roll 106 (for curriculum); 1930, frame 0014, M1011, roll 107 (for expenses); 1925, frame 0726, M1011, roll 106 (for families), NARA-W. See Szasz, *Education*, 89, for enrollment.
30. Elaine Goodale Eastman's *Sister to the Sioux* is an entertaining account of her years on the prairie. (See pages 37, for door-knocking; 43, for dancing; 82–84, for returned students and agriculture; 123, for language and tipi.)
31. The Indian Office is quoted in Eastman, *Sister to the Sioux*, 124.
32. Eastman's brief stay at Carlisle is recounted in Wilson, *Ohiyesa*, 105–6.
33. See Charles Eastman to R. H. Pratt, January 27, 1911, WA MSS S-1174, box 3, folder 85, "R. H. Pratt Incoming Letters," Richard Henry Pratt Papers, BL.
34. Eastman, *Pratt*, 250. For letters to Pratt, see Elaine Goodale to R. H. Pratt, July 14, 1890, and Elaine Goodale Eastman to R. H. Pratt, December 16, 1910, WA MSS S-1174, box 3, folder 85, "R. H. Pratt Incoming Letters," Richard Henry Pratt Papers, BL.
35. Pratt, *Battlefield and Classroom*, 265.
36. The quotation is from *Pierre Indian Industrial School*, 9, Pierre Indian Learning School Research Materials, H2014-028, South Dakota State Archives (SDSA).
37. See *Pierre Indian Industrial School*, 15, 17, 25, SDSA.
38. For tuberculosis and Carlisle, see ARCIA, 1883, 222; for intermarriage, see ARCIA, 1894, 290; for general causes of disease, see Robinson, "Tuberculosis Among the Sioux Indians," *Oglala Light*, April 1906 (7, 1), in "The Oglala Light," Zc16 O25+Og4 f.7_1, BL; for medicine men, see ARCIA, 1902, 339.
39. *Reports of Indian Agents and Superintendents in South Dakota, Washington, and Utah to Commissioner of Indian Affairs*, ARCIA, 1907, 18, Sudoc: 120.15:907. For number of doctors, see ARCIA, 1898, 277; and Sniffen, "Pine Ridge," *Oglala Light*, May 1906 (7, 2), in "The Oglala Light," Zc16 O25+Og4 f.7_2, BL; for mortality rates, see ARCIA, 1899, 337; ARCIA, 1901, 367. Don Southerton provides a detailed account of his efforts in "James R. Walker's Campaign Against Tuberculosis on the Pine Ridge Reservation."
40. The facts on Louisa's funeral are reported in the *Oglala Light*, March 1908 (9, 1), 25.
41. For the suit of clothes and John Grass, see Robinson, "Tuberculosis Among the Sioux Indians," *Oglala Light*, April 1906 (7, 1), in "The Oglala Light," Zc16 O25+Og4 f.7_1, 1–2, BL; see *Superintendent's Annual Narrative and Statistical Reports, Pine Ridge, 1910–1929*, 1915, frame 0154 (for sanatorium); 1920, frame 0326; 1922, frame 0524; 1923, frame 0601, (for mortality estimates), M1011, roll 106, NARA-W; the contests are noted in the *Oglala Light*, June 1912 (13, 4), 35.
42. The poem was published in the *Oglala Light*, March 1908 (9, 1), 25, in "The Oglala Light," Zc16 O25+Og4 f.9_1, BL.

9. A Place Called Pine Ridge

1. This chapter is a composite view of the reservation between 1880 and 1930. Since the reservation wasn't officially established until 1889, any sources from before that year come from the agency of Pine Ridge on the Great Sioux Reservation. Not every law and regulation noted was in force throughout this fifty-year span, but the details in aggregate give an idea of the general contours of reservation life. As for land mass, I have used figures for acreage and square miles that include Bennett County. Although the county incorporated as a separate government in 1912, it is still, in the eyes of the Interior Department, within the boundaries of the reservation.
2. For McGillycuddy, see ARCIA, 1879, 143. For Pine Ridge village, see ARCIA, 1893, 289, 291; and *Superintendent's Annual Narrative and Statistical Reports, Pine Ridge, 1910–1929*, 1915, frame 0143, M1011, roll 106, NARA-W.
3. For a study of worldwide concentration camps and their progenitors, see Pitzer, *One Long Night*, esp. 5–16.
4. For AWOL punishment, see Mails, *Fools Crow*, 75.
5. Indian Territory is mentioned as an alternative home for Lakotas in the 1877 Black Hills agreement. See *An Act to Ratify an Agreement*.
6. ARCIA, 1886, 294. For a detailed explanation of the *tiyospaye*, see White Hat, *Life's Journey—Zuya*, 37–49; also, Hämäläinen, *Lakota America*, 200–201.
7. ARCIA, 1881, 104–5.
8. ARCIA, 1880, 163. For early housing, see ARCIA, 1885, 261; and ARCIA, 1880, 104. For later living arrangements and density, see *Superintendent's Annual Narrative*, 1926, frame 0797, M1011, roll 106, NARA-W; for strategy of substations, see ARCIA, 1892, 454; for kinship and rations, see Robertson, *Power of the Land*, 60–61.
9. The 1886 census is described in ARCIA, 1886, 294; double counting is also noted in ARCIA, 1892, 458.
10. For districts and boss farmer, see ARCIA, 1884, 82; allotting crews are described in the *Oglala Light*, March 1907 (7, 12); see Eastman, *Sister to the Sioux*, 82–83, for dispersal of allotments.
11. ARCIA, 1894, 289; ARCIA, 1903, 309.
12. See *Superintendent's Annual Narrative*, 1910, frame 005 (for quotation); 1920, frame 0344 (for tillable land); 1932, frame 0172 (for machinery); and 1911, frame 0067 (for land-poor allottees), from M1011, roll 106, NARA-W.
13. The visitor quotation is from Eastman, *Sister to the Sioux*, 81; the Clapp quotation is from ARCIA, 1899, 335. Most of the weather details are from ARCIA, 1893, 287; 1899, 335; 1901, 366; 1903, 309; 1906, 354; information on various plagues is taken from *Superintendent's Annual Narrative*, 1927, frame 0862, M1011, roll 106; and 1930, frame 0024, and 1931, frame 0111, M1011, roll 107, NARA-W.
14. Lewis, *Wo'Wakita Reservation Recollections*, 161–62; and Bennett County Historical Society, *70 Years*, 515.

15. *Reports of Indian Agents and Superintendents in South Dakota, Washington, and Utah to Commissioner of Indian Affairs*, ARCIA, 1907, 16, Sudoc: 120.15:907; *Superintendent's Annual Narrative*, 1926, frame 0830, M1011, roll 106, NARA-W.
16. All of the following are from *Superintendent's Annual Narrative and Statistical Reports, Pine Ridge*, 1910–1929: 1910, frame 008; 1911, frame 0065; 1915, frame 0156, 0158; 1910, frame 007; 1929, frame 1088, M1011, roll 106, NARA-W. Additional references are to ARCIA, 1882, 96; and ARCIA, 1889, 156.
17. ARCIA, 1895, 293; and Mails, *Fools Crow*, 109.
18. *Superintendent's Annual Narrative*, 1918, frame 0219; 1919, frame 0234, M1011, roll 106, NARA-W. The details on Indian Office and trespassing are from Robertson, *Power of the Land*, 128–29, 136–37.
19. See McDonnell, *Dispossession*, 48–49, 110, 94, 97, 104, 112, 117. Three Stars's role is from Resolution, Indian Protective Association, CCF 1907–1939, 20644—1925 Pine Ridge—312, Pine Ridge, RG 75, NARA-W.
20. *Superintendent's Annual Narrative*, 1916, frame 0202; quote is from 1922, frame 0516, M1011, roll 106, NARA-W. Selling of useless machinery is noted in Mekeel, *Economy*, 8n5.
21. ARCIA, 1896, 294. Most details regarding labor are from ARCIA reports: 1892, 196–97; 1901, 365; 1904, 329; 1905, 338; 1902, 337. Information regarding the removal from ration rolls is from *Reports of Indian Agents*, ARCIA, 1907, 15, Sudoc: 120.15:907; field labor is from *Superintendent's Annual Narrative*, 1921, frame 0492, and 1928, frame 0932, M1011, roll 106, NARA-W.
22. *An Act to Ratify an Agreement*. Information on rations is from ARCIA, 1903, 353; ARCIA 1901, 367; and Robertson, *Power of the Land*, 71.
23. For feasting and sharing cycle, see Nurge, "Dakota Diet," 55. For sharing and family, see ARCIA, 1896, 294; and *Superintendent's Annual Narrative*, 1922, frame 0513, M1011, roll 106, NARA-W.
24. Details regarding punishment can be found in ARCIA, 1892, 30; ARCIA, 1904, 330; Mails, *Fools Crow*, 71; and *Oglala Light*, June 1917 (18, 10), 18–19.
25. For details concerning marriage and divorce, see *Superintendent's Annual Narrative*, 1915, frame 0145; 1922, frame 0498; 1910, frame 0020; 1921, frame 0408; and 1923, frame 0597, M1011, roll 106, NARA-W.
26. ARCIA, 1892, 457. See ARCIA, 1891, 409; ARCIA, 1890, 54; and ARCIA, 1899, 335. Information on horse thieves is in Lewis, *Wo'Wakita Reservation Recollections*, 64.
27. See ARCIA, 1894, 290–91, for quotation and birth details; ARCIA, 1879, 336 [mispaginated as 236]–337, for early population; *Superintendent's Annual Narrative*, 1928, frame 0910, for later population; and 1923, frame 0601, for doctors, M1011, roll 106, NARA-W.
28. For *tiyospaye*, see Powers, *Oglala Religion*, xiv; for *tiyospaye* and schools, see Andrews, "Turning the Tables," 428. Shinny is described in Lewis, *Wo'Wakita Reservation Recollections*, 139–40; for the telegraph, see ARCIA, 1888, 50.

29. For gum quote and smoking, see ARCIA, 1894, 291; for intoxicants, see *Superintendent's Annual Narrative*, 1915, frame 0146, and 1925, frame 0719, M1011, roll 106, NARA-W.
30. Elaine Goodale Eastman describes the early beef issues in *Sister to the Sioux*, 59–60. See also ARCIA, 1892, 454; and Lewis, *Wo'Wakita Reservation Recollections*, 75, 142.
31. The fair is described in the *Oglala Light*, September–October 1915 (17, 1, 2), 6–8; for July 4, see Lewis, *Wo'Wakita Reservation Recollections*, 19–20, 22.
32. Albert Kneale discusses rotation policy of personnel in *Indian Agent*, 71–72.
33. Efficiency Record, October 11, 1912, and April 5, 1911, Personal Record of Clarence Three Stars, OPF, NARA-STL.
34. See ARCIA, 1879, 144 (for two masters); 1883, 93 (for treaties, Washington hotel, and ridiculous assumption); and 1882, 96 (for gastric region).
35. ARCIA, 1888, 49; ARCIA, 1889, 153 (for Wild West); and Lame Deer and Erdoes, *Lame Deer*, 41.
36. W. H. Clapp to Commissioner of Indian Affairs, April 24, 1897, "Letters Sent to Office of Indian Affairs by Pine Ridge," roll 27, vol. 26, March 30, 1897–March 1, 1898, frame 49–50, NARA-W.
37. Mails, *Fools Crow*, 69–70; *Superintendent's Annual Narrative*, 1912, frame 0093, and 1916, frame 0192, M1011, roll 106, NARA-W; and Robertson, *Power of the Land*, 105, 167.

10. Lightning Creek

1. My main source for the Lightning Creek incident is U.S. Senate, *Encounter Between Sioux Indians*. See page 24 for travel permits.
2. Accounts of the October 30 meeting differ in some details, and my version is a composite of the eyewitness testimony of William Brown, a summary made by Pine Ridge agent Brennan, and a letter written by Three Stars himself. See Clarence Three Stars to Edgar Allen, November 30, 1903, 2, WA MSS S-1174, box 8, file 291, R. H. Pratt Incoming Letters, Richard Henry Pratt Papers, BL; and U.S. Senate, *Encounter Between Sioux Indians*, 46.
3. U.S. Senate, *Encounter Between Sioux Indians*, 22–24, 47.
4. U.S. Senate, *Encounter Between Sioux Indians*, 27.
5. For fatalities and injuries, see U.S. Senate, *Encounter Between Sioux Indians*, 6–7, 16, 51; the death song is from Bad Heart Bull and Tish, *Pictographic History*, 500.
6. U.S. Senate, *Encounter Between Sioux Indians*, 16, 22–23.
7. U.S. Senate, *Encounter Between Sioux Indians*, 18–19, 29.
8. Clarence Three Stars to Edgar Allen, November 30, 1903, 2, WA MSS S-1174, box 8, file 291, R. H. Pratt Incoming Letters, Richard Henry Pratt Papers, BL.
9. Clarence Three Stars to Edgar Allen, November 30, 1903, 1, WA MSS S-1174, box 8, file 291, R. H. Pratt Incoming Letters, Richard Henry Pratt Papers, BL. See *Red Man and Helper*, December 11, 1903 (19, 20), 2, CCHS, for a publication of the

Three Stars letter; see also Deloria, *Indians in Unexpected Places*, 23–24 (on the issue of Indians firing first), 28, 50 (on how various terms like *outbreak* and *pacification* came to characterize struggles with Indian groups during the period).

10. Quotations are from Clarence Three Stars to Edgar Allen, November 30, 1903, 5, 4, 6, WA MSS S-1174, box 8, file 291, R. H. Pratt Incoming Letters, Richard Henry Pratt Papers, BL.
11. Quotations and recounting are from Clarence Three Stars to Edgar Allen, November 30, 1903, 7, WA MSS S-1174, box 8, file 291, R. H. Pratt Incoming Letters, Richard Henry Pratt Papers, BL. Hope Clear's account of this meeting appears in U.S. Senate, *Encounter Between Sioux Indians*, 50.
12. Clarence's graduation speech appears in *Red Man*, February–March 1899 (15, 5), 8, CCHS.

11. A Taste of the Law

1. J. A. George to Indian Commissioner, August 10, 1893, file 30368, "Letters Received by the Office of Indian Affairs, 1881–1907," entry 91, RG 75, NARA-W.
2. See "Instruction by Mail," in *The Columbian Views of Washington*, Printed Materials Collection, DC History Center (DCHC).
3. Kett, *Pursuit of Knowledge*, 234–35.
4. Kett, *Pursuit of Knowledge*, 238–39.
5. "Instruction by Mail," in *The Columbian Views of Washington*, Printed Materials Collection, DCHC; and Kett, *Pursuit of Knowledge*, 256.
6. Washington facts gathered from *Boyd's City Directory*, n.p., District of Columbia Public Library, Washingtoniana Division (DCPLW).
7. "Department of Law," in *The Columbian Views of Washington*, 65, Printed Materials Collection, DCHC.
8. Remondini, "Charles A. Ray," 77–79.
9. See Personal Record of Clarence Three Stars, OPF, NARA-STL; and Remondini, "Charles A. Ray," 79–80.
10. Ray, *Quiz Book*, 10, 46, 77, 87.
11. *Washington Evening Star*, May 12, 1937, A-12.
12. The work of the Columbian Information Bureau is described at length in the *Washington Evening Star*, January 19, 1922, 2.
13. For the 1900 suit, see *Washington Evening Star*, April 19, 1900, 2; Edwards's defense is reported in the *Washington Evening Star*, January 19, 1922, 2.
14. See Hoxie, *A Final Promise*, 126, 145, 152, for limitations on full assimilation and equality.

12. The Pipe, the Cross, and the Eagle

1. Sneve, *That They May Have Life*, 19–20, 26; for more on Hinman, see Hyde, *A Sioux Chronicle*, 114, 139, 143–44.

2. Sneve, *That They May Have Life*, 59; for Clarence's work and singing, see *Spirit of Missions*, 112.
3. The summary of Lakota religious beliefs and the importance of the pipe is from Standing Bear, *Spotted Eagle*, 197–203.
4. Sneve, *That They May Have Life*, 9–10, 74–78, 128; for convocation numbers, see Cochran, *Dakota Cross Bearer*, 18.
5. For the church committee report, see Missionary District of South Dakota, *Journal of the Convocations* (1916), 41; for the Sun Dance, see ARCIA, 1884, 81; for general dances, see *Superintendent's Annual Narrative*, 1916, frame 0174, M1011, roll 106, NARA-W.
6. Missionary District of South Dakota, *Journal of the Convocations* (1916), 41.
7. See Stewart, *Peyote Religion*, 3–6, 130–33.
8. Maroukis, "Peyote Controversy," 162.
9. For Pine Ridge numbers, see Stewart, *Peyote Religion*, 175; for peyote habit, see *Superintendent's Annual Narrative*, 1915, frame 0147; for poison, see 1922, frame 0501; and for addicts, see 1923, frame 0598, all M1011, roll 106, NARA-W.
10. See U.S. House of Representatives, *Peyote Hearings*, 139–40 (for Eastman quote), 135 (for Bonnin quote), 141 (for Pratt quote). The Harry Black Bear case is discussed in Stewart, *Peyote Religion*, 215–16; for Paul Black Bear, see Paul Black Bear student file, CISDRC.
11. See Stewart, *Peyote Religion*, 65 (for Carlisle), 178–80 (for Lone Bear and Blue Bird), and 196–97, 200–201 (for Lone Bear). For an alternative account of Lone Bear that disputes Stewart's telling, see Friesen and Chaladiuk, *Lakota Performers in Europe*, 68–73. Another mystery: the Lone Bear who went to Carlisle is described as deceased on his student information card, which would have been noted before the school closed in 1918, but Friesen argues that both of the Lone Bears lived into the 1930s.
12. For Carlisle details and quotation, see James Blue Bird student file, CISDRC. Further details on his life are available in Stewart, *Peyote Religion*, 180–82, 274.
13. For Clarence's church participation, see Missionary District of South Dakota, *Journal of the Convocations* (1895), 5; *Living Church Annual*, 289; Missionary District of South Dakota, *Journal of the Convocations* (1917), 13; *Sioux City Journal*, August 12, 1927, 2; and *Wausau Daily Herald*, August 21, 1926, 12. For priesthood, see Herbert T. Hoover, "Forbidden Culture," *South Dakota Magazine*, accessed September 16, 2023, https://www.southdakotamagazine.com/forbidden-culture.
14. "Report of the 10th Annual Institute of Pine Ridge Agency, S.D., October 3–5, 1905," and "Teaching Indian Pupils to Speak English in the Day School Work," in "Day School Lessons," 1154511, "Essays and Reports on Indian Education," Pine Ridge, NARA-KC; *Hymnal*, 332.
15. Walker, *Lakota Belief and Ritual*, 3–4.
16. Walker, *Lakota Belief and Ritual*, 4–6.

17. Walker, *Lakota Belief and Ritual*, 12–13.
18. Walker, *Lakota Belief and Ritual*, 13–15, 18–19, 44–45.
19. DeMallie, "'George Sword Wrote These,'" 247–48; for warrior details, see Red Shirt, *George Sword's Warrior Narratives*, 58–59, 69.
20. Walker, *Lakota Belief and Ritual*, 74–75; Ricker, *Indian Interviews*, 326–30; Red Shirt, *George Sword's Warrior Narratives*, 77.
21. Walker, *Lakota Belief and Ritual*, 23; for translating troubles, see Red Shirt, *George Sword's Warrior Narratives*, 76.
22. "There is a house" quotation is from "Translation from a text," 1, W 355, box 2, folder 20, James Walker Collection, American Museum of Natural History (AMNH). See Walker, *Lakota Belief and Ritual*, 21, for a formal version of Lakota; the letter to Wissler is quoted on page 23. For payment, see *Native America: A Primary Record*, series 4, James R. Walker Collection on the Oglala Sioux, reel 1, frame 0100, Zimmerman Library, University of New Mexico (UNMZ); for *house* and *sin* translations, see DeMallie, "'George Sword Wrote These,'" 249–50.
23. Garner, *What Sort of Indian*, 75–87. For Edgar Fire Thunder, see *Native America*, series 4, James R. Walker Collection on the Oglala Sioux, reel 4, frame 0467, UNMZ; on Sword, see Red Shirt, *George Sword's Warrior Narratives*, 68.
24. For Clarence's membership, see *Report of the Executive Council*, 180.
25. Hertzberg, *American Indian Identity*, 79, 100. For more on the motto, see Rosier, *Serving Their Country*, 45.
26. See Hertzberg, *American Indian Identity*, 81, 96, 109, 134.
27. Hertzberg, *American Indian Identity*, 153, 265; Maroukis, "Peyote Controversy," 177–78.

13. Citizen Three Stars

1. For a brief summary of the Lone Wolf case, see C. Blue Clark, "Lone Wolf v. Hitchcock," *Encyclopedia of the Great Plains*, accessed September 16, 2023, http://plainshumanities.unl.edu/encyclopedia/doc/egp.law.027.
2. Proceedings of April 5, 1909, council, pp. 1–4, box 589, "1909 Land Transfer," MS6, Richmond Clow Collection, OLCA. For specific speeches, see *Oglala Light*, May 1909 (10, 5), 7–9, in "The Oglala Light," Zc16 O25+Og4 f.10_5, BL.
3. Proceedings of April 5, 1909, council, pp. 6–15, box 589, "1909 Land Transfer," MS6, Richmond Clow Collection, OLCA. See page 14 for the quote from Industrious.
4. For McLaughlin quote, see Proceedings of April 5, 1909, council, p. 19, box 589, "1909 Land Transfer," MS6, Richmond Clow Collection, OLCA. For September 1 meeting, see H722, folder 3, "Surplus Reservation Land 1909," September 4, 1909, John Brennan Family Papers, SDSA; for September 7, see petition, Gamble, South Dakota, box 589, "1909 Land Transfer," MS6, Richmond Clow Collection,

OLCA; for congressional statute, see *Act to Authorize the Sale*. For treaty provision, see Gonzalez and Cook-Lynn, *Politics of Hallowed Ground*, 243.

5. For branding and ranching, see U.S. Senate, *Statements of a Delegation*, 18–19.
6. U.S. Senate, *Statements of a Delegation*, 18–19.
7. ARCIA, 1905, 338.
8. For land patent SDMTAA 208649, see The Land Patents (website), accessed September 16, 2023, https://thelandpatents.com/gallery/obeqggla#google_vignette. The rainfall quotation is from *Superintendent's Annual Narrative*, 1930, frame 0002, M1011, roll 107, NARA-W.
9. For the Burke Act and some of its consequences, see Prucha, *Great Father*, 298–302. The public notice is from September 19, 1910, CCF 1907–1939, 93955—10 Pine Ridge—312, Pine Ridge, RG 75, NARA-W.
10. See Wagoner, "*They Treated Us*," 39. The quotation is from McDonnell, *Dispossession*, 95.
11. Patent application for allotment 2058, CCF 1907–1939, 93955—10 Pine Ridge—312, Pine Ridge, RG 75, NARA-W.
12. Clarence Three Stars to Secretary of the Interior, August 27, 1910, patent application for allotment 2058, CCF 1907–1939, 93955—10 Pine Ridge—312, Pine Ridge, RG 75, NARA-W.
13. Letter from Henry A. Dawson, August 29, 1910, patent application for allotment 2058, CCF 1907–1939, 93955—10 Pine Ridge—312, Pine Ridge, RG 75, NARA-W; see also U.S. Senate, *Statements of a Delegation*, 26, 31–32.
14. Wagoner, "*They Treated Us*," 39–46.
15. For details on the homestead drawings, see Bennett County Historical Society, *70 Years*, 18.
16. On dueling jurisdictions, see Wagoner, "*They Treated Us*," 39–40. To this day, the status of Bennett County is disputed. A Rand McNally map will show the county as off-reservation, but numerous court decisions since the 1950s have recognized that the county is within the boundaries of Pine Ridge Reservation.
17. For Lakotas as "disciplined opportunists," see Hämäläinen, *Lakota America*, 195–97.
18. Bennett County Historical Society, *70 Years*, 423; Lewis, *Wo'Wakita Reservation Recollections*, 94.
19. Lewis, *Wo'Wakita Reservation Recollections*, 95.
20. Lewis, *Wo'Wakita Reservation Recollections*, 17, 93–95.
21. See Standing Bear, *My People the Sioux*, 228–29 (on Stronghold), 234 (on Wanamaker), 235–37 (on school, council, and store).
22. See Standing Bear, *My People the Sioux*, 248–67 (on foreign travels), 270–71 (on train wreck), 273–74 (on chieftainship), 278 (on allotment), 282 (for quotation).
23. See Standing Bear, *My People the Sioux*, 282 (for chieftainship), 277 (for fighting the agent), and 278–82 (for allotment process).

24. Clarence Three Stars to C. F. Hauke, November 18, 1911, Pine Ridge, CCF 1907–1939, 100271—11 Pine Ridge—253, Pine Ridge, RG 75, NARA-W; Standing Bear, *My People the Sioux*, 284–85.
25. For letterhead, see Luther Standing Bear to General H. R. Pratt, n.d., WA MSS S-1174, box 8, file 290, Richard Henry Pratt Papers, BL; for quotation, see Standing Bear, *My People the Sioux*, 277.
26. For coal, see *Gordon Journal*, January 1, 1904, 5.
27. For a record of Three Stars's public service, see *Inventory of the County Archives*, 79; and *Fourth Biennial Report*, 184. For the bar exam, see *Madison Daily Leader*, April 4, 1913; and *Pierre Weekly Free Press*, April 10, 1913. For the auditor position, see *Lead Daily Call*, October 5, 1916, 6. Some accounts say he was elected state's attorney; others say he was appointed. I could find no confirmation of whether Three Stars actually passed the bar exam; his obituary in the *Martin Messenger*, September 3, 1931, 1, says he did. It would seem, from the *Madison Daily Leader* source, cited above, that passing would have been a requirement for obtaining his future judicial positions, as is also noted in *Dakota Farmers' Leader*, April 18, 1913, 6.
28. For the sodomy case, see #34, South Dakota vs. [Defendant], June 24, 1913; for the lewd picture, see #139, South Dakota vs. [Defendant], September 9, 1916; for the horse thief, see #134, South Dakota vs. [Defendant], September 2, 1916, #135, September 2, 1916, and #136, August 5, 1916; for embezzlement, see #176, South Dakota vs. [Defendant], August 15, 1912, and #35, South Dakota vs. [Defendant], April 22, 1918. All cases from file 1-260, Register of Actions, Bennett County Courthouse, Martin, South Dakota (BCC).
29. For the Townsite Company, see *Sioux Falls Argus Leader*, May 16, 1913, 5; for Bates-Foster, see *Bennett County Booster*, April 28, 1915, 8; for loss of allotments, see *Superintendent's Annual Narrative and Statistical Reports, Pine Ridge*, 1910–1929, 1919, frame 0272, M1011, roll 106, NARA-W. For deeds, the following are the dates for land deeded and indicates where notation exists in deed books held at BCC: Three Stars land patent, December 7, 1912, Patent Records, deed book 1, 76; for Nash, September 4, 1916, deed book 2, 303; for Omaha businessman, July 6, 1918, deed book 2, 501; for Townsite Company, May 22, 1913, deed book 2, 30, and May 3, 1916, deed book 2, 270; for No Necks, February 14, 1916, deed book 2, 343; for Red Wing, December 12, 1918, deed book 2, 601; for Volz, October 10, 1918, deed book 2, 568. For status of chief, see *Cody Cow Boy*, May 26, 1916, 4.
30. Martin School District, October 16, 1914, deed book 2, 97, and June 2, 1919, deed book 3, 29–30; for Calvary Cathedral, January 7, 1922, deed book 4, 535; Episcopal Church, August 5, 1918, deed book 2, 520, BCC.

14. Politics and the War Years

1. The Oklahoma Historical Society has a brief biography of Oklahombi: Corie Delashaw, "Oklahombi, Joseph," *Encyclopedia of Oklahoma History and Culture*,

accessed September 16, 2023, https://www.okhistory.org/publications/enc/entry.php?entry=OK091. See also Britten, *American Indians*, 81.

2. For Civil War draft, see Kennedy, *Over Here*, 151.
3. See Kennedy, *Over Here*, 148 (for congressional resistance), 156–57 (for deferments and dependents), 162 (for African Americans), 163 (for conscientious objectors), 166 (for dragnet).
4. For Indian resistance, see Britten, *American Indians*, 67–71; for deferments, see Barsh, "American Indians," 281.
5. Kennedy, *Over Here*, 167–69.
6. Britten, *American Indians*, 14, 62–63.
7. Britten, *American Indians*, 14, 140–41.
8. For citizenship, see Britten, *American Indians*, 52; for Indian participation and volunteers, Indian schools, and Carlisle, see Barsh, "American Indians," 277–78, 278–79. The Library of Congress has a photograph of Wilson's speech script at Echoes of the Great War, accessed September 16, 2023, https://www.loc.gov/exhibitions/world-war-i-american-experiences/about-this-exhibition/arguing-over-war/for-or-against-war/wilson-before-congress/; also see Rosier, *Serving Their Country*, 47.
9. Russell Lawrence Barsh discusses casualties in "American Indians in the Great War," 278. Also see Britten, *American Indians*, 77, 106.
10. Barsh, "American Indians," 298n7. Thomas A. Britten notes Oklahombi's plight after the war in *American Indians in World War I*, 165–66. For Lakota perspective on alcohol, see Mails, *Fools Crow*, 110–11.
11. Britten, *American Indians*, 133, 136–38; Barsh, "American Indians," 280.
12. See Britten, *American Indians*, 144–46 (for livestock herds), 135 (for Liberty bonds). For consequences of selloff, see MacGregor, *Warriors Without Weapons*, 39.
13. For competency commissions, see McDonnell, *Dispossession*, 94–110; and for number of patents, see Britten, *American Indians*, 149.
14. For Pine Ridge leasing, see *Superintendent's Annual Narrative*, 1918, frame 0227, and 1919, frame 0234, M1011, roll 106, NARA-W; and for restrictions, see McDonnell, *Dispossession*, 48–49, 62.
15. Henry Tidwell to Commissioner of Indian Affairs, October 3, 1918, CCF 1907–1939, 48365—18 Pine Ridge—926, Pine Ridge, RG 75, NARA-W. See also Britten, *American Indians*, 56.
16. Prucha, *Great Father*, 272–73.
17. Henry Tidwell to Commissioner of Indian Affairs, May 10, 1918, CCF 1907–1931, 4309—1918 Pine Ridge—926, Pine Ridge, RG 75, NARA-W.
18. E. B. Merrit to Oliver Leftheron, June 3, 1918, CCF 1907–1931, 4309—1918 Pine Ridge—926, Pine Ridge, RG 75, NARA-W; Henry Tidwell to Commissioner of Indian Affairs, August 8, 1918, CCF 1907–1939, 48365—18 Pine Ridge—926, Pine Ridge, RG 75, NARA-W; and Henry Tidwell to Commissioner of Indian Affairs,

July 23, 1918, CCF 1907–1939, 4309—1918 Pine Ridge—926, Pine Ridge, RG 75, NARA-W.

19. For council, see Robertson, *Power of the Land*, 92; and *Superintendent's Annual Narrative*, 1915, frame 0168, M1011, roll 106, NARA-W. Also see John Brennan to Commissioner of Indian Affairs, June 24, 1909, "OST 1909," MS6, Richmond Clow Collection, OLCA.
20. "To Citizens of the Oglala Sioux Tribe on the Pine Ridge Reservation," Henry Tidwell, March 9, 1918, 064, "Councils, Claims, etc.," 1918–1922, NAID: 285586, NARA-KC; *Oglala Light*, February–March 1918, 30.
21. For treasurer, see Henry Tidwell to Clarence Three Stars, May 10, 1918, 064, "Councils, Claims, etc.," 1918–1922, NAID: 285586, NARA-KC; and for council payment, see "To Citizens of the Oglala Sioux Tribe on the Pine Ridge Reservation," Henry Tidwell, March 9, 1918, 064, "Councils, Claims, etc.," 1918–1922, NAID: 285586, NARA-KC.
22. For Paul's eligibility, see Clarence Three Stars to Henry Tidwell, July 18, 1918; for deferments, see M. T. Benham to W. A. Morris, May 31, 1918, both CCF 1907–1939, 48365—18 Pine Ridge—926, Pine Ridge, RG 75, NARA-W. Paul's year of birth on his grave headstone at Inestimable Gift Cemetery, Allen, South Dakota, is given as 1894; however, his birth year is sometimes listed as 1895, as in Jennie Three Stars probate, August 8, 1929, CCF 1907–1939, E 121, 36457—29 Pine Ridge—350, Pine Ridge, RG 75, NARA-W.
23. Henry Tidwell to Commissioner of Indian Affairs, August 8, 1918, and Henry Tidwell to Commissioner of Indian Affairs, October 3, 1918, both CCF 1907–1939, 48365—18 Pine Ridge—926, Pine Ridge, RG 75, NARA-W.
24. Henry Tidwell to Commissioner of Indian Affairs, August 8, 1918, CCF 1907–1939, 48365—18 Pine Ridge—926, Pine Ridge, RG 75, NARA-W. Paul's unit is inscribed on his grave headstone at Inestimable Gift Cemetery.
25. *Superintendent's Annual Narrative*, 1921, frame 0416–0417; 1920, frame 0324, M1011, roll 106, NARA-W.
26. U.S. House of Representatives, *Complaint*, 54.
27. U.S. House of Representatives, *Complaint*, 54.
28. Lepore, *These Truths*, 395.
29. *American Indian Magazine*, January–March 1918 (6, 1), 5.
30. For the story of Pettigrew and Darrow, see "Hidden Treasures from the Stack," *National Archives at Kansas City Newsletter*, May 2019, 3–5, https://www.archives.gov/files/kansas-city/press/newsletter/2019-may.pdf.
31. See Rosier, *Serving Their Country*, 50, 58–60.
32. For car, see *Gordon Journal*, March 21, 1918, 1.
33. For Pine Ridge deaths, see *Superintendent's Annual Narrative*, 1919, frame 0248, M1011, roll 106, NARA-W. For national American Indian mortality figures, see Crosby, *America's Forgotten Pandemic*, 228; and "Influenza among American Indians,"

1008–9. For doctors, see *Superintendent's Annual Narrative*, 1923, frame 0628, M1011, roll 106, NARA-W.

34. For a riveting description of Philadelphia during the epidemic, see Barry, *Great Influenza*, 220–27; for city numbers, see Thomas Wirth, "Influenza ('Spanish Flu' Pandemic, 1918–19)," *The Encyclopedia of Greater Philadelphia*, accessed September 16, 2023, https://philadelphiaencyclopedia.org/archive/influenza-spanish-flu-pandemic-1918-19/; and for overall Native numbers, see "Influenza among American Indians," 1009.
35. *Weekly Pioneer Times*, November 7, 1918, 4; Bennett County Historical Society, *70 Years*, 425; and *Lead Daily Call*, November 7, 1918, 4.
36. See Spinney, *Pale Rider*, 170–71 (on mortality numbers), 218–22 (on survivors).

15. Canton

1. H. R. Hummer to Commissioner of Indian Affairs, August 26, 1922, CCF 1907–1939, E 121, 70005—Canton Asylum 1922, Canton Asylum, RG 75, NARA-W; and Silk, "Survey of Asylum for Insane Indians," March 20–26, 1929, CCF 1907–1939, E 121, 7448—Canton Asylum 1929—150, part 1, Canton Asylum, RG 75, NARA-W.
2. Sophia Three Stars admissions summary, n.d., CCF 1907–1939, E 121, 7448—Canton Asylum 1929—150, part 2, Canton Asylum, RG 75, NARA-W.
3. Putney, "Canton Asylum," 1–2.
4. Putney, "Canton Asylum," 3–4, 12.
5. Joinson, *Vanished in Hiawatha*, 289; and Indian Census, 1915, roll M595_370, p. 180, line 16, Pine Ridge, NARA-W. For flu diagnosis, see Sophia Three Stars admissions summary, n.d., CCF 1907–1939, E 121, 7448—Canton Asylum 1929—150, part 2, Canton Asylum, RG 75, NARA-W; and for subsequent conditions, see Yudofsky, "Contracting Schizophrenia," 324. Carla Joinson provides a gruesome but even-handed account of the asylum, by far the most comprehensive work on the subject.
6. Jennie Three Stars, South Dakota Certificate of Death, 79491, October 24, 1921, SDDH; Fourteenth Census of the United States, 1920, Bennett County, South Dakota, Township 38 North, Range 36 West of 6th Meridian, Enumeration District 8, 134.
7. Jennie Three Stars probate, August 8, 1929, CCF 1907–1939, E 121, 36457—29 Pine Ridge—350, Pine Ridge, RG 75, NARA-W. Application and Report on Application for Patent in Fee, July 10, 1911, CCF 1907–1939, E 121, 88393—11 Pine Ridge—312, Pine Ridge, RG 75, NARA-W.
8. Sophia Three Stars admissions summary, n.d., CCF 1907–1939, E 121, 7448—Canton Asylum 1929—150, part 2, Canton Asylum, RG 75, NARA-W.
9. Putney, "Canton Asylum," 12.
10. H. R. Hummer to Commissioner of Indian Affairs, August 26, 1922, CCF 1907–1939, E 121, 70005—Canton Asylum 1922, Canton Asylum, RG 75, NARA-W.

11. Fourteenth Census of the United States, 1920, Bennett County, South Dakota, Township 38 North, Range 36 West of 6th Meridian, Enumeration District 8, 134; Fifteenth Census of the United States, 1930, Canton Township, South Dakota, Supervisor's District 6, 46; and Twelfth Census of the United States, 1900, Pine Ridge Indian Reservation, South Dakota, Enumeration District 46-7, 140B.
12. Shorter, *Brief History*, 34, 45–46, 49–50, 59, 65.
13. Ward dimensions are from Joinson, *Vanished in Hiawatha*, 24–25. Other details are from Silk, "Survey of Asylum for Insane Indians," 3, 5, 18.
14. Riney, "Power and Powerlessness," 60–61, 53–54; and Silk, "Survey of Asylum for Insane Indians," 42.
15. Riney, "Power and Powerlessness," 53–55; and Joinson, *Vanished in Hiawatha*, 138, 250–51, 243.
16. Silk, "Survey of Asylum for Insane Indians," 19, 38, 24–25.
17. Silk, "Survey of Asylum for Insane Indians," 17, 6–7.
18. Silk, "Survey of Asylum for Insane Indians," 10, 14, 33–34.
19. Joinson, *Vanished in Hiawatha*, 33–34, 64–65, 200.
20. Silk, "Survey of Asylum for Insane Indians," 7, 13, 15–17, 33, 41. For radiators, see Inspection Sheet, Dr. Emil Krulish, March 23, 1929, CCF 1907–1939, Canton Asylum, E 121, 10814—Canton Asylum 1929—155 (1 of 2), RG 75, NARA-W.
21. Joinson, *Vanished in Hiawatha*, 257–58; Putney, "Canton Asylum," 30; and Riney, "Power and Powerlessness," 49, 59–61.
22. Grob, *Mental Illness*, 171–75. American Indian women were among the most vulnerable to sterilization. Estimates suggest that as late as the 1970s the Indian Health Service sterilized 25 percent or more of Native women through the use of inadequate and misleading consent forms, violation of waiting periods, and sheer surgical profit motive, rather than prescribing other means of birth control. See Lawrence, "Indian Health Service," 410.
23. Joinson, *Vanished in Hiawatha*, 141–42, 198–99.
24. Silk, "Survey of Asylum for Insane Indians," 14, 15, 23–24, 49.
25. Riney, "Power and Powerlessness," 47.
26. Silk, "Survey of Asylum for Insane Indians," 30–33, 48; and Putney, "Canton Asylum," 10, 18–19.
27. Joinson, *Vanished in Hiawatha*, 61–62, 79, 89–90.
28. Putney, "Canton Asylum," 18–19.
29. Joinson, *Vanished in Hiawatha*, 134, 258, 269, 335–43.
30. Emil Krulish memorandum, March 22, 1929, CCF 1907–1939, Canton Asylum, E 121, 10814—Canton Asylum 1929—155 (1 of 2), RG 75, NARA-W; and Joinson, *Vanished in Hiawatha*, 231–32, 242.
31. Silk, "Survey of Asylum for Insane Indians," 21, 93, 95.
32. Silk, "Survey of Asylum for Insane Indians," 95–108.

33. Clarence Three Stars probate 48966-31, June 10, 1976, personal communication, Harold Compton, Rosebud, South Dakota, March 8, 2017; Clarence Three Stars, #28, April 14, 1925, PI 163, entry 762, box 28, "Reports of Industrial Surveys, 1922–1929," Pass Creek District, Pine Ridge, RG 75, NARA-W.
34. Clarence Three Stars, #28, April 14, 1925, PI 163, entry 762, box 28, "Reports of Industrial Surveys, 1922–1929," Pass Creek District, Pine Ridge, RG 75, NARA-W; *Superintendent's Annual Narrative*, 1930, frame 0014, and 1931, frame 0106, M1011, roll 107, NARA-W.
35. Clarence Three Stars, #28, April 14, 1925; and Paul Three Star, #63, May 25, 1925; Edgar Fire Thunder, #82, April 16, 1925, all in PI 163, entry 762, box 28, "Reports of Industrial Surveys, 1922–1929," Pass Creek District, Pine Ridge, RG 75, NARA-W. Clarence Three Stars probate 48966-31, June 10, 1976, Harold Compton, personal communication, March 8, 2017. The 1930 federal census shows Clarence living with a Mary Three Stars, perhaps his daughter Mary, who would have been about eighteen at the time, and not Mary Emery, if indeed he had divorced her by Indian custom as noted above. Still, Mary's age is given as fifty-five in the census, and she is described as Clarence's wife.

16. The Black Hills

1. Sundstrom, "Sacred Black Hills," 200–205.
2. For sacred geography and implications, see Ostler, *Lakotas*, 4, 10, 21, 26, 183–84.
3. Hämäläinen, *Lakota America*, 169, 191, 235. On diversity, see Ostler, *Lakotas*, 75.
4. *Report of the Commission Appointed*, 13.
5. Lazarus, *Black Hills, White Justice*, 83, 90.
6. U.S. Senate, *Message From the President*, 36 (for Little Wound), 22 (for Oglala signatories). For Fire Thunder, see Ostler, *Lakotas*, 100–101; and Bennett County Historical Society, *70 Years*, 423.
7. Lazarus, *Black Hills, White Justice*, 92.
8. U.S. Senate, *Statements of a Delegation*, 17; Hämäläinen, *Lakota America*, 92–93, 191.
9. For seven generations, see *Report of the Commission Appointed*, 7–8; and DeMallie, *Sixth Grandfather*, 168–69. For Red Cloud, see Ricker, *Indian Interviews*, 346; and Ostler, *Lakotas*, 92.
10. Ostler, *Lakotas*, 128, 137. For the quotation, see "Claims of Sioux," *Pioneer Press*, June 3, 1897, 3.
11. Lazarus, *Black Hills, White Justice*, 124.
12. Black Hills Council decree, 1913, "OST 1913," MS6, Richmond Clow Collection, OLCA.
13. Lazarus, *Black Hills, White Justice*, 131; and Committee to Commissioner of Indian Affairs, June 24, 1915, Main Decimal Files, 062, "Treaties, Claims, Agreements 1912–1918," NAID: 285586, RG 75, Pine Ridge, NARA-KC.

14. Petition to Commissioner of Indian Affairs, April 6, 1918, box 5, folder 25, "Sioux Black Hills Council," MSI, Jeanne Smith Collection, OLCA; Lazarus, *Black Hills, White Justice*, 144; and *Madison Daily Leader*, April 10, 1918, 2.
15. Lazarus, *Black Hills, White Justice*, 138, 146–47; *Martin Messenger*, September 28, 1923, 1; and Ostler, *Lakotas*, 133.
16. Lazarus, *Black Hills, White Justice*, 156–57. For a detailed timeline of the case, see Gonzalez and Cook-Lynn, *Politics of Hallowed Ground*, 41, 340–41, 353.
17. Gonzalez and Cook-Lynn, *Politics of Hallowed Ground*, 41, 251, 260. For history of ICC, see U.S. Indian Claims Commission, *Final Report*, 1978.

17. The End of It All

1. Clow, "Indian Reorganization Act," 127–28.
2. Clow, "Indian Reorganization Act," 128–29; and petition, n.d., CCF 1907–1939, 1131—1924, Pine Ridge, part 1—054, Pine Ridge, RG 75, NARA-W.
3. James LaPointe to Commissioner of Indian Affairs, March 8, 1931, and Hermus Merrival to Commissioner of Indian Affairs, March 6, 1931, CCF 1907–1939, 1131—1924, Pine Ridge, part 1—054, Pine Ridge, RG 75, NARA-W.
4. Clow, "Indian Reorganization Act," 129.
5. *Martin Messenger*, September 3, 1931, 1.
6. John Collier to Secretary of Interior, October 8, 1934, estate of Clarence Three Stars, probate 48966-31, Harold Compton, personal communication, March 8, 2017.
7. "Statement in Re Making and Execution of The Last Will and Testament of Clarence Three Stars Sr. #2058," John Thompson, Examiner of Inheritance, August 24, 1931; Last Will and Testament of Clarence Three Stars, August 24, 1931, estate of Clarence Three Stars, probate 48966-31, both Harold Compton, personal communication, March 8, 2017.
8. The Lakota name of the moon is from Neihardt, *Black Elk Speaks*, 101. Many different winter counts exist, but Red Horse's was an Oglala count that is in possession of the Fire Thunder family and is chronicled in Karol, *Red Horse Owner's Winter Count*, 59–65.
9. Clarence Three Stars, South Dakota Certificate of Death, 139578, August 28, 1931, SDDH. His gravestone says August 22, 1931, and so there is some disagreement about the date.
10. Details are compiled from the *Martin Messenger*, September 3, 1931; and the *Shannon County News*, September 3, 1931.
11. John Collier to Secretary of Interior, October 8, 1934; and A. B. Melzner to Secretary of Interior, September 19, 1936, estate of Clarence Three Stars, probate 48966-31, Harold Compton, personal communication, March 8, 2017.
12. Clow, "Indian Reorganization Act," 125, 132; and Biolsi, *Organizing the Lakota*, 60.
13. For *ikce wicasa*, see Lame Deer and Erdoes, *Lame Deer*, 14.

14. *Superintendent's Annual Narrative*, 1928, frame 0962, M1011, roll 106, NARA-W. See Bennett County Historical Society, *70 Years*, 109, for quotation.
15. Joinson, *Vanished in Hiawatha*, 261–63; and Putney, "Canton Asylum," 27–28.
16. Joinson, *Vanished in Hiawatha*, 345–47; *Asylum for Insane Indians, Canton, S.D.*, 9, 14, September 1933, Samuel Silk, CCF 1907–1939, E 121, Canton Asylum, 7448—Canton Asylum 1929—150, part 1, RG 75, NARA-W; and Yudofsky, "Contracting Schizophrenia," 324.
17. Sophia Three Stars admission, December 22, 1933, CCF 1907–1939, E 121, Canton Asylum, 7448—Canton Asylum 1929—150, part 2, lot 2, RG 75, NARA-W.
18. Clinical Director to W. O. Roberts, May 31, 1938; Riley Guthrie to Clarence Three Stars, January 2, 1940; Riley Guthrie to Clarence Three Stars, March 26, 1940; Riley Guthrie to Clarence Three Stars, October 27, 1941; Riley Guthrie to Mary Allman, March 2, 1942; and Samuel Silk to W. O. Roberts, June 23, 1938, all in CCF 1907–1939, E 121, Canton Asylum, 7448—Canton Asylum 1929—150, parts 2 and 3, RG 75, NARA-W.
19. Gambino, "Mental Health," 194–201. The discharge reference is included in a personal email from Carla Joinson, September 3, 2015.

Bibliography

Archives and Manuscript Materials

AMNH. American Museum of Natural History, New York, New York.
James Walker Collection.
BCC. Bennett County Courthouse, Martin, South Dakota.
County Clerk Files.
Register of Deeds Office.
BL. Beinecke Rare Book and Manuscript Library, Yale University, New Haven, Connecticut.
Yale Collection of Western Americana.
Richard Henry Pratt Papers.
CCHS. Cumberland County Historical Society, Carlisle, Pennsylvania.
CISDRC. Carlisle Indian School Digital Research Center, Dickinson College, Carlisle, Pennsylvania.
DCHC. DC History Center, Washington DC.
Printed Materials Collection.
DCPLW. District of Columbia Public Library, Washingtoniana Division, Washington DC.
NARA-KC. National Archives and Records Administration, Kansas City, Missouri.
Record Group 75—Records of the Bureau of Indian Affairs.
NARA-STL. National Personnel Records Center, National Archives and Records Administration, St. Louis, Missouri.
NARA-W. National Archives and Records Administration, Washington DC.
Record Group 75—Records of the Bureau of Indian Affairs.
OLCA. Oglala Lakota College Archives, Kyle, South Dakota.
Jeanne Smith Collection.
Richmond Clow Collection.
PHS. Pennsylvania Historical Society, Philadelphia.
John Wanamaker Collection.
SDDH. South Dakota Department of Health, Pierre.

SDSA. South Dakota State Archives, Pierre.
John Brennan Family Papers.
UNMZ. Zimmerman Library, University of New Mexico, Albuquerque.
James R. Walker Collection on the Oglala Sioux.

Published Works

An Act to Authorize the Sale and Disposition of the Surplus and Unallotted Lands in Bennett County. 61st Congress, 2nd session. S.2341, chap. 257. May 27, 1910.

An Act to Ratify an Agreement with Certain Bands of the Sioux Nation of Indians. 44th Congress, 2nd session. Chap. 72. February 28, 1877.

Adams, David Wallace. *Education for Extinction: American Indians and the Boarding School Experience, 1875–1928*. Lawrence: University Press of Kansas, 1995.

Ahern, Wilbert. "An Experiment Aborted." *Ethnohistory* 44, no. 2 (Spring 1997): 263–304.

Allen, Shannen K., and Richard D. Semba. "The Trachoma 'Menace' in the United States, 1897–1960." *Survey of Ophthalmology* 47, no. 5 (September–October 2002): 500–509.

Andrews, Thomas. "Turning the Tables on Assimilation: Oglala Lakotas and the Pine Ridge Day Schools, 1889–1920s." *Western Historical Quarterly* 33, no. 4 (Winter 2002): 407–30.

Annual Reports of the Commissioner of Indian Affairs.

Annual Reports of the Department of Interior.

Arnold, Sarah Louise, and Charles B. Gilbert. *Stepping Stones to Literature: A Second Reader*. New York: Silver, Burdett, c. 1897. http://hdl.handle.net/2027/hvd.32044097054662.

Bad Heart Bull, Amos, and Helen H. Blish. *A Pictographic History of the Oglala Sioux*. 1967. Lincoln: University of Nebraska Press, 2017.

Baldwin, James. *School Reading by Grades: Baldwin's Readers, Third Year*. New York: American Book Company, 1897. http://hdl.handle.net/2027/hvd.32044097054639.

Ball, Eve. *Indeh: An Apache Odyssey*. With Nora Henn and Lynda Sánchez. Provo UT: Brigham Young University Press, 1980.

Barry, John M. *The Great Influenza: The Epic Story of the Deadliest Plague in History*. New York: Viking, 2004.

Barsh, Russell Lawrence. "American Indians in the Great War." *Ethnohistory* 38, no. 3 (Summer 1991): 276–303.

Bell, Genevieve. "Telling Stories Out of School: Remembering the Carlisle Indian Industrial School, 1879–1918." PhD diss., Stanford University, 1998.

Bennett County Historical Society. *70 Years of Pioneer Life in Bennett County, South Dakota, 1911–1981*. Pierre SD: State Publishing Company, 1981.

Biolsi, Thomas. *Organizing the Lakota: The Political Economy of the New Deal on the Pine Ridge and Rosebud Reservation*. Tucson: University of Arizona Press, 1992.

Book of Common Prayer. New York: New York Bible and Common Prayer Book Society, 1871.

Boyd's City Directory. Washington DC: R. L. Polk and Company, 1910. City Directories, DCPLW.

Britten, Thomas A. *American Indians in World War I: At War and at Home*. Albuquerque: University of New Mexico Press, 1999.

Brown, Joseph Epes, ed. *The Sacred Pipe: Black Elk's Account of the Seven Rites of the Oglala Sioux*. 1953. Baltimore: Penguin, 1972.

Buecker, Thomas R. *Last Days of Red Cloud Agency: Peter T. Buckley's Photograph Collection, 1876–1877*. Lincoln: Nebraska State Historical Society, 2016.

Buecker, Thomas R., and R. Eli Paul, eds. *The Crazy Horse Surrender Ledger*. Lincoln: Nebraska State Historical Society, 1994.

Burt, Nathaniel, and Wallace E. Davies. "The Iron Age: 1876–1905." In *Philadelphia: A 300-Year History*, edited by Russell F. Weigley, 471–523. New York: W. W. Norton, 1982.

Cahill, Cathleen D. *Federal Fathers and Mothers: A Social History of the United States Indian Service, 1869–1933*. Chapel Hill: University of North Carolina Press, 2011.

Carter, Harvey. "Chat Dubray." In *Mountain Men and the Fur Trade of the Far West*, vol. 6, edited by Leroy Hafen, 143–46. Glendale CA: Arthur H. Clark and Company, 1968.

Champney, Elizabeth W. "Another Indian Invasion." *St. Nicholas: An Illustrated Magazine for Young Folks* 11, part 2 (October 1884): 944–52. https://babel.hathitrust.org/cgi/pt?id=mdp.39015020061712&view=1up&seq=454.

Child, Brenda J. *Boarding School Seasons: American Indian Families 1900–1940*. Lincoln: University of Nebraska Press, 1998.

Clow, Richmond L. "The Indian Reorganization Act and the Loss of Tribal Sovereignty: Constitutions on the Rosebud and Pine Ridge Reservations." *Great Plains Quarterly* 7, no. 2 (Spring 1987): 125–34.

Cochran, Mary E. *Dakota Cross Bearer: The Life and World of a Native American Bishop*. Lincoln: University of Nebraska Press, 2000.

Coel, Margaret. *Chief Left Hand, Southern Arapaho*. Norman: University of Oklahoma Press, 1981.

Coleman, Michael C. *American Indian Children at School, 1850–1930*. Jackson: University Press of Mississippi, 1993.

Coleman, William S. E. *Voices of Wounded Knee*. Lincoln: University of Nebraska Press, 2001.

The Columbian Views of Washington. Washington DC: Columbian Correspondence College, 1902. Printed Materials Collection, DCHC.

Crosby, Alfred. *America's Forgotten Pandemic: The Influenza of 1918*. Cambridge: Cambridge University Press, 2003.

Deloria, Philip. *Indians in Unexpected Places*. Lawrence: University Press of Kansas, 2004.

DeMallie, Raymond J. "'George Sword Wrote These': Lakota Culture as Lakota Text." In *Theorizing the Americanist Tradition*, edited by Lisa Philips Valentine and Regna Darnell, 246–58. Toronto: University of Toronto Press, 1999.

———, ed. *The Sixth Grandfather: Black Elk's Teachings Given to John G. Neihardt*. Lincoln: University of Nebraska Press, 1984.

———. "Touching the Pen: Plains Indian Treaty Councils in Ethnohistorical Perspective." In *Ethnicity on the Great Plains*, edited by Frederick C. Luebke, 38–53. Lincoln: University of Nebraska Press, 1980.

Eastman, Charles Alexander. *From The Deep Woods to Civilization*. 1916. Chicago: Lakeside Press, 2001.

Eastman, Elaine Goodale. *Pratt, the Red Man's Moses*. Norman: University of Oklahoma Press, 1935.

———. *Sister to the Sioux: The Memoirs of Elaine Goodale Eastman, 1885–1891*. 1978. Lincoln: University of Nebraska Press, 2004.

Eighteenth Annual Report of the Board of Indian Commissioners, 1886. Washington DC: Government Printing Office, 1887.

Fear-Segal, Jacqueline. *White Man's Club: Schools, Race, and the Struggle of Indian Acculturation*. Lincoln: University of Nebraska Press, 2007.

Fifteenth Annual Report of the Board of Commissioners of Public Charities of the State of Pennsylvania. Harrisburg PA: Lane S. Hart, 1885. https://babel.hathitrust.org/cgi/pt?id=pst.000060102126&view=1up&seq=144.

Finkelstein, Barbara. *Governing the Young: Teacher Behavior in Popular Primary Schools in 19th Century United States*. New York: Falmer, 1989.

Fourth Biennial Report of the Executive Accountant of the State of South Dakota, 1917–18. Pierre SD: State Publishing Company. https://babel.hathitrust.org/cgi/pt?id=uc1.b2994601&view=1up&seq=1.

Friesen, Steve, and Francois Chaladiuk. *Lakota Performers in Europe: Their Culture and the Artifacts They Left Behind*. Norman: University of Oklahoma Press, 2017.

Gambino, Matthew J. "Mental Health and Ideals of Citizenship: Patient Care at St. Elisabeths Hospital in Washington, D.C., 1903–1962." PhD diss., University of Illinois, 2010.

Garner, Sandra. "What Sort of Indian Will Show the Way? Colonization, Mediation, and Interpretation in the Sun Dance Contact Zone." PhD diss., Ohio State University, 2010.

Geffen, Elizabeth. "Industrial Development and Social Crisis, 1841–1854." In *Philadelphia: A 300-Year History*, edited by Russell F. Weigley, 307–62. New York: W. W. Norton, 1982.

Gonzalez, Mario, and Elizabeth Cook-Lynn. *The Politics of Hallowed Ground: Wounded Knee and the Struggle for Indian Sovereignty*. Urbana: University of Illinois Press, 1999.

Greene, Jerome A. *American Carnage: Wounded Knee, 1890*. Norman: University of Oklahoma Press, 2014.

Grob, Gerald N. *Mental Illness and American Society, 1875–1940*. Princeton NJ: Princeton University Press, 1983.

Hämäläinen, Pekka. *Lakota America: A New History of Indigenous Power*. New Haven CT: Yale University Press, 2019.

Hassrick, Royal B. *The Sioux*. 1964. Norman: University of Oklahoma Press, 1977.

Hertzberg, Hazel. *The Search for an American Indian Identity: Modern Pan-Indian Movements*. Syracuse NY: Syracuse University Press, 1971.

Hoxie, Frederick. *A Final Promise: The Campaign to Assimilate the Indians, 1880–1920*. Cambridge: Cambridge University Press, 1989.

Hyde, George E. *Red Cloud's Folk: A History of the Oglala Sioux Indians*. 1937. Norman: University of Oklahoma Press, 1975.

———. *A Sioux Chronicle*. 1956. Norman: University of Oklahoma Press, 1980.

The Hymnal, As Authorized and Approved for Use by the General Convention of the Protestant Episcopal Church. New York: J. Pott, 1920. https://hdl.handle.net/2027/nyp.33433068259617.

"Influenza among American Indians." *Public Health Reports (1896–1970)* 34, no. 19 (May 9, 1919): 1008–9.

Inventory of the County Archives of South Dakota: No. 3, Bennett County. Mitchell: South Dakota Historical Records Survey, 1940. https://babel.hathitrust.org/cgi/pt?id=mdp.39015041076335&view=1up&seq=3.

Joinson, Carla. *Vanished in Hiawatha: The Story of the Canton Asylum for Insane Indians*. Lincoln: University of Nebraska Press, 2016.

Karol, Joseph S., ed., *Red Horse Owner's Winter Count: The Oglala Sioux 1786–1968*. Martin SD: Booster, 1969.

Keep, John R. *First Lessons for the Deaf and Dumb*. Hartford CT: Press of the Case, Lockwood, and Brainard Company, 1875. https://babel.hathitrust.org/cgi/pt?id=hvd.hn1rpw&seq=7.

Kennedy, David. *Over Here: The First World War and American Society*. New York: Oxford University Press, 1980.

Kett, Joseph F. *The Pursuit of Knowledge Under Difficulties*. Stanford CA: Stanford University Press, 1994.

Kneale, Albert. *Indian Agent*. Caldwell ID: Caxton Printers, 1950.

LaFrance, Daniel. *An Indian Boy's Story*. New York, 1903. http://etext.lib.virginia.edu/modeng/modengJ.browse.html.

Lame Deer, John (Fire), and Richard Erdoes. *Lame Deer, Seeker of Visions: The Life of a Sioux Medicine Man*. New York: Simon and Schuster, 1972.

Larson, Robert W. *Red Cloud: Warrior-Statesman of the Lakota Sioux*. Norman: University of Oklahoma Press, 1997.

Lawrence, Jane. "The Indian Health Service and the Sterilization of Native American Women." *American Indian Quarterly* 24, no. 3 (Summer 2000): 400–419.

Lawson, Michael. "The Fractionated Estate: The Problem of American Indian Heirship." In *The Sioux in South Dakota History: A Twentieth Century Reader*, edited by Richmond Clow, 45–84. Pierre: South Dakota State Historical Society Press, 2007.

Lazarus, Edward. *Black Hills, White Justice: The Sioux Nation versus the United States, 1775 to Present*. New York: Harper Collins, 1991.

Lepore, Jill. *The Story of America: Essays on Origins*. Princeton NJ: Princeton University Press, 2012.

———. *These Truths: A History of the United States*. New York: W. W. Norton, 2018.

Lewis, Emily. *Wo'Wakita Reservation Recollections: A People's History of the Allen Issue Station District on the Pine Ridge Reservation of South Dakota*. Sioux Falls SD: Center for Western Studies, 1980.

Littlefield, Daniel F., and Lonnie E. Underhill. "Renaming the American Indian: 1890–1913." *American Studies* 12, no. 2 (Fall 1971): 33–45.

The Living Church Annual and Whittaker's Churchman's Almanac. Milwaukee WI: Young Churchman, 1910. https://babel.hathitrust.org/cgi/pt?id=hvd.hw29py&view=1up&seq=11.

Lomawaima, K. Tsianina. *They Called It Prairie Light: The Story of Chilocco Indian School*. Lincoln: University of Nebraska Press, 1995.

MacGregor, Gordon. *Warriors Without Weapons: A Study of the Society and Personality Development of the Pine Ridge Sioux*. Chicago: University of Chicago Press, 1946.

Mails, Thomas E. *Fools Crow*. 1979. Lincoln: University of Nebraska Press, 1990.

———. *The Mystic Warriors of the Plains*. 1972. New York: Marlowe and Company, 1996.

Maroukis, Thomas C. "The Peyote Controversy and the Demise of the Society of American Indians." *Studies in American Indian Literatures* 25, no. 2 (Summer 2013): 159–80.

Matthews, Jessica. "Killing a Culture to Save a Race: Writing and Resisting the Discourse of the Carlisle Indian School." PhD diss., George Washington University. 2005.

McDermott, John D., R. Eli Paul, and Sandra Lowry, eds. *All Because of a Mormon Cow: Historical Accounts of the Grattan Massacre*. Norman: University of Oklahoma Press, 2018.

McDonnell, Janet A. *The Dispossession of the American Indian, 1887–1934*. Bloomington: Indiana University Press, 1991.

McGillycuddy, Julia B. *Blood on the Moon: Valentine McGillycuddy and the Sioux*. 1941. Lincoln: University of Nebraska Press, 1990.

Mekeel, H. Scudder. *The Economy of a Modern Teton Dakota Community*. Yale University Publications in Anthropology, no. 6. New Haven CT: Yale University Press, 1936.

Miller, David Humphreys. *Ghost Dance*. New York: Duell, Sloan, and Pearce, 1959.

Missionary District of South Dakota. *Journal of the Convocations with the Annual Address of the Bishop*. 1895. https://babel.hathitrust.org/cgi/pt?id=uiuo.ark%3A%2F13960%2Ft4zg9kp6q&view=1up&seq=307&q1=clarence+three+stars.

———. *The Journal of the Convocations, and Reports of the Officers and Committees*. Sioux Falls SD: Will Beach Printing Company, 1916. https://babel.hathitrust.org/cgi/pt?id=nyp.33433081979522&view=1up&seq=247.

———. *The Journal of the Convocations, and Reports of the Officers and Committees*. Hobart

IN: Parish Leaflet Company, 1917. https://babel.hathitrust.org/cgi/pt?id=nyp.33433081979522&view=1up&seq=345.

Morgan, Thisba Hutson. "Reminiscences of My Days in the Land of the Ogallala Sioux." In *South Dakota Department of History Report and Historical Collections*, vol. 29, 23–62. Pierre: South Dakota Historical Society, 1958.

Neihardt, John G. *Black Elk Speaks: Being A Life Story of a Holy Man of the Oglala Sioux*. 1932. Lincoln: University of Nebraska Press, 2004.

Nurge, Ethel. "Dakota Diet: Traditional and Contemporary." In *The Modern Sioux: Social Systems and Reservation Culture*, edited by Ethel Nurge, 35–91. 1970. Lincoln: University of Nebraska Press, 1977.

Ostler, Jeffrey. *The Lakotas and the Black Hills: The Struggle for Sacred Ground*. New York: Penguin, 2010.

———. *The Plains Sioux and U.S. Colonialism from Lewis and Clark to Wounded Knee*. Cambridge: Cambridge University Press, 2004.

Phenix, George P. "Day School No. 27." *Southern Workman*, March 1907. https://babel.hathitrust.org/cgi/pt?id=hvd.32044010020618&view=1up&seq=161&q1=Clarence%20Three%20Stars.

Pierre Indian Industrial School. Pierre SD, 1909.

Pitzer, Andrea. *One Long Night: A Global History of Concentration Camps*. New York: Little Brown, 2017.

Powers, Marla N. *Oglala Women: Myth, Ritual, and Reality*. Chicago: University of Chicago Press, 1986.

Powers, Thomas. *The Killing of Crazy Horse*. New York: Alfred Knopf, 2010.

Powers, William K. *Oglala Religion*. 1975. Lincoln: University of Nebraska Press, 1977.

Pratt, Richard Henry. *Battlefield and Classroom: An Autobiography*. Norman: University of Oklahoma Press, 2003.

Price, Catherine. *The Oglala People, 1841–1879: A Political History*. Lincoln: University of Nebraska Press, 1996.

Prucha, Francis Paul. *The Great Father: The United States Government and the American Indians*. Abridged ed. Lincoln: University of Nebraska Press, 1986.

Putney, Diane T. "The Canton Asylum for Insane Indians, 1902–1934." *South Dakota History* 14, no. 1 (1984): 1–30.

Ray, Charles A. *Quiz Book: Questions and Answers on the Subject of Criminal Procedure*. Washington DC: Columbian Correspondence College, 1900.

Red Cloud. *Autobiography of Red Cloud: War Leader of the Oglalas*. Edited by R. Eli Paul. Helena: Montana Historical Society Press, 1997.

Red Shirt, Delphine. *George Sword's Warrior Narratives: Compositional Processes in Lakota Oral Tradition*. Lincoln: University of Nebraska Press, 2016.

Reinhardt, Akim D., ed. *Welcome to the Oglala Nation: A Documentary Reader in Oglala Lakota Political History*. Lincoln: University of Nebraska Press, 2015.

Remondini, David J. "Charles A. Ray." In *Justices of the Indiana Supreme Court*, edited by Linda C. Gugin and James E. Clair, 77–80. Indianapolis: Indiana Historical Society, 2011.

Report of the Commission Appointed to Treat With the Sioux Indians for the Relinquishment of the Black Hills. Washington DC: Government Printing Office, 1875.

Report of the Executive Council on the Proceedings of the Annual Conference of the Society of American Indians. Washington DC, 1912. http://hdl.handle.net/2027/mdp.39015003696468.

Ricker, Eli S. *The Indian Interviews of Eli Ricker, 1903–1919*. Vol. 1 of *Voices of the American West*. Edited by Richard Jensen. Lincoln: University of Nebraska Press, 2005.

———. *The Settler and Soldier Interviews of Eli S. Ricker, 1903–1919*. Vol. 2 of *Voices of the American West*. Edited by Richard Jensen. Lincoln: University of Nebraska Press, 2005.

Riney, Scott. "Power and Powerlessness: The People of the Canton Asylum for Insane Indians." *South Dakota History* 27, nos. 1–2 (Spring and Summer 1997): 41–64.

Robertson, Paul. *The Power of the Land: Identity, Ethnicity, and Class Among the Oglala Lakota*. New York: Routledge, 2002.

Rosier, Paul C. *Serving Their Country: American Indian Politics and Patriotism in the Twentieth Century*. Cambridge MA: Harvard University Press, 2009.

Ross, Ralph H. *The Pine Ridge Reservation: A Pictorial Description*. 1909. https://babel.hathitrust.org/cgi/pt?id=loc.ark:/13960/t19k4g15w&seq=7.

Seventeenth Annual Report of the Executive Committee of the Indian Rights Association. In *Annual Report of the Board of Directors of the Indian Rights Association, no. 10–17, 1892–1899*, 19–21. Philadelphia: Wm. Fell & Co., 1900. https://babel.hathitrust.org/cgi/pt?id=wu.89060399821&view=1up&seq=629.

Shorter, Edward. *A Brief History of Psychiatry*. New York: John Wiley and Sons, 1997.

Sidney, Margaret. "The Carlisle School for Indian Pupils." *Wide Awake* 18, no. 4 (March 1884): 227–37. https://babel.hathitrust.org/cgi/pt?id=hvd.hxp1sv&view=1up&seq=247.

Sneve, Virginia Driving Hawk. *That They May Have Life: The Episcopal Church in South Dakota, 1859–1976*. New York: Seabury, 1977.

Southerton, Don. "James R. Walker's Campaign Against Tuberculosis on the Pine Ridge Reservation." In *The Sioux in South Dakota History: A Twentieth Century Reader*, edited by Richmond Clow, 141–56. Pierre: South Dakota State Historical Society Press, 2007.

Spack, Ruth. *America's Second Tongue: American Indian Education and the Ownership of English, 1860–1890*. Lincoln: University of Nebraska Press, 2002.

Spinney, Laura. *Pale Rider: The Spanish Flu of 1918 and How It Changed the World*. New York: Public Affairs, 2017.

The Spire on the Square: A History of St. John's Episcopal Church, Carlisle, Pennsylvania. Carlisle PA: St. John's Episcopal Church, 2002.

The Spirit of Missions Issued by the Board of Missions of the Protestant Episcopal Church. New

York, 1886. https://babel.hathitrust.org/cgi/pt?id=wu.89064897119&view=1up&seq=151.
Standing Bear, Luther. *Land of the Spotted Eagle*. 1933. Lincoln: University of Nebraska Press, 1978.
———. *My People the Sioux*. 1928. Lincoln: University of Nebraska Press, 1975.
Stewart, Omer C. *Peyote Religion: A History*. Norman: University of Oklahoma Press, 1987.
Sundstrom, Linea. "The Sacred Black Hills: An Ethnohistorical Review." *Great Plains Quarterly* 17, no. 3/4 (Summer/Fall 1997): 185–212.
Swinton, William. *Primary Geography: An Introduction to Swinton's Grammar School Geography*. New York: Ivison, Blakeman, Taylor, 1881. http://hdl.handle.net/2027/hvd.32044097021315.
Szasz, Margaret Connell. *Education and the American Indian*. 1974. Albuquerque: University of New Mexico Press, 1999.
Treaty with the Sioux—Brule, Oglala, Miniconjou etc. April 9, 1868. 15 Stats, 635. https://dc.library.okstate.edu/digital/collection/kapplers/id/29721.
U.S. House of Representatives. *Complaint of the Pine Ridge Sioux*. Hearings Before the Committee on Indian Affairs. 66th Congress, 2nd session. April 6, 1920. Washington DC: Government Printing Office, 1920.
———. *Engagement Between United States Troops and Sioux Indians*. 33rd Congress, 2nd session. 788 House Executive Document 63. 1855. Washington DC, 1855.
———. *Peyote Hearings Before a Subcommittee of the Committee on Indian Affairs of the House of Representatives on H.R. 2614*. Parts 1 and 2. Washington DC: Government Printing Office, 1918.
U.S. Indian Claims Commission. *Final Report*, August 13, 1946–September 30, 1978. Washington DC: Government Printing Office, 1979.
U.S. Senate. *Encounter Between Sioux Indians of the Pine Ridge Agency, South Dakota, and a Sheriff's Posse of Wyoming*. 58th Congress, 2nd session. Senate Executive Document 128. 1904. Washington DC, 1904.
———. *Memorial of Sioux Indians*. 55th Congress, 1st session. Senate Document 90-55. 1897. Washington DC, 1897.
———. *Message From the President of the United States Communicating the Report and Journal of Proceedings of the Commission Appointed to Obtain Certain Concessions from the Sioux Indians*. 44th Congress, 2nd session. Senate Executive Document 9. 1876. Washington DC, 1876.
———. *Report of the Secretary of War*. 34th Congress, 1st session. Executive Document 91. 1856. Washington DC, 1856.
———. *Report Relative to Opening a Part of the Great Sioux Reservation*. 50th Congress, 2nd session. Senate Executive Document 17. 1888. Washington DC, 1888.
———. *Reports Relative to the Proposed Division of the Great Sioux Reservation*. 51st Congress, 1st session. Senate Executive Document 51. 1890. Washington DC, 1890.

———. *Statements of a Delegation of Ogalalla Sioux Before the Chairman of the Committee on Indian Affairs*. 55th Congress, 1st session. Senate Document 61. 1897. Washington DC, Government Printing Office, 1897.

———. *To Examine into the Condition of the Sioux and Crow Indians*. 48th Congress, 1st session. Senate Report 283. March 7, 1884. Washington DC, 1884.

Utley, Robert M. *The Last Days of the Sioux Nation*. New Haven CT: Yale University Press, 1963.

Viola, Herman J. *Diplomats in Buckskins: A History of Indian Delegations in Washington City*. Washington DC: Smithsonian Institution Press, 1981.

Vitale, Frank, IV. "Counting Carlisle's Casualties: Multiple Methods for Measuring Mortality at the Carlisle Indian Industrial School, 1879–1918." Master's diss., University of Oxford, 2018.

Wagner, Fredric C., III. *Participants in the Battle of the Little Big Horn: A Biographical Dictionary of Sioux, Cheyenne, and United States Military Personnel*. Jefferson NC: McFarland, 2011.

Wagoner, Paula. *"They Treated Us Just Like Indians": The Worlds of Bennett County, South Dakota*. Lincoln: University of Nebraska Press, 2002.

Walker, James R. *Lakota Belief and Ritual*. Edited by Raymond J. DeMallie. 1980. Lincoln: University of Nebraska Press, 1991.

———. *Lakota Society*. Edited by Raymond J. DeMallie. 1982. Lincoln: University of Nebraska Press, 1992.

Waring, George E., Jr., ed. *Report on the Social Statistics of Cities*. Part 1, *New England and the Middle States*. 1886. New York: Arno, 1970.

White, Louellyn. "White Power and the Performance of Assimilation: Lincoln Institute and Carlisle Indian School." In *Carlisle Indian Industrial School: Indigenous Histories, Memories and Reclamations*, edited by Jacqueline Fear-Segal and Susan D. Rose, 106–23. Lincoln: University of Nebraska Press, 2016.

White Hat, Albert, Sr. *Life's Journey—Zuya: Oral Teachings from the Rosebud*. Salt Lake City: University of Utah Press, 2012.

Wilson, Raymond. *Ohiyesa: Charles Eastman, Santee Sioux*. Urbana: University of Illinois Press, 1983.

———. "The Writings of Ohiyesa—Charles Alexander Eastman, M.D., Santee Sioux." *South Dakota History* 6, no. 1 (December 1975): 55–73.

Witmer, Linda F. *Changing Images: The Art and Artists of the Carlisle Indian Industrial School*. Carlisle PA: Cumberland County Historical Society, 2008.

Yudofsky, Stuart C. "Contracting Schizophrenia: Lessons from the Influenza Epidemic of 1918–1919." JAMA 301, no. 3 (January 21, 2009): 324–26.

Index